CRITICAL EXPLORATIONS IN SCIENCE FICTION AND FANTASY
(a series edited by Donald E. Palumbo and C.W. Sullivan III)

I SEE YOU

The Shifting Paradigms of James Cameron's Avatar

Ellen Grabiner

McFarland & Company, Inc., Publishers
Jefferson, North Carolina, and London

In memory of my father,
who taught me to see,
and for my son Alex,
who keeps my eyes wide with wonder.

LIBRARY OF CONGRESS CATALOGUING-IN-PUBLICATION DATA

Grabiner, Ellen, 1950–
    I see you : the shifting paradigms of James Cameron's *Avatar* /
Ellen Grabiner.
        p.   cm. — (Critical explorations in science fiction and
        fantasy ; 34)
    [Donald E. Palumbo and C.W. Sullivan III, series editors]
    Includes bibliographical references and index.

    ISBN 978-0-7864-6492-0
    softcover : acid free paper ∞

    1. Avatar (Motion picture : 2009)   I. Title.
PN1997.2.A94G83 2012
    791.43'72 — dc23   2012018796

BRITISH LIBRARY CATALOGUING DATA ARE AVAILABLE

On the cover: A scene from the 2009 film *Avatar* depicting Jake
Sully's avatar (left) with Neytiri. Front cover design by David
Landis (Shake It Loose Graphics)

Manufactured in the United States of America

McFarland & Company, Inc., Publishers
  Box 611, Jefferson, North Carolina 28640
   www.mcfarlandpub.com

Table of Contents

Acknowledgments

This book would not have come into being without the loving and extra-ordinary generosity of Bruce and Renae Perry who midwifed the nascent project into existence. Thanks to my readers and dear friends, Ellen Balis and Susan Fleischmann, and especially to Marla Zarrow for her careful and patient reading and copyediting.

With particular gratitude to my fellow *Avatar* scholars and panelists who presented at the Northeast Modern Languages Association Conference, University of Rutgers, New Jersey, April 2011: Chris Dilworth, Aaron Tucker, Jennifer Nesbitt, Jennifer Miller, Seung-hoon Jeong, Jonathan Foltz, and Sonja Georgi, as well as Paul Chafe, the panels' organizer. Thinking along with this group was a heady, inspiring experience.

Finally, with appreciation for the support and confidence of my editor, Donald Palumbo.

Introduction

James Cameron's blockbuster film *Avatar* has had the unique effect on spectators of throwing us backward and forward in time all at once. Backward, to a time when audiences were awed simply by the spectacle of the moving image, and forward, to the possibility of the experience of completely immersive entertainment, along the lines of the *Star Trek* "holodeck."

Avatar is a film that affects people. The critics have extolled and crucified it in equal measure. Cameron's masterpiece has been labeled sexist, anti-imperialist, anti-militaristic, racist, anti-capitalistic, leftist, reactionary, and pro-environment.

There have been accusations of it being a rehash of tired narratives, notably the *Pocahontas/Dances with Wolves/Last Samurai* motif, or as David Brooks of the *New York Times* suggested, another white messiah movie.[1] It could be argued, however, that the lack of originality and subtlety in the narrative is, in fact, beside the point.

Despite critical pans, one would be hard pressed to find anyone who has seen Cameron's technological breakthrough in 3-D and who claims not to have enjoyed the sheer visual delight of the thing. Yes, *Avatar* is a spectacle, is simulacra, but even those who bemoan the triteness of its plot or the paucity of its dialog deign to admit that they loved the "experience" of the film. As *New York Times* film critic Manohla Dargis noted, Cameron "uses 3-D seemingly to close the space between the audience and the screen. He brings the movie to you."[2]

Avatar is, at this writing, the highest grossing film of all time, having raked in over 2.7 billion dollars worldwide. During a time when DVD sales are in a free fall, *Avatar* sold 4+ million DVDs in the week following its release on disc. As audiences shift toward watching films that stream into their homes instantly on Netflix rather than building up their DVD libraries, *Avatar* is a film that viewers want to possess.[3] With a gestation of several decades and actually four years in the making, the film embraces a revolutionary motion capture technique in which live action is melded with CG animation. Nominated for nine Academy Awards, including Best Picture and Best Director, *Avatar* won those for Art Direction, Cinematography and Visual Effects, highlighting the visual sumptuousness of the world Cameron and his team brought to viewing audiences.

This volume coalesces around theoretical and philosophical issues brought to bear by *Avatar*. The world of science fiction and the technological prowess of Mr. Cameron meet in a heady concoction that while visually ravishing could easily be dismissed as "eye candy." Under closer scrutiny, the film elicits provocative questions about the relationship between mind and body, between appearance and reality. It brings into focus the relationships between humans and their technology, between humans and their planet and each other. But it also zooms in on the nature of film itself and its future potential. In some ways, the "avatar" comes to signify the same absence/presence dichotomy that Christian Metz articulated as being intrinsic to the motion picture itself.[4]

Avatar makes the case for a revisioning of the prevalent visual paradigm, moving it away from a "power-over," reifying gaze in favor of a more holistic, embodied approach to the practice of looking. It also presents, in bold strokes, a picture of the construction of otherness. And on the meta level, *Avatar* blazes a trail that will move the cinematographic experience forward in dramatic and novel ways.

In the pages that follow, the interstitial aspect of *Avatar*'s filmic space will be examined. By way of a close reading of the film, this book excavates the gaps between human and machine, between technology and nature, between chick flick and action-packed adventure, between old-fashioned storytelling and new-fangled technology. Most important is the exploration of the question to what extent *Avatar* melds together the seer and the seen, illuminating an alternative visual paradigm. What makes this an even more exciting venture is that the film ends up being performative. The narrative, the technology used to create the film, and the moviegoer experience are all three interlaced; the meaning is imparted in the form that the film takes.

Chapter One looks at our modernist visual paradigm and the ways in which *Avatar* alternately offers a way of seeing that shimmers instead of solidifies. It brings into relief our own visuality and the extent to which current technologies — video games, simulations, virtual reality — designed to show us more, actually place us at a greater remove from our embodied experience of seeing. *Avatar* blatantly links power/might to a greater technological vision, echoing the paradigm of a totalizing, single-pointed gaze that has reigned in Western cultures since the Enlightenment. The film offers as an alternative a practice of embodied vision.

Cameron has taken on no less than the entrenched and dualistic Cartesian model, and in Chapter Two, we look at the ways he has transformed this way of thinking, particularly in relation to traditionally paired oppositions like mind/body, nature/technology, appearance/reality. Diegetically, technology plays a complex role in Cameron's *Avatar*. On the one hand, we are shown that the highly advanced use of all manner of surveillance, recording, sensing, imaging and modeling equipment come to stand for a one-pointed reifying vision which prevents the corporation from truly seeing the Na'vi. Yet here Cameron embraces a paradox. He is clearly not anti-technology. Advanced biotechnology is necessary for the linkup to the avatar, making possible the inhabiting of the Na'vi body, the embodied experience of their world. And the Na'vi themselves are fiber optically wired to their world, their goddess, and each other. Embedded in their braids are lively fiber optic cables with which they can connect to the beasts that they ride, to the Tree of Souls, and to each other for ritual and prayer. As the film tackles the tension that exists between technology and nature, we can place Cameron in a lineage that draws on Marshall McLuhan's tribal man and Martin Heidegger's observations about our relationship to technology.

In Chapter Three we examine how Cameron's technological inventions and priorities in the making of *Avatar* mirror the ways in which he is transforming a dualistic paradigm and revisioning the relationship between technology and nature. Here a history of the use of computer-generated characters is recounted, as well as the complex innovations Cameron himself brought about. In the making of *Avatar*, Cameron invented three unique contraptions to achieve the highly realistic 3-D characters generated by performance capture. This chapter explores the SimulCam system, the virtual camera and the head-rig system that Cameron developed and the ways in which these devices undergird his shifting vision.

One of the most prevalent complaints or critiques of the movie is that it rehashes the same old story. *Avatar* has been panned for being a remix of a tired narrative that can be traced all the way back to the 1950 James Stewart film *Broken Arrow*. Versions of the white man saving a native people have proliferated in film. Chapter Four examines the thread of this narrative as it runs through films such as Disney's *Pocahontas*, Costner's *Dances with Wolves*, *The Last Samurai*, *Dune*, and more recently, *District 9* and the deviations it takes along these paths. Here we look at storytelling, repetition, the value of remediation, and what this offers a viewing audience. Has the diegesis been "dumbed down" to meet the diminishing standards of a blogged, social-mediated, multi-tasked spectatorship?[5]

To what extent are there advantages to using a familiar story as a vehicle to bring to light new ideas? And, in an age of sampling and remixing as de rigueur, how does "knowing the story" change spectator expectations and offer opportunities for meaning making?

Chapter Five approaches the film through a psychoanalytic lens, examining the dream and the dreamer, illusions and reality, and whether the employment of the 3-D motion capture alters the traditional sense of the cinematic apparatus. Revisiting Plato's allegory of the cave and its application in Jean-Louis Baudry's apparatus theory, we consider the "apparatus" of the avatar link. Also in examining the role played by Cameron's radical use of 3-D motion capture, we become aware of its doubling effect. The avatar itself stands in for Cameron's immersive technology and forces questions of transformed subjectivity. If Dargis is correct in thinking that this groundbreaking technology closes the gap between the screen and the viewer, we can ask whether the trajectory from emulsion to bits and bytes, from movie camera to virtual camera, actually does transform what has come to be known as the cinematographic apparatus.

Responding to critiques of *Avatar* as a racist, sexist, able-ist, heterosexist film, Chapter Six looks at the constructions of identities in the movie and the ways in which it reinforces encoded stereotypes, as well as the ways in which it upends them. This chapter pulls apart some of the more salient threads crisscrossing through cyberspace, an appropriate method for investigating a film that envisions a future networked existence. Identity politics has always been deeply encoded in cinema, and unpacking representations of race, gender, and ability in *Avatar* leads to the overarching question of how otherness is constructed. This chapter draws heavily on Stuart Hall's notions of encoding, meaning making, and of culturally constructed representations, as well as on Judith Butler's work on gender. Finally, this chapter concludes by evoking from the archive of filmic representations *The Jazz Singer*, which like *Avatar* incorporated groundbreaking technological innovation in the service of poignantly focusing on the construction of otherness.

Finally, in Chapter Seven, Cameron himself comes into the spotlight. This chapter follows Cameron's parallel interests in the technology of cinema as tool and fodder for his narrative exploits. Investigating his narrative, cinematographic, and directorial achievements, we glance backward at *The Terminator*, *Aliens*, *Terminator 2: Judgment Day*, *The Abyss*, *True Lies*, *Strange Days* (for which Cameron wrote the screenplay, but which was directed by Kathryn Bigelow), and of course his other blockbuster, *Titanic*, for the seeds of the genesis of *Avatar*. Tracing his work as a screenwriter, director, producer and inventor, we examine these films leading up to the production of *Avatar* to see the extent to which it emerges as the culmination of a life's work, so far. It is well known that he is working on sequels to *Avatar*, as well as several other projects, and thus the "so far" qualification is necessary.

James Cameron is a master of mixology who, by combining disparate elements, whips up concoctions that by their very nature blur the boundaries that heretofore have bound genres. *Avatar*—love story and shoot-'em-up, sci-fi epic and western saga, hero's quest and anti-war film, tech-noir and *Fern-Gully*—is no doubt his finest visual cocktail.

Chapter One

Did You See That?

The magic of the Hollywood style at its best (and of all the cinema which fell within its sphere of influence) arose, not exclusively, but in one important aspect, from its skilled and satisfying manipulation of visual pleasure. — Laura Mulvey[1]

Visual Pleasure

From the awe-inspiring, iridescent landscape of Pandora, to the richly regal blue of the skin of the Na'vi, to the eye-popping pyrotechnics of the battle scenes, *Avatar* is nothing if not a satisfying manipulation of our visual pleasure. And while in her seminal essay Mulvey's self-avowed intent is to destroy the problematic pleasure she perceives in cinema by discussing it, the intent here is quite the opposite.

This first chapter brings to light a redoubled paradigm shift. In the less-than-unique story line of *Avatar* there is a motif that suggests an embodied, soft gaze as antidote to the phallocentric, dominant gaze against which Mulvey rails. This latter is represented in the film by the corporate/military installation as it goes about the business of annihilating the indigenous population of Pandora. Shaping a narrative that critiques what Mulvey and others have identified as a totalizing "gaze" are the transcendent technological advances of Cameron's 3-D motion capture, wowing audiences and ultimately directing awareness to the pleasure we take in seeing.

Mulvey's essay is just the tip of an iceberg constituted by a passel of Western thinkers who have seen seeing as problematic and, in a large part, as responsible for the mess we find ourselves in today. Historically, responses to visuality have always been fraught, emerging out of a kind of "iconoclastic suspicion of the image,"[2] alternately elevating and demonizing it. Looking back we uncover ripples of a vast and brash distaste for the visual in Western

7

thought, beginning with biblical injunctions against graven images. A particular blend of the one-pointed, geometric perspective that emerged during the Renaissance, coupled with a philosophical tendency built upon a mind/body split has yielded the hegemonic gaze with which we are all too familiar.[3]

It is this totalizing, power-over way of looking that Cameron's *Avatar* makes visible in the guise of a militarily bolstered corporation poised to commit genocide. But in its own stunning way *Avatar* does its best to underscore the broad notion that to reject the visual altogether does us a disservice. In an attempt to upend the dehumanizing effects of objectification which the film makes clear, *Avatar* brings to light practices of looking that have long been obscured by the shadows of a historically hypostatized gaze. In spite of the fact that *Avatar*'s narrative trajectory has drawn the fire of claims that it lacks originality, the film surfaces complex philosophical issues that challenge habitual practices of looking. A close reading of the film calls to mind Maurice Merleau-Ponty's descriptions of the relationship between the seer and what is seen as "an intimacy as close as between the sea and the strand."[4] Located in *Avatar* are traces of Martin Heidegger's *Aletheia*,[5] an approach to the visual in which the object of our gaze is forever in the process of uncovering itself and never ultimately becoming hard-edged or discretely defined, an approach in which letting go of knowing precedes *seeing*. In *Avatar* the linkage between seeing and knowing has been re-formed.

In the pages that follow, the extent to which the film shifts the paradigm of the seer and the seen will be examined. The sci-fi technology of the fantasy moon Pandora brings into high relief current visual technologies — video games, simulations, virtual reality — all of which claim to reveal more and yet in actuality place us at a greater remove from the "natural" embodied experience of seeing.

Same Old Story

In order to unpack the ways in which an embodied practice of looking resides in the narrative of *Avatar*, a brief synopsis is offered. Perhaps this distilled summary of the narrative looks oh so familiar: White man infiltrates native peoples to gain intelligence and to convince them to yield to imperialist adversaries. White man falls in love with native princess, her way of life, her world. White man leads natives to victory over their would-be annihilators. The story smacks of Disney's *Pocahontas* or Costner's *Dances with Wolves*. It is the white man as savior that David Brooks objected to in his *New York Times* Op-Ed column, "The Messiah Complex,"[6] and which has many claiming that the story line is intrinsically racist. There are, however, inherent differences here that merit attention.

Protagonist Jake Sully's voice-over narration opens *Avatar*, and for a short while the film flips back and forth between the current day—Jake awakening from a cryogenically induced sleep—and the cremation of his twin brother six years earlier. The visual similarity between the "cryo-pod," from which Jake emerges, and the casket in which his brother's body is being burned cements the connection between the two. Jake's brother had been senselessly murdered just prior to departing for Pandora where he was a key member of a scientific expedition. Because Jake, a paraplegic ex-marine, shares his twin's DNA, he is the perfect replacement for his brother. A grieving, wounded, limp-legged young man in a wheelchair, Jake's white male privilege is somewhat diminished and his pathos enlarged.

The "company," while never explicitly named in the film, is identified by the logo "*RDA*," and in extra-textual discourse, such as *Pandorapedia: The Official Field Guide*, one learns that the whole expedition is financed by this Resources Development Administration, a powerful "quasi" governmental agency. The RDA is primarily there to mine an ore invaluable to its corporate stockholders. The story proper begins when Jake arrives along with a convoy of mercenaries at a high-tech military/industrial installation surrounded by surveillance towers. The company's base is shot in muted shades of gray, foreboding hints that life is not all that rosy here on Pandora.

During a welcome briefing, head of security Colonel Miles Quaritch is introduced to us from the feet up, his military-issue boots walking the waxy floors, echoing throughout the large briefing room. The camera tilts upward to the gun on his hip, to the jagged scars on his scalp, before his face is revealed. With a self-reflective nod at one of his favorite films, Cameron lets the mercenaries and the audience in on the fact that they are *not in Kansas anymore*. Along with the new arrivals, we learn that Pandora is inhabited by living things that "crawl, fly and squat in the mud and want to kill you and eat your eyes for jujubes."[7] According to the colonel, hell would provide a respite from Pandora, where the indigenous population, the Na'vi, are hostile, hard to kill, and fond of aiming their arrows tinged with deadly neurotoxins at humans.

The clan of Na'vi known as Omaticaya is not only hostile and deadly but, simply put, in the way. They live in a gargantuan deciduous "Home Tree" that grows out of an "unobtanium"[8] rich site. Obtaining the irresistibly lucrative ore is the human poachers' primary purpose for being on Pandora. By the time Jake arrives, the company has already lost faith in famous botanist Grace Augustine and the potential diplomatic success of her "avatar" project. Despite her attempts to study the Omaticaya, to learn their language and culture, thus far she has been unable to convince them that they are in real danger. Under Colonel Quaritch's watch the corporation is poised to exterminate them.

The struggle that ensues between the corporate/military "baddies" and the blue-skinned Na'vi is a familiar story that evokes our collective American historical guilt at the slaughter of Native peoples across our continent, in Southeast Asia, and the Middle East. But in the tradition of the classical Hollywood narrative, this is just one of two intertwined plots.

Much to Grace's dismay, Jake joins her team of researchers, replacing his dead twin as an "avatar driver." Jake "links" to his avatar, ostensibly to learn enough about the Na'vi to gain their trust and induce them to move from Home Tree, hence avoiding the impending genocide. At the same time, though, Jake is secretly reporting to Colonel Quaritch, surreptitiously gathering intelligence to facilitate the annihilation of the Omaticaya. The night that Jake becomes stranded on Pandora he is rescued by and becomes smitten with Neytiri, the Na'vi warrior princess. Eventually he comes to feel that his time spent in the avatar and with Neytiri is more real than his real life, and he incites the Omaticaya to defend their home and defeat the imperialist incursion. He switches sides and, as the colonel later accuses, betrays his race.

One doesn't have to scratch the surface of *Avatar* very hard to find flickers of the Pocahontas story or perhaps that of *The Last Samurai*.[9] This familiar narrative, however, is simply the armature on which Cameron has draped his story and in which an embodied practice of looking resides. Within the diegetic world of *Avatar* the reifying gaze of Mulvey is usurped.

Did You See That?

Parker Selfridge is practicing his putting in the midst of an array of high-tech imaging equipment: there is a three-dimensional model of the surface of Pandora, a 180-degree simulation of the skies above the moon facilitating air traffic control, and multiple computer screens with multiple windows open on each. Serried screens line the upper limits of this control center like clerestory windows; later on in the film they will replicate in 360 degrees the infernal destruction of the Na'vi's Home Tree. Selfridge, who is in charge of the corporate operation, is surrounded not only by screens but also by technologically savvy employees who make the entire enterprise go. Sinking his putt in the makeshift hole of his overturned coffee mug, he shouts, "Did you see that!?" To which a sycophantic lackey immediately responds, "Yes, sir."

Without looking up from his ersatz putting green, Selfridge replies, "No you didn't. You were looking at the monitor."

While Selfridge is undeniably portrayed as the bad guy and is ultimately responsible for the razing of the Na'vi's home, he is not unaware. In this microcosmic snippet it appears that on some level he knows that the extensive technology which purports to help his team see more, better, and deeper, keeps them, in effect, from really seeing at all. With eyes on the machine, with a screen between us and the world in which we live, we miss the experience of living. Susan Sontag addressed this removal from direct experience in her book *On Photography*, when she suggested that photography "is mainly a social rite, a defense against anxiety, and a tool of power."[10] The sheer ubiquity of and increase in the number of screens that separate us from experience and enhance the illusion of a power-over perspective today and in this futuristic rendition of Cameron's has raised the stakes exponentially.

The corporation and its military "security" arm patently point to the "ugly American." Wielding an ethnocentric, technology driven, power-over gaze, the preparation for the genocide of the Na'vi evokes George Bush's "Shock and Awe" campaign, with much the same underwhelming results. Mercenaries run blindly ahead, Colonel Quaritch in the lead, not heeding the havoc they will wreak nor the lives they will destroy. It is a sobering moment in the film when the surveillance cameras — in a panoramic 360 degrees — broadcast the firestorm that topples the mammoth Home Tree in which the Na'vi had made their lives.

The colonel, especially when he is suited up in his Amplified Mobility Platform, or AMP suit, personifies the invincible human who is impervious to his surroundings. The AMP suit resembles nothing as much as it does the "mecha," a mechanical robot familiar to audiences of Japanese anime. The pilot sits inside this elaborate weapon, navigating from inside like a *virtual* driver. Small arm and fist gestures are writ large; the driver can smash and stomp and activate weapons from within his armored "bridge." Ensconced in his metallic shell, the colonel doesn't need to see the Na'vi or their world or the beauty that surrounds him. But he "knows." He knows they are hostile and savage and that it is incumbent upon him to destroy them. The colonel and his military legions link might to a greater technological vision, resulting in the rigidly frozen gaze that has characterized Western culture's scopic regime since the Enlightenment. When mind is pitted against body, reason against sense, the results are an unnecessary conflation of knowing and seeing such that a reified gaze comes to obscure all other possible manners of seeing.

The Old Paradigm

Laying the philosophical ground out of which these questions have emerged magnifies their articulation within *Avatar*.

In critiquing a dualistic model that has held sway for centuries, the over-arching *visual* paradigm — in which knowledge of the world is understood through the metaphor of visual perception — has been found culpable.[11] Thought to be responsible for promoting, propagating and institutionalizing a stultifying Cartesian worldview, the "spectator theory of knowledge," as John Dewey has referred to it,[12] has been targeted in an attempt to disrupt and dismantle what has been perceived as a prevailing, objectifying vision. It did not appear overnight. It is the result of centuries of thought and centuries of thinkers thinking about thought and its relationship to looking and seeing.[13]

Martin Jay, for example, tells his version of the story of "ocularcentrism," by which he refers to the privileging of the visual in Western thought. As he scans the horizon of twentieth-century thinkers he sees

> that the visual has been dominant in modern Western culture in a wide variety of ways. Whether we focus on the prevalence of surveillance with Michel Foucault, bemoan the society of the spectacle with Guy Debord, or emphasize "the mirror of nature" metaphor in philosophy with Richard Rorty, we confront again and again the ubiquity of vision as the master sense of the modern era.[14]

Visual metaphor has shown us the ways we understand what it is that we know. Some contemporary thinkers — including Foucault, Debord and Rorty, among others — have therefore concluded that it is the *visual* in the model that is the culprit. If we rid ourselves of the need to "represent" or to "picture," we could undo the dehumanizing effects of an insidious objectification that constricts our thinking.

But it is *not* the visual frame that is at the root of the problem of how we approach experience. It is this one particular *kind of looking*—a linear, menacing, dominating gaze, which can be recognized in the stance of Colonel Quaritch in *Avatar*— that separates us from experience and from one another. Adhering to this reifying gaze is a powerful need to know in advance how life will unfold that keeps us from being able to actually experience the unfolding.

No one likes to be in the position of not knowing. No one likes the feelings of being lost or confused or out of our element. We certainly don't like the feeling of not understanding what is going on. To know is to have power. Looking out from an either/or, black/white perch, we are tempted to choose — out of habit, out of fear, out of ignorance — to paste preexisting pictures of what we *believe is* over actuality, thereby flattening, homogenizing, thinning, and ultimately missing the richness that potentially dwells in experience as it unveils itself. Our attachment to knowing in advance, to being in control, while comforting and bolstering to our confidence, freezes and immobilizes our conceptual structures and keeps us from a more authentic way of being in our world.

Most of us move through life on autopilot. We walk into the same kitchen each morning, open the same refrigerator door, pull out the same orange from the same fruit bin and slice it with the same knife on the same cutting board. We go through these motions, most of us, without "seeing." But if we could step outside of our habits and take the opportunity to really look at the orange sitting there whole and not quite round in its bumply skin, a nub of the stem that once held it to a tree branch and now offers a way into the juicy fruit, we are bound to see something we hadn't noticed before. No matter how many oranges we have seen, this orange on this cutting board in this morning's light is unique and if we take the time to be with it, let it show itself to us, it will reveal something new.

If we decouple our already knowing from our active seeing, if we dismantle the hierarchical oppositions that parallel a "power-over" gaze,—body/mind, sense/reason, appearance/reality—then we might engender a look that allows for a kind of seeing that shimmers instead of solidifies, that fosters connection not domination; we might see with a loving, open eye.

Martin Heidegger would locate this kind of looking in an *Aletheic* tradition rather than subscribing to the "truth as correspondence" theory that grew out of the Cartesian project. Instead of a world where we grasp at the clarity that certainty assures us, where truth exists out there and it is our rational, thinking mind's job to circumscribe, define, or contain it, Heidegger suggests that if we embrace a soft gaze it would radically alter us and challenge our "everyday" way of being the world. A quick glance at the headlines of today's newspaper provides reason enough to think that changing "our way of being the world" is a useful strategy.

Throughout Heidegger's earlier writing, the Greek notion of *Aletheia* provides a way to think about truth as unconcealment rather than correspondence and draws on the language of the visual to reflect what we know. From Greek mythology, *a-letheia* is literally "not Lethe," Lethe being one of the rivers that flows through Hades, the underworld. Souls journeying to Hades were made to drink from the river Lethe, or Oblivion, in order to forget the details of their lives here on earth. *A-letheia*, then, embodies *not*-forgetting, coming out of being hidden. With *Aletheia* Heidegger points to the movement that inheres in this word. It is not just that we can see the orange, but if we sit with it, it reveals itself to us.

When Neytiri first encounters Jake, she is present to the unfolding moment. He is alone in the Pandoran jungle, and Neytiri recognizes him as one of the "Sky People" from her bird's-eye view in a tree branch above him. She raises her bow and aims, intent on killing him. But before she can shoot, an iridescent seed floats down and lands on the tip of her arrow. In that moment Neytiri waits for the seed to disclose itself. She has seen these seeds before. She could have shorthanded her experience and just nodded to the fact that a seed came to rest on her bow. She could have been in an "everyday," habitual mode, moving on autopilot. But instead she saw the seed that touched down as a sign, as something with meaning. She was willing at that moment to not know: she didn't know yet what the sign meant, and she didn't know why she should not just go ahead and kill Jake, but she was willing to let her initial intent go, suspend her action and relinquish her attack.

Circumscribed versus Circumspect

In *Being and Time,* Heidegger carefully examines this idea of a habitual mode or "everydayness."[15] In order to function we rely on habit, codes, and short cuts. Imagine if every morning upon waking we had to begin at the beginning, trying to decipher our visual experience the way we did when we were infants. We spent our earliest years of our lives cataloging, matching what we saw to what we felt, smelled, tasted, and heard. We reached for the rattle and when we successfully grasped it we noted that this splotch of red felt smooth and made a shushing sound; it was light enough for us to hold in our tightly closed fist. It tasted a little like the strained peaches we spilled on it earlier that day. The whole of our experience is mapped, in sighted individuals, to the visual stimulus recorded by light sensitive receptors in our retinas, interpreted by our visual cortex, and stored in what amounts to a visual data bank from which we can retrieve what we need on demand. We rely on this process, this "circumscribing" our world so that we can function, but we have become so enamored with our functional "database" that we forget that these bits of data are just shorthand and not the world at hand.

Whether we label it objectification, enframing, or circumscription, this approach "serves the development of knowledge."[16] The infant needs to *know* how to think about that red plastic globe that rattles when she grasps it, so she circumscribes it with her conceptual apparatus and labels it to help her make sense of her world. But the name and the idea don't come close to the delight she experiences when her tiny fingers close around it and the sound ripples through her body as she flails her arms with joy.

Heidegger's famous hammer can help us to get to the heart of this kind of apprehension. When Heidegger looks at the hammer he suggests, contrary to what most of us take for granted, that it cannot really be known simply by staring at it. "No matter how keenly we *just* look at the 'outward appearance' of things constituted in one way or another, we cannot discover handiness."[17] This "handiness" is a broad concept that perhaps we already have constructed and into which we have placed those things we deem "useful." We can look and look at the figure of the hammer and never approach an understanding of the thing. But if we bother to pick it up, if we feel its heft in our hands, if we let fall the weight of it on the head of a nail, if we sense the nail being driven into the wood that becomes a shelf of our bookcase, then we begin to uncover the "handiness" of the hammer.

It is only against a ground of nail, of heft, of wood, of swinging the tool in order to do the work of building, that the figure of the hammer emerges. Heidegger calls this *kind of seeing* circumspection (*Umsicht*) and links it with the notion of "taking care of." "Observation is a kind of taking care just as primordially as action has its own kind of seeing."[18] Here Heidegger shows us his circumspect view in process. He can't look at the figure of observation without also seeing how it emerges out of the ground of a kind of taking care. And he can't see action without noticing that it contains within it its own way of seeing. This back and forth, figure to ground and back again, presence and absence, concealing and revealing, are all contained in the notion of *Umsicht*, a circumspect way of looking.

Umsicht *and the Na'vi*

The application of *Umsicht*, a circumspect approach to our experience that arises from adopting a stance of not knowing, is exemplified in myriad ways in *Avatar*. What follows are a series of narrative cues that illustrate the connection between the suspension of knowing and the soft, circumspect gaze of Umsicht.

Linking into an avatar is only possible if you suspend knowing. Grace tells Jake when he attempts his first link to his avatar, "Let your mind go blank. That shouldn't be too tough for you."[19] While this is a gratuitous comic moment in which we are reminded that Jake is unprepared for the linkup — he has had no previous "link" time, has done no research, and hasn't learned the language of the Na'vi — it is precisely his *lack* of knowing that facilitates his success. He is in some respects like the child described above reaching for her rattle.

Having lost the use of his legs, Jake's first experience of embodiment in the avatar is a heady ride. In his childlike impulsivity he tears outside, disregarding the warnings of the medical team, the IVs and sensors still connected to his avatar's body. He begins to run, his feet make contact with the ground, his toes curl in the soil, and we too experience his exhilaration. He tastes the fruit Grace tosses at him as if it is the first food he has ever enjoyed. The spectator is left to wonder, is it the fruit that is extraordinary or is it Jake's experience of his avatar's superior taste buds?

On the expedition with Grace into the jungle, he can't help but touch everything, including the iridescent parasol-shaped plants that retract into the ground when they are approached. Like a child, he runs and looks and touches, not knowing but attempting to learn through the perceptions of his avatar body.

His exuberance and curiosity get him into trouble. Out in the jungle at night, separated from his expedition, he is surrounded by a pack of viper-wolves—wild doglike critters. With only a makeshift torch whittled into a spear at one end to fend off the rabid creatures, he is losing ground. His torch is wrenched from him by one of the viperwolves, and he is forced to wrestle with them, slicing at them with his hunting knife. Neytiri, fortuitously nearby, shoots an attacking beast with her arrow and then in an impressive show, reminiscent of the classic martial arts master effortlessly fighting off the masses, she artfully slays a number of viperwolves before the rest of the pack retreats. Grateful for his life, Jake tries to show his appreciation while she is praying over each fallen wolf. Lashing out angrily and striking him with her bow, she tells him not to thank her, for it is his childish carelessness that has caused her to unnecessarily take the lives of the viperwolves in the first place.

In the hunting rituals of the Na'vi we find evidence of the kind of taking care that Heidegger describes for us. The Omaticaya kill creatures only when it is necessary, and they remain present to the taking of a life.

While Jake doesn't really understand this, he is mindful of his mission and pleads with Neytiri to teach him the ways of the Na'vi. She tells him that "Sky People" can't learn. They are not able to see. It is clear to Neytiri that "Sky People" approach their encounters with rigid conceptual structures, circumscribing instead of letting what comes, come. Seeing for the Na'vi is not simply a visual experience. To see is to be present to, to be in contact with. Neytiri sees very clearly the limitations of the humans who have invaded her world and are destroying it in their blinkered search for the valuable ore.

Pressing her further, Jake insists that she teach him to see.

"No one can teach you to see," is Neytiri's answer.

Jake is intrepid. He follows her, although she insists that he "go back." Suddenly the seeds of the Tree of Souls, the sacred tree of the Na'vi, float down from above them—the same seed that earlier signaled Neytiri to put down her bow. At first Jake swats reflexively at them as if they were pesky mosquitoes, but Neytiri stays his hand. The luminescent seeds—reminiscent of some kind of jellyfish—descend, alighting on Jake's arms and torso, anointing him. Neytiri watches in awe. As suddenly as they appeared, the seeds leave, swimming off into the air. Although Neytiri doesn't know what it means that the seeds would choose Jake as their resting perch, she is willing to change course midstream and take him with her, patient until some meaning reveals itself.

When finally at Home Tree, Jake negotiates with Neytiri's parents, hoping they will agree to take him on as an apprentice. Moat, Neytiri's mother and a powerful shaman, circles around Jake as he is encircled by the Na'vi. The camera dizzily follows her inspection, emphasizing the circularity of the shot. Moat explains to Jake that they have tried to teach Sky People before, but in her experience the humans approach everything as if they always already know. She tells Jake, "It is hard to fill a cup which is already full."

"My cup is empty," Jake responds. "Trust me."[20]

Again, there is the intended comic relief here in the obvious fact that Jake is, in most ways, unprepared for this mission. This empty cup image evokes the Buddhist concept of *śūnyatā*, emptiness. It is this emptiness, this beginner's mind, that makes Jake uniquely prepared to learn: he has no preconceptions. To learn to speak and walk like a Na'vi, Jake will have to see their speaking and walking with a soft gaze, circumspectly, with *Umsicht*. As Grace tells him this during his apprenticeship to Neytiri, "You need to listen to what she says. Try to see the forest through her eyes."[21] The triteness of the dialogic prose notwithstanding, Jake can't be *told* how to see, it can't be *explained* to him. He must actually live in the experience of seeing.

Jake's Apprenticeship

Neytiri begrudgingly agrees to take Jake on as her apprentice and teaches him how to ride the direhorses. As soon as he makes the bond with the beast, a change in both the creature and in Jake is visible. The horse's eyes dilate and open wide. Jake closes his eyes. He feels the animal's heartbeat, her breath, the strength of her legs, and his own toes curl with sensual pleasure. Throughout the film Cameron employs the opening and closing of the eye to direct the attention to what is without and what is within. When the eye closes, it signals a shift of focus. In order to really *feel* the horse, Jake must shut out his vision, which for many is the dominant sense. We may recognize this reflex as often present when we smell or taste something extraordinary or hear exquisite music. We close our eyes to focus more intently on these sensory experiences without the distraction of vision.

When his horse dumps him in the mud after Jake makes his initial bond, Tsu'tey, the warrior next in command to Neytiri's father, tells Neytiri that this "alien" will learn nothing. "A rock sees more."[22] Here we are reminded of how, for the Na'vi, the capacity to learn is melded with the capacity to see. Norm, a well-studied avatar driver who trained with Jake's brother tries to help Jake improve his command of the Omaticayan language. He explains to Jake why understanding the Na'vi greeting, "I see you," is so essential. He tells Jake that it is not just seeing the person standing there in front of him, but it is about seeing into a person, and ultimately understanding them. Perhaps as Robert Heinlein would say, it is "grokking" them.[23]

Doubling the importance of the visual on the filmic level, Jake recounts his lessons with Neytiri via a video log: Jake peers into the lens as he describes his adventures. This video is shot in muted grays, reflective of the high-tech, scientific environment in which he finds himself. A red *record* button blinks at the spectator. A close-up of Jake's face, simulating what Jake is able to see as he records his observations, displaces the camera eye and hence our point of view. As the film alternates between this monochromatic video log and a montage of Jake's vivid memories of his adventures with Neytiri, Cameron contrasts Jake's dull, grayed-out "real" existence with the intensity of the full-spectrum color of his life when he is linked into his avatar and with Neytiri. The only thing in Jake's "real" world that is *not* shot in muted sci-fi gray or military-issue brown is the inside of his linkup pod. A bright florescent green mirrors the bioluminescence that illuminates the nighttime world of Pandora as it connects Jake to it.

"Every day," Jake tells the video log, "it's reading the trails, the tracks of the water hole, the tiniest scents and sounds."[24] As he becomes more proficient in the ways of the Na'vi warriors, he begins to understand the deep connection the people have to the forest. When he successfully wounds his prey with his bow and arrow, he moves quickly to plunge his hunting knife into the creature, reciting the words of prayer that Neytiri taught him. The people, the animals, the plants, the trees, the planet, are all held in awe. Here a circumspect vision can be located in which the tiniest traces are allowed to presence and are wrapped up in the kind of taking care articulated by Heidegger.

Jake's clean kill readies him for his initiation. He must chose and be chosen by an ikran, a banshee, to truly become a warrior. The stunning scape of sky and moons, floating mountains and trailing vines in this scene is enhanced by James Horner's sweeping musical score, adding an auditory thrill to the intensely vivid panoramic. Reminiscent of the epic scene in *E.T.* where Eliot's bicycle is silhouetted across the full moon, Cameron offers infinitesimally small Na'vi warriors leaping across massive vines that bisect the enormous planet around which Pandora revolves.

When Jake finally makes a bond with the ikran, this animal too reacts — it feels the interior change to itself and is wide eyed.

The Omaticaya warrior thinks and the creature reacts. Here Cameron doubles our sense of the body/mind connection: Jake is linked into the avatar body, the avatar body is linked now to ikran. Jake thinks "fly," and the ikran responds. Is it his mind, resting in the linkup pod that relays this message, or has his embodiment of the avatar transformed and transferred his perceptions? Thought enacted undoes our rigid concept of a discrete separation between thought and sense.

It is in this breathtaking scene when Neytiri and Jake soar over and under the floating mountains, around waterfalls that pour themselves into the void of the Pandoran sky, that Cameron's technological prowess asserts itself and the viewer soars along with them. Critic Daniel Mendelsohn was "literally gasping with pleasure" the first time he saw the movie.[25] Carrie Rickey, of the *Philadelphia Enquirer*, explains that she felt transported.[26] The fantastical computer-generated world spins beneath the powerful wings of the banshee. The audience feels muscles that strain as Jake and Neytiri maintain their balance on the ikran, diving down the sides of the floating mountains. We sense the wind rushing up to meet them. We are beside them on this dizzying ride and merge with their joy and exhilaration. The bond between Jake and his ikran is not the only bond in the making here. This ride that Jake shares with Neytiri seals their connection as well. As if performing a mating ritual, they dance in and out of the mountains and jungles on their ikran.

But yet another shift is occurring. There exists an even bigger banshee than the ikran, "a great Leonopteryx," or Toruk, "the Last Shadow." As Neytiri spins the yarn of her ancestor's riding of the great beast, the camera zooms in on a hot orange close-up of the skeletal eye of the last Toruk. Cameron quickly cuts to a grayed-out shot of Jake's small human eye, blinking open in his link pod, foreshadowing his future link to Toruk. Having completed his apprenticeship, Jake's sense of reality has also been transformed. He appears smaller, paler, even less substantial as he lifts his shriveled white legs out of the linkup pod. He thinks aloud that everything is backward now. "Like out there is the true world, and in here is the dream."[27]

The Seer and the Seen

When Jakes links into the body of his avatar he is having a phenomenological experience of embodied vision, much like that posited by Maurice Merleau-Ponty. In his essay "The Intertwining—The Chiasm," Merleau-Ponty offers us a kind of vision that itself has substance. Breaking down the dichotomy of outside/in, he posits a kind of membrane, a fleshy dimensionality, an actual substance that connects the seer to what is seen. "Vision," which Merleau-Ponty understands as a word that doubles for both the experience of seeing and the thing seen, is a medium connecting these polarities. We can consider that Grace Augustine's entire immersive research method rests on a foundation of Merleau-Ponty's approach, including his pronouncements that "he who looks must not himself be foreign to the world that he looks at,"[28] and "we do not mean to do anthropology, to describe a world covered over with all our own projections."[29] A world covered over with our own projections is what Heidegger alludes to when he describes our everydayness, our circumscribing of experience. A world covered over with our projections is all Colonel Quaritch is able to see through the multiple readout screens and sensors of his AMP suit or his scorpion copter, and it is what keeps him from experiencing what unfolds in front of him.

In the act of inhabiting his avatar Jake transforms the paradigm in which the seer and what is seen are polar opposites of one another and discrete. Thinking about Jake's embodied experience of Pandora forces us to look at the ways in which we have inherited an Enlightenment legacy that encourages us to consider mind and body to be another pair of discrete oppositions. As Jake moves the limbs of his strong, healthy, long-legged avatar, as he sees through the large luminous catlike eyes, as he touches the plants and weapons and world of the Na'vi with elongated fingers (this seems to be the one place the DNA of the humans is dominant: Jake has five fingers and Neytiri and other Na'vi only four), the question of whether his phenomenological experience comes *through* his avatar body arises. How does his avatar body filter his perceptions? Does it challenge/enhance the limits of what his human mind is capable of apprehending? Are his "senses" — his human mind and the avatar's body working in concert — sharper, more acute? Does living in an avatar body allow him to be more open to his experience, more like a Na'vi?

The melding of mind/body that Jake exemplifies might be understood in the way Merleau-Ponty describes our looking. "The look ... envelops, palpates, espouses the visible things."[30] Here there is no separation between eye and hand, between seeing and touching. As in Merleau-Ponty's vision, the act of looking actually *fluxes* the relationship between seer and seen.

A Word About Flux

In thinking about words that are descriptive of a lack of discreteness, we tend toward the metaphorical. In an attempt to undo the Cartesian rigidness of those traditionally paired opposites — mind/body, appearance/reality, found/made, inside/out — Merleau-Ponty gives us the lovely vision of the intimacy of sea meeting the shore. It is something with which most of us are familiar and can easily envision. This helps us to apply it to the less familiar notion of an object and a subject that are not quite separate, discrete entities. If we visualize a wave overlapping the sand, its edge in perpetual motion, constantly changing shape and therefore redefining where sand ends and water begins, we might start to have a sense of what Merleau-Ponty means. We might begin to experience an alternative to the black-and-white way of thinking to which most of us have become accustomed.

In the sentence above, the word *flux* is used to describe the movement inherent in Merleau-Ponty's model, movement to which Heidegger calls our attention when he gives us an Aletheic version of the truth. This movement is imbricated in the idea of circumspection. We don't encase or enframe; our gaze is soft and unfocused; it *fluxes*.

With his clear and accessible prose Richard Rorty must be credited with bringing the notion of "fluxing" into focus to describe the activities of a group of thinkers engaged in a project similar to his, one that upends a fundamentally dualist approach to thinking. In his book *Philosophy and Social Hope*, Rorty gathers under the umbrella of "anti-dualist"[31] a diverse group of philosophers who share overlapping projects.[32] While he grabs the label "anti-dualist" for these thinkers because it is handy, he is quick to point out that it does not mean what we might think. It does not categorize this motley crew as being *against* binary oppositions. Rorty would no doubt have agreed that it is not entirely clear that we would be capable of any thought at all without these conceptual couples.[33]

Instead, Rorty's group of thinkers is engaged in the project of refiguring Heidegger's inflexible "circumscribing" by "shaking off the influences of the peculiarly metaphysical dualisms" and substituting a version in which the relationships between polarities are, in Rorty's words, *"a picture of a flux of continually changing relations."*[34]

Although this sentence is taken out of context, it dovetails nicely with both Heidegger's and Merleau-Ponty's thinking, and it bears looking more closely at what Rorty is saying and precisely how he went about saying it.

It is curious that he chose the word *flux* to stand for the relationships between traditionally antithetical poles. Flux is generally thought to mean "constant change," which would suggest, in Rorty's sentence, a somewhat absurd redundancy. *A picture of a constant change of constantly changing relations.* Perhaps this is in fact what he intended. Perhaps he wanted to deliberately overemphasize the fluxi-ness of the flux. Or perhaps he just liked the sound of the word *flux*. There are just so many ways to make this fluidity visible.

But *flux* has several other meanings: something added to ore to form slag, a material added to ceramic glazes to increase their flow, or in physics, the amount/rate at which water or energy flows. There is one meaning of the word, though, in which resides a vivid picture of a relationship that acknowledges alterity but erases the impregnable barrier between opposites. Flux is a material that is used in jewelry making and welding to promote the fusion of two substances or surfaces. When you solder together the two ends of a band of silver in order to make a ring, you apply flux to the joint. The work of flux is as a catalyst that eases the joining, eases the melding of differences, the movement from one side to the other and back again.

This "fluxual" metaphor infuses *Avatar*, and multiple layers of meaning emerge. Of particular salience is the shift from the black/white, on/off paradigm that permeates Western culture, to what Heidegger has given as Aletheic, a perceptual mode that oscillates and isn't locked into rigid conceptual cells. For some, this has been problematic. Critic Daniel Mendelsohn found what he perceives as Cameron's inconsistency more troubling than the clichéd portrayal of an indigenous people.

> The problem here is not a patronizingly clichéd representation of an ostensibly primitive people; the problem is the movie's intellectually incoherent portrayal of its fictional heroes as both admirably precivilized and admirably hypercivilized, as atechnological and highly technologized. *Avatar*'s desire to have its anthropological cake and eat it too suggests something deeply unself-aware and disturbingly unresolved within Cameron himself.[35]

Mendelsohn's observation lucidly demonstrates the difficulty many have with a fluxual, circumspect approach. He wants to know, are the Na'vi pre- or hyper-civilized? Are they atechnological or highly technological? Clearly it is easier to interpret this as "incoherence" on Cameron's part, rather than as a deliberate portrayal of an oscillation, in which polar opposites comfortably co-exist in a shared space. Mendelsohn finds the fact that Cameron wasn't decisively clear on these points further evidence of something deeply disturbing, instead of granting that perhaps Cameron, like Rorty above, intended to have the Na'vi embody these apparently paradoxical qualities to disrupt our everyday, habitual approach to his film and to our perceptual apparatus in general.

The colonel and his minions can be said to signify this circumscribed approach, as well as the imperialistic, entitled tendencies that are reminiscent of the ways in which Western civilizations generally have reacted to the indigenous peoples that they have encountered. We might recognize, here, the blind pursuit of our own *unobtaniums* and the ways in which our ancestors forged ahead without care for the consequences of their actions to native peoples or to their environs. As Cameron noted in an interview with NPR's Terry Gross, "(Our) sense of entitlement is what causes us to bulldoze a forest and *not blink an eye*."[36]

The colonel in *Avatar* commands his own bulldozers and initiates a full-scale attack on the Na'vi. Coincidentally it is within the Pandoran "flux vortex" that his fleets' technological supremacy is upended. When the bombers fly into this mystical airspace, their instruments no longer work. In the flux vortex, it is VFR — visual flight rules. Having become dependent on screens and dials, beeps and blips, when they enter Pandoran air space they fly blind. The changeable, movable, ethereal energy of the vortex — the spiral representing yet another figure of unending, continuous movement — scrambles the signals received by the military's instruments, providing the Na'vi with an advantage.

Trudy, a sympathetic pilot who flies all the "science sorties," transports the trailers containing the linkup pods to an area near the Tree of Souls, a luminescent willow through which the Na'vi can connect to their ancestors and to the goddess Eywa. Around its dangling branches, the *vortex* intensifies, sensors are stymied, and tracking functions fail. The "flux vortex" thus comes to symbolize the undoing of a rigid perspective that has been mapped to imperialist, power-over tendencies, fluxing concretized conceptual structures by removing the screens from between us and what we gaze upon.[37]

Jake and the Colonel

In the textual relationship between Jake and the colonel we can locate the antithetical approaches of Heidegger's circumscription and circumspection as well as the tension between these articulated modes of seeing.

In the first scene in which we find Jake and Colonel Quaritch together, marine to marine, we are aware of the colonel's regulation black leather and high-top boots, as described above. When the colonel stops his pacing and turns to face Jake, their difference is exaggerated by the way this scene is shot. The colonel stands strong, legs astride, arms akimbo. Sully looks up at him from his wheelchair, and the camera tilts up mirroring his "lower-than-thou" point of view. His lifeless legs hang limply in place.

In their second encounter this discrepancy is even more pronounced. Quaritch is pumping iron when Jake rolls up to him, responding to the colonel's summons.

At first they sit eye to eye, the camera located just behind Jake's shoulder. We see his flaccid legs juxtaposed to the colonel's camouflage-clad muscular thighs that straddle the workout bench. The colonel lets his gaze travel down to Jake's useless limbs resting in the chair, and then he looks into Jake's eyes and observes, "You've got some heart, kid." It is here that Quaritch is his most empathic, most human, here that we are forced to let go of our black-and-white, good guy/bad guy paradigm and see that even within this macho, Na'vi-hating character, there is some small nuance that resists the spectator's tendency toward circumscription.

Leaving Jake to follow behind him in his wheelchair, the colonel saunters over to his enormous AMP suit, climbs up and in. Jake manually rolls his chair along behind him, and the colonel reverts to what is comfortable and predictable, bad-mouthing the avatar program. The colonel drones on from his seat in the AMP suit, towering above the floor of the facility, and Jake is invited to move his chair onto a hydraulic lift that stops just short of matching the height of the colonel's seat in the cab of the AMP. The comparison between the colonel's strength and agility as he clambers up the outside of the metallic warrior and Jake's limitations on the lift are stark. Despite the aid of the mechanical lift, Jake still looks up at the colonel. The camera zooms out, and we see Jake small and vulnerable in his low-tech wheelchair, the colonel strapped into his metal behemoth. The colonel's instructions to Jake are to infiltrate and ultimately gain the trust of the Na'vi from the inside, convince them to move their home. Even with his constrained view of the Na'vi as savages, the colonel is wise enough to understand the value of implanting Jake in their midst. Yet it is outside of the bounds of his circumscribed expectations that Jake might experience something through his avatar that would forever change him.

When Jake eagerly agrees to work for Quaritch, the colonel fires up his AMP suit and flexes his armored, mechanical muscles. As the AMP moves forward it fills the entire screen, dwarfing Jake in his wheelchair and forcing him to duck his head in order to avoid being struck by the mechanical man's air punches. The colonel pauses just long enough to make Jake an offer he can't refuse. If he cooperates with Quaritch, Jake is promised a pair of legs, "real legs," the implication being that the avatar's legs that have been carrying him on Pandora are something less. As Jake watches from the hydraulic lift, the colonel slaps down the windshield of his AMP, signaling his separation from all that surrounds him, and within the safety of his metallic shell he lumbers off.

By the time Jake and the colonel next come together, Jake has begun his apprenticeship. Jake confers with the colonel and Selfridge in the control center, updating them with his "covert report." Although still seated in his wheelchair, we notice that the discrepancy between Jake's size and that of the colonel and Selfridge is now minimized. Sitting in close proximity to the camera, Jake appears larger, as the colonel and Selfridge recede into the picture plane. He has grown in their esteem and he has gained some power. The three share an optimism that Jake will succeed in moving the Na'vi away from their Home Tree. The enormous tabletop three-dimensional simulation of Home Tree is projected in this scene in such a way that Jake's body serves as its screen. The enormous tree and its surroundings are projected onto Jake's arms and shoulders, a visual suggestion of his beginning immersion into their world.

When Jake meets again with the colonel, after his three-month initiation into the world of the Omaticaya, Quaritch is suspicious and asks him if he might not have gotten lost in the woods. They meet in what appears to be the empty mess hall, rife with metallic gray tables and a steely blue cast to the room. The colonel straddles his chair and they are for the first time face to face, eye level to eye level, as equals. Colonel Quaritch gives Jake the news that he can be on a flight out that very evening on his way to getting his legs. But Jake is neither ready nor willing to go. Jake half believes that if he goes through with the planned initiation that the Na'vi will accept him and he will be able to negotiate the terms of their relocation. There is also the unspoken bond with Neytiri, which Jake is loath to reveal to the colonel. Quaritch is no fool and mistrusts Jake's motives. He abruptly stands, rupturing their equal "footing," once more putting Jake beneath him as he turns and strides away.

In the intervening scenes between this one and the final encounter between Jake and the colonel, their activities and significations are mapped out once removed through video surveillance and parallel battle preparations. The first of these video interactions occurs after Selfridge, ignoring the inroads Jake has made toward gaining the trust of the Na'vi, has ordered the bulldozers to raze Home Tree. Following his elaborate initiation ceremony, Jake and Neytiri consummate their relationship and fall asleep together in the forest. The bulldozers move forward, startling Neytiri, who tries desperately to wake Jake. She shakes his lifeless avatar shell to no avail, and as the dozers close in, she drags it out of harm's way. Back at the camp in his "real" body, Jake is wolfing down some scrambled eggs at Grace's insistence. When he finally links back in, the bulldozers are upon them.

Enraged, Jake gestures wildly for the dozers to stop. The remote driver—yet another example of the controller once removed—piloting the bulldozer from the safety of the base camp, informs Selfridge that a native is blocking the blade of the bulldozer. Unfazed and more interested in the snack upon which he is munching than the life of a Na'vi, Selfridge orders the driver to keep going. He assists the hesitant bulldozer driver by pushing forward the remote throttle himself. When the dozer starts up again, Jake leaps up on top of it and smashes the reconnaissance cameras with a stone. The dozer driver stops, reporting to Selfridge that he is now *blind*.

As the camera is shooting from the dozer driver's perspective, we are granted a succession of screens, insets and readouts, guiding the demolition. When Jake destroys the video feed, the efficacy of that dozer is terminated. When the technology fails, there is no driver present in the bulldozer, no backup option. We are made aware of the distance afforded in this situation, of the lack of connection between the remote bulldozer pilot and the damage he inflicts. There is no one present to the destruction as it actually occurs. It all is about as real and as present to the drivers as killing in a video game. The reference doesn't escape us. But before Jake can disable all the cameras on all the dozers, soldiers accompanying the bulldozers begin to pepper him with machine-gun spray, and he is forced to grab Neytiri and run.

Cameron then cuts to a scene in which we find the colonel reviewing the surveillance videos. He recognizes that it is Jake who has disabled the cameras. In the commands that Quaritch barks to the technician — "Freeze it right there; scale up; enhance"[38] — the language of visual technologies has now become a language of battle.

A fleet of armed military vehicles hovers at the base of Home Tree, awaiting Quaritch's orders to proceed. The colonel in the lead chopper zooms in on the Omaticaya below with his video surveillance camera, finds the avatars of Jake and Grace, bound and held at knifepoint, and surmises that diplomacy has failed. When the base of Home Tree is fire bombed and the Na'vi flee in retreat, the colonel sits back in his chopper with satisfaction. To the colonel, from the remove of the air and the reduction of the video screen, these living, breathing, caring beings are nothing more than the equivalent of insects. It does not take a giant leap to connect Cameron's less-than-subtle references to the effects of *technology* on the wars carried out in Iraq and Afghanistan, to the unpiloted drones that are guided from afar as they drop their missiles. Even some of Cameron's dialog, particularly lines like "We'll fight terror with terror," or "It's some kind of shock-and-awe campaign,"[39] seem as if they could have been cribbed directly from George W. Bush's press conferences. And there is no question that Cameron is directing the spectators' attention toward the dangers of this kind of removed and reifying vision.

As the spreading fires cause the Na'vi to disperse and retreat, the columns that support Home Tree come crashing down. Cameron cuts from the wailing Na'vi, keening among the falling fiery embers, to Selfridge and his sobered group of employees monitoring the inferno in a panoramic 360-degree display and surround sound. Saddened and stunned, albeit removed, at least the workers are reacting humanely with compassion. Cameron then cuts to a smug and satisfied colonel against a backdrop of the ravaged fallen tree enveloped in flames. Encased in his metal transport, the colonel is untouched. In scenes like this it is not too much of a leap to read Cameron's anti-war sentiment — and paradoxically his love of warlike pyrotechnics — as well as his spot-on representation of the extent to which if we intend to perpetrate such atrocities, we must find a way to inure ourselves to the ramifications of these acts.

In these last two encounters Jake is "caught" on video, the colonel responding to the surveillance. But now the antagonism between Jake and the colonel has escalated.

What follows might be identified as *parallel syntagma*, in which we are shown alternating montages of the war preparation of each side. The scenes in which Jake and Neytiri ride out on the giant Toruk, meet with clan leaders, and invite them to join the fray are shot in brilliant firelight, hot orange against the deep rich blue of the Na'vi, enhanced by the swelling choral music of the soundtrack.

In contrast, when Cameron cuts to the colonel preparing his troops for the incursion, the music abruptly stops, and all the color is washed out of the image. The colonel shuts the slatted blinds in the mess hall, blotting out any natural light in order to enhance the projections of his tactical slides. On a screen in the front of the room we see a map of the area lit up with hot spots, signifying the "aboriginal horde massing for an attack." We don't see living beings. We see quantified, circumscribed, orbital images, a heat-sensitive representation, adding to the dehumanization and the objectification of the Na'vi. They become just so many swarming dots on a map.

As the battle lines are drawn and the military mercenaries line up against the Na'vi, both the troops in their AMP suits on the ground and the scorpion copters in the sky are relying on their instrument panels to detect the heat signatures of the approaching Na'vi. But the flux vortex distorts their readings. The action speeds up, becoming more intense and much like the finale in Fourth of July fireworks — the kitchen sink is thrown in. Cuts come faster, there is more smoke, louder, more frequent violent explosions. When Trudy's damaged scorpion copter loses altitude, she falls to a fiery death. Neytiri's ikran is shot and killed by a pursuing scorpion. Norm is shot and barely escapes to his linkup pod in the base camp. Tsu'tey dies heroically in battle. Just when it looks as if all is lost, the cavalry, stretching credulity, arrives in the form of Pandora's wild beasts, and it seems as if Jake's prayers for help from the goddess Eywa have been heard and answered.

It is at this point that Jake and the colonel meet one last time, AMP to avatar.

Before Jake arrives, the colonel finds himself outside of the trailer housing Jake's linkup pod and sees an opportunity to destroy the apparatus symbolic of the whole avatar program and kill Jake in the process. But just in the nick of time Neytiri rides in on the back of a ferocious Thanator and interrupts the colonel. What is fascinating is that with all the incredibly high-tech screens and sensors and mind boggling 3-D imaging that we have seen throughout the film, in this one scene the colonel becomes aware of Neytiri's approach from behind in what appears to be a simple rearview mirror attached to the windshield of his AMP suit! (Even today's SUVs have video imaging capability when in reverse, so one wonders if this was an oversight, a lack of imagination, or a deliberate reverse anachronism. A visual representation of Quaritch's backward thinking, perhaps?) Quaritch turns and relatively quickly kills the beast. As it falls to its death it pins Neytiri beneath it immobilizing her. Happily, Jake arrives — yes, also just in the nick of time — to lure the colonel away from finishing off Neytiri.

In this last dance between Jake, the driver of the avatar, and Colonel Quaritch, the driver of the AMP, we are aware of the clank of metal versus the silence of skin, the grace and agility of Jake's avatar versus the clumsiness of the metal man. Jake uses his environment like a true martial artist, while the colonel just smashes everything in his wake. When Jake punctures a hole in the AMP windshield, poisonous Pandoran air seeps in. Quaritch abruptly turns away from Jake and again makes his way to the trailer, this time succeeding in flooding it with toxic air. Jake's consciousness flickers back to his human body encased in his linkup pod. He gasps for air and then forces himself to return to his avatar. Weakened, Jake is no match for the colonel. Quaritch easily lifts him up and dangles him by his braid. It is particularly telling here that we see the colonel's real hand making the empty gesture of grabbing at the air, in order to move the mechanical AMP arm that actually holds Jake within its grasp. Here again is this doubling of which Cameron is so fond. What is real here, what is simulated? Is the colonel driving the AMP suit any less or more of a simulation than Jake in his avatar? His real hand is empty, it grasps at nothing. He gestures, his closed, empty fist moving toward him, pointing to the emptiness of his power. But in spite of this lack, he succeeds in stopping Jake cold. Still, the contrast is stark. Jake in his avatar seems infinitely more human, more animal, more organic, than the dehumanizing hunk of metal in which Quaritch is sheathed. As the colonel is about to slit Jake's throat, Neytiri frees herself from under the carcass of the beast and shoots Quaritch with two of her enormous poisoned arrows. Quaritch's AMP suit crashes to the ground with him in it.

Neytiri leaps into the trailer, scoops up Jake's lifeless body and just as we believe he has breathed his last, she places the oxygen mask on his face. With a Pieta-like embrace, Neytiri cradles Jake, tiny in her arms. Larger than (human) life, she is protector/mother/lover all at once. They reach for each other's faces and say "I see you" to each other. This reiteration of the Omaticaya greeting has extra power here, as Neytiri *sees* Jake — his real human form — for the very first time, but acknowledges something beyond his frail skin and bones.

In spite of the romantic, expected happy ending, the spectator can read deeper questions of essentialism: what are we *really*— our bodies, our souls, our minds or some combination thereof? And can we, do we, look past the containers in which we come?

The Eyes Have It

While with an eye made quiet by the power
Of harmony, and the deep power of joy,
We see into the life of things.
—William Wordsworth, from the poem "Tintern Abbey"

The eye motif infuses *Avatar* as well as serving to bracket the film. Cameron deliberately employs it, but to what end is not entirely clear. Whether or not he intended to develop an alternative to the dominant visual paradigm, it is clear that dialogically and visually he is pointing to the ways that we do or don't see: ourselves, one another, our worlds, our natural resources. Cameron underscores this effort by asserting that *Avatar* doesn't look like anything that we have ever seen before.[40] The particular significations of images of the eye that are dispersed throughout the film are reflected here.

While the actual opening scene is a dreamscape that Jake Sully flies through while recuperating in the VA hospital from the wound that paralyzed him, the scene functions more like a prologue. Fade to black as Sully's voice-over intones, "Sooner or later, though, you always have to wake up." A quick cut, in the theatrical release, brings us to a close-up of a human eye, blinking open. We are in tight enough to see creases in the skin around the eye, tight enough to watch the eyeball circle its environs, as we imagine the mind, still dull from what we soon learn is a six-year cryo-sleep, is trying to grasp where it is and what it is doing there. This scene inside the cryo-pod in which Jake has been traveling is shot monochromatically in a rich blue, foreshadowing what is to come, and a perfect color match to the final scene in *Avatar*. After the "aliens" are sent home and the "time of sorrow" on Pandora has ended, Jake decides to attempt to transfer his consciousness into the body of his avatar so that he can remain on Pandora and build a life with Neytiri. A similar ceremony was performed earlier in the film when Grace becomes mortally wounded, but she is too weak to survive the transfer. Jake's mind/soul/consciousness moves through Eywa and enters the body of the avatar. Cameron visually represents this transfer with a psychedelic computer graphic—a wormhole effect—that is identical to that of the linkup each time Jake inhabited his avatar.

It will be obvious to the viewer that the eyes of the Na'vi are particularly brilliant. Wide and luminous, they sit proportionately large in the Omaticaya face. Children, puppies and kittens, have eyes that dominate their faces. It is no coincidence that we react similarly to the Na'vi eye, the cornerstone of the collateral advertising material for the film, gracing posters and the cover of the DVD sleeve. But it is also true that one of the most powerful moments in the film's end is when, during the transfer of Jake's consciousness into that of his avatar, Neytiri leans down to kiss his small, less than brilliant human eyes, one at a time, before moving over to his avatar's body to await his arrival there. This gesture of acknowledgment, of seeing through the facade of the avatar, embodies the underlying meaning of the Na'vi "I see you." Jake will no longer see with his limited human eyes.

It is no coincidence that the image of the eye — literal, significant, metaphorical — has come to stand for the film. As we take in the eye — ancient, powerful, pregnant with associations and a long history predating this filmic context — we can't help but consider that the eye *in* film also signifies the eye *of* film.

The final scene of the film bookends the opening shot of Jake's eyes. The camera is zoomed in on the face of Jake's avatar, eyes closed, and the hint of Neytiri's palm cupping his cheek. Jake's avatar eyes, unlike his small human eyes that open at the film's start, are yellow, feline, luminous. They flash open, glittering with a hint of expectancy — the happy possibility of a sequel? — and before we can even take in the look that beholds us, a quick cut to black ends the film.

Chapter Two

Thinking Technology: Technology in the Art

Throughout history technology has alternately been perceived as demon or as savior, as racing ahead of its own volition like a small child on a steep hill who can't keep her feet underneath her or as something to be resisted at all cost. Technological prowess was famously embodied in ancient myth by the characters of Daedalus and Icarus, who exemplify the myriad qualities associated with technology's far-reaching impact: in the creations of Daedalus his artisanship is paramount. In the success of his flight lie the pursuit of freedom and the expansion of boundaries. In Icarus' fall, the dangers of soaring come to light — actually and metaphorically — and so, too, the ruin associated with the hubris that frequently accompanies invention.

Technology — part science, part art — has often been perceived as a threat to the powers that be and at times has proven to have the capacity to alter the way in which we conceive of our universe, as evidenced by Galileo's discoveries and his support of Copernican theories. Derived from the Greek *techne*, technology originally concerned itself with art, skill or craft. It was not until the 19th century that its connotation was imbued with the scientific or mechanical emphasis of modernity.

In the broadest sense, technology has included the mundane — the pencil, the can opener, Velcro — and the fantastical: artificial limbs and organs, data streaming invisibly through the ether, walking on the moon. In the 20th century we witnessed a shift toward what was initially called "high technology,"[1] or high tech. This concept, which moved toward that which was on the cutting edge, is obviously not a static locus — it slips and slides in whatever direction technology is exploding. At one moment it might be atomic energy, at another, artificial intelligence. On the coattails of whichever of the high techs we choose ride the benefits and risks of their development. Atomic energy, on the one hand, presents the possibility of cheap, clean energy weighed against nuclear holocausts and the destruction of the planet on the other. AI presents the opportunity for advancements in almost any arena imaginable — health care, warfare, entertainment, education — and carries with it the scary prospect of displacing an entire human workforce, as well as the possible development of sentience and rebellion, an idea that has been fodder for many a sci-fi scenario, *2001: A Space Odyssey*, *The Matrix*, *I, Robot*, or *Battlestar Galactica*, to name just a few.

Today it is almost unthinkable to run a business, a law office, a university, or a hospital without an entire "technology department" which has almost exclusive responsibility for issues related to the 24/7 use of our personal and business technology: desktops, laptops, handhelds, smartphones, networks, databases, servers, and so forth.

Some tend to bemoan the ubiquitousness of these devices, while others thrill to their touch. We rue the fact that our younger people — and many not so young people — are perpetually plugged in. We worry that brains will no longer function, that they are no longer capable of sustained, deep thinking, and we express our concern that they have lost some of the primary capacities associated with basic literacy. Can our children born in the latter portion of the 20th century and early 21st do computations or understand mathematics without a calculator? Can they write in complete sentences when they have become accustomed to shorthanding their personal communiqués while texting? Can they read difficult, complex texts and comprehend them when they have become acclimated to abridged and simplified, reductive versions of the classics made for YouTube? Can they read at all? Sven Birkets, author of *The Gutenberg Elegies*, worries that we are "most willing to accept a life hurried and fragmented on every front by technology."[2] A case in point is Vishal Singh, a 17-year-old from Redwood City, California, recently spotlighted in a *New York Times* article about growing up digital. It seemed that Vishal was only able to get through the first 43 pages of his summer reading assignment, Kurt Vonnegut's *Cat's Cradle*. He was incapable of applying himself to the sustained task of reading the relatively short novel, but he had no trouble shooting, editing and uploading several videos to YouTube that same summer.[3]

These worries that we — parents, educators, concerned citizens — sustain are not all that different in kind or degree from concerns that emerged with the arrival of the first automobile, the first radio program, the first television, the first moving pictures. During the Renaissance, skepticism greeted several mechanical devices designed to assist the artist in mastering the "science of perspective." In his book *The Science of Art*, Martin Kemp points to the thinking that these "perspective machines" yielded nothing but "mechanical artlessness."[4]

Artist Drawing a Nude in Perspective by **Albrecht Dürer (1471–1528). Dürer was able to represent the practices that were compelling to artists in the 16th century and at the same time embed his thinking on these practices as commentary in his etching. Woodcut from "Unterwysung der Messung" [Treatment in Perspective], Nuremberg, 1527 (Foto Marburg/Art Resource, NY).**

Beginning with a look at our ambivalence toward technology, this chapter opens up the role of technology in narrative. Martin Heidegger's thinking about what remains problematic in modernity's approach to technology serves as a lens through which we see the part technology plays in the narrative of *Avatar*. Additionally, Cameron's technological inventions and priorities in the making of *Avatar* mirror his diegetic transformation of the relationship between technology and nature. It becomes apparent that technology is not only the happy subject around which a narrative may dance, but it is also instrumental in supporting the creation of the art in which its story is being choreographed. *Avatar* is a film that rethinks technology, and the technology specifically employed in the making of *Avatar* buttresses the ways in which Cameron presents these possibilities.

The Question Concerning Technology

In order to appreciate the ways in which technology is disclosed in Cameron's film, it is necessary to unpack what, precisely, we mean by *technology*. Martin Heidegger gives an Aletheic definition of technology that is made visible in and by *Avatar*. Following Heidegger along his thinking paths is not for the faint of heart, but zooming in on the way that he "thinks technology" will be useful in grounding the figure of technology that emerges in the story of *Avatar*.

Heidegger takes on the task of interrogating technology, at least in part, so that he may have the privilege of seeing it disclose itself. In the process of seeking the "essence of technology," in his essay "The Question Concerning Technology," Heidegger offers the following definitions: "Technology is a means to an end. Technology is a human activity."[5] And then he declares his definition to be "correct." The astute reader, however, suspects that "correct" is not all that it is cracked up to be. This definition may be instrumental and anthropological and therefore *correct*.[6] But Heidegger is not nearly content with a correct or a *circumscribed* definition of anything. This is simply the springboard from which he jumps out into "thinking technology."

The rigor of his questioning of technology is camouflaged by Heidegger's use of language. When hearing words like revealing, unconcealing, *poiesis*, and *Aletheia*, the reader is hard pressed to connect them to our modern-day, circumscribed understanding of technology. But that is precisely what Heidegger does. His deliberately unusual application of language is intentional. When he tells us, "Technology is ... no mere means. Technology is a way of revealing,"[7] it is so unexpected that it brings the reader up short and forces him to drop his expectations, to let go of already knowing and pay attention in perhaps a deeper and more thoughtful way. Language can assist us in a process of circumscription, a process of encapsulating our experience. But it can also aid us in approaching an attitude of circumspection and Heidegger uses it to just that end.

Heidegger characterizes the definition of technology "as a means and as a human activity" *as* being instrumental, *as* a definition which circumscribes and "fixes" the meaning but won't lead to the essence of technology. To understand instrumentality it is necessary to understand the philosophical causes of a means. The ends act in such a way as to shape or cause or bring into being the means. Heidegger offers the low-tech example of the silversmith fashioning a chalice so that his reader might see instrumentality reveal itself.

There are four causes which together share responsibility for bringing something about. In the case of the chalice, the first cause, the actual matter, is the silver out of which the chalice is crafted. The second cause is the chalice itself, the "form," into which the silver is poured. Thirdly, we have the circumscribed idea of a chalice as a "sacrificial vessel." It is this circumscribing that shapes or "gives bounds to the thing."[8]

The "fourth participant" in bringing the chalice into existence is the silversmith. But here Heidegger cautions us. The silversmith is not a cause of the chalice coming to be. But by considering and gathering the other three causes — the silver, its form, and its function — the silversmith gathers what is necessary, what "becomes responsible" for the "chalice lying ready before us, a sacred vessel."[9] The essence of these four causes together being responsible for the Being of the silver chalice is that by "being responsible" they have started the incipient chalice on its way. The figure of the chalice begins emerging against a ground of silver, a cuplike shape, a ritual in which the chalice serves a sacred function, and an artisan who works with precious metals.

Figure/Ground

In order to more fully understand this *Aletheic* notion of truth on which Heidegger relies, one in which perpetual movement is key, it is necessary to look at the notion of figure/ground. A concept with which visual artists frequently grapple, figure/ground assists us in organizing our visual world. We are trained early on, particularly those of us for whom the two-dimensional picture plane is paramount, to consider not just the figure but also the ground, commonly referred to as the "background." Novice aspiring artists are often guilty of placing their renderings of a vase, a nude figure, a copse of trees, plop! in the middle of the paper so that the figure often appears to float disembodied in an invisible ether. Any teacher worth her salt will insist early on that her students deal with the entire page; she will point out that the so-called "negative space" is as, if not more, important than the figure we are attempting to represent. In nonobjective art, it is a no-brainer. The entire canvas is one's field.

Seeing figure/ground as a pulsing, shifting field, as an example of coming to presence, serves as a useful paradigm for *Aletheia* and the kind of visioning Heidegger suggested we employ.

Consider the moment when we dive into a pond on a hot summer afternoon. What follows is an explosion of sensory input. Cold! Wet! Silky! Fresh! Choosing to express that experience by saying, "Brrr ... the water is *sooo* cold!" the water's silkiness, its freshness, the warmth of the sun, are all erased by their omission. Cold becomes a figure against a ground of wet, silky, fresh. If a fish flits against a thigh and startles, if a toe touches the scummy pond bottom, all of this is left out of the initial ejaculation. It becomes the ground out of which *cold* emerges. Eventually each one of the observations might be uttered, yet here in clauses, one after the other, each impression or thought becoming a solitary, closed bit.

In *Being and Time*, Heidegger talks about "being-in-the-world," a compound expression, which he maintains stands for a "unified phenomenon." In reality, like diving into the pond, "being-in-the-world" can't be broken up into bits. But in talking about it, it is necessary to do just that. "This primary datum must be seen as a whole. But while being-in-the-world cannot be broken up into components that may be pieced together, this does not prevent it from having several constitutive structural factors."[10]

It helps, then, in our quest for understanding, to break things up into their constituent parts. It helps us to *see* it in pieces, in blacks *and* whites. And because language is linear, we are trained to follow one thought after the next. In language we can't articulate the "all at once" that is figure *and* ground. We recognize the pieces. And we carry these pieces around with us as thoughts, as "pictures." When necessary they are recalled, and in the repetition of their retrieval they become calcified, standing in for what once was an all-of-a-piece experience.

One way of "patterning experience" is to try to fit it into already existing mental pictures. This way of thinking relies on circumscription, the arbitrary outline within which we categorize.[11] Like the Venn diagrams suffered while learning set theory in math class, each category becomes an enclosure.[12] For example, a tomato might be found in the intersection of a *red* circle, a *fruit* circle, a *grows-on-vine* circle, a *juicy* circle, an *acidic* circle and so forth.

These enclosed categories suggest the objectifying tendencies of our time. Heidegger saw this process of "enframing" (*Gestell*) as inhibiting our field of vision. "'Enframing blocks [verstellt] the shining-forth and holding sway of

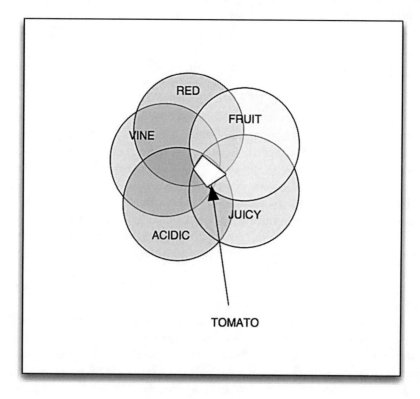

Venn diagram of a tomato.

truth' [i.e., the moment or event, of Aletheic unconcealment by grace of which there is a visual field]."[13]

Comparing the experience of the Venn diagram with the image of *Dana Tomatoes*, a viewer might find that the image transcends the circumscription of the diagram and sidesteps the ways in which *labeling reduces experience.*

In Marshall McLuhan's paradigm of the evolution from Tribal Man to Gutenberg Man, he understood the fragmentation of the enframing process in a somewhat similar way. McLuhan's rather romantic understanding of primitive cultures included the picture of nonliterate peoples as somehow enjoying a much richer experience. Before phonetic language, McLuhan believed, primitive peoples were tuned into a collective consciousness, in a "magical integral world patterned by myth and ritual, its values divine and unchallenged."[14] In creating the Na'vi, Cameron has torn a page straight out of McLuhan.

McLuhan argued that with the advent of phonetic alphabets, people became fragmented, "individualistic, ... detached."[15] He saw the advent of literacy as undoing the connectivity of the tribal web; although it facilitated abstract thinking, in much the same way that circumscribing aids us episte-

***Dana Tomatoes* by Ellen Grabiner.**

mologically, McLuhan bemoaned the lack of a sense of belonging to one's social milieu. In incising sight from sound McLuhan saw people as losing their imaginations, their access to their emotions, and to their sensory experience.[16] When the phonetic alphabet appeared and was dispersed it enabled primitive peoples to categorize and classify, in much the same way as was possible with the Venn diagram above. But these abilities, McLuhan asserts, were gained at the expense of the ways in which tribal cultures enjoyed a full and embodied sensory experience.

Whether we label it objectification, enframing, fragmentation, or circumscription, this approach expands what it is that we think we know, but it doesn't bring us closer to an understanding of an essence, doesn't bring us closer to truth. Heidegger therefore suggests that a more appropriate model is one that is *Aletheic*, a model in which "concepts are not enclosures but perspectives which bring something into being or into the open, which make something stand out against a background."[17]

Standing out against a background returns us to the idea of figure/ground. Heidegger describes the ground as a sort of openness without which we can't really "see" the figure. It is only because there is a windowsill on which the tomatoes rest, glass windowpanes in front of which they sit, that we are able to make out the figures of the tomatoes in the image above.

Technology as Poetry

To the question of what is the *essence* of the four causes of the silver chalice together Heidegger answers that it is "to occasion ... to let what is not yet present arrive into presencing ... a bringing that brings what presences into appearance."[18] Again, Heidegger is not content to let this "occasioning" or "presencing" ultimately stand for technology. Plato tells us that this *bringing forth* is, in essence, *poiesis*. And this is just about as far from our modern understanding of technology as one could imagine. Is Heidegger equating technology with poiesis—the Greek word for "making," laden with connotations of creativity and from which our modern word *poetry* originates? Technology as poetry? Yes, but Heidegger doesn't leave it at that.

Bringing forth is a kind of making, but not simply making, not just the artist crafting her ware. *Physis*, what grows, changes and becomes, is also a form of poiesis — in fact, for Heidegger, the highest form. He offers, by way of example, the flower bursting into bloom as the essence of physis *as* poiesis. The flower erupts without anyone making it so; it brings itself forth into being. Heidegger contrasts this with the making of the chalice. Here the poiesis, the bringing forth, irrupts *in* the artist, not in the chalice or in what is brought forth. Again, Heidegger's thinking has taken an unexpected swerve as he pairs technology *with* nature, when all the while most of us would be tempted to see nature and technology as antithetical to one another.[19]

In seeking the essence of technology, Heidegger sees it first as a means, a means that is caused by its ends. These causes come together to occasion or bring forth, understood as poiesis *and* physis. But how does this bringing forth happen? Heidegger takes another surprising turn suggesting that "bringing forth brings out of concealment into unconcealment." The reader may recognize this as the definition of *Aletheia*, described earlier in this volume. *Aletheia*, understood as revealing, is also translated as *truth*, but not the kind of truth that is equated with correspondence, a matching of what we perceive out there with a representation of our making. Truth as correspondence maps nicely to what Heidegger repeatedly calls a "correct" definition, but not what he perceives as a true one. An *Aletheic* truth is a truth which moves freely as it presences or reveals itself. But what does technology have to do with revealing?[20]

According to Heidegger, technology is ultimately a way of revealing. To discover its essence, it is necessary to approach technology by allowing it to reveal itself to us. In other words, we think technology the way that Heidegger has demonstrated for us in his approach to uncovering its essence. If we are willing to do this, we might see technology open itself as the "realm of revealing, i.e., of truth."[21]

Heidegger's insistent method accepts no point in his wandering as a final destination, but instead is committed to walking his path, following it further and deeper, spiraling into the brambles, paying attention to every scratchy thorn in his way. He takes no shortcuts, and he doesn't walk on autopilot. He is alert to what presents itself, and the reader might be struck by how his method is performative. It illustrates in the way that he proceeds precisely what he is instructing us to do. He is *showing* what he is doing by doing it as he shows us. It is up to us to learn to see.

On this path we find reflections of the Na'vi approach to learning, to living, to seeing. Hopefully, through following in Heidegger's footsteps, we have a sense of how this kind of *Aletheic* seeing is not simply visual, but applies to our thinking and experiencing as well. The Na'vi greeting "I see you," or Jake's apprenticeship in which he learned to see in the ways of the Na'vi, are more all encompassing than simply a visual experience.

Technology Revealing Nature

As if to comfort his perplexed reader, Heidegger confirms that we have indeed come to a strange place when we think technology *as* truth, technology *as* revealing. Perhaps, he posits, it is easier to accept this way of thinking technology if we apply it to ancient technologies or the pre-modern, but what about modern technology? When trying to ascertain the difference between the "old" technology and the new, between mechanical and electric, between industry and information, we may have a sense or a feeling for a difference in quality, in speed, in immediacy. But it remains difficult to tease out specific criteria that make one substantially different in kind from the other. When we think windmill versus hydroelectric power plant, as Heidegger does, we may be struck again, by their differing qualities. Both are technologies. Both are a means of generating power by harnessing nature. Yet they *feel* different. The windmill, aside from being picturesque and perhaps even evoking a kind of romantic nostalgia, is easy to fathom. Its technology is comprehensible to even the least technical among us. The hydroelectric plant less so, but possibly still within our grasp. When we consider Wi-Fi technology, for most of us, it may as well be magic. That information can be stored as numbers is difficult to grasp in the first place. Bits and bytes of data traveling through the air without wires to be converted into more bits and bytes when they reach their destination — it feels as if these things are of a significantly different order.

Heidegger addresses this difference in feel and quality by looking at the "revealing that holds sway" in modern technology.[22] He supports our sense of this difference by acknowledging that the *revealing* that we may find in modern technology does have a quality unlike that of poiesis. Instead of bringing forth in the way that nature brings forth, it *challenges* nature. It *demands* of nature. And here is where we run into trouble.

It is *the nature of what is revealed by modern technology that reveals our challenge to nature.* We make a demand of nature, and that demand changes the nature of nature. Nature appears differently to us when we harness, when we attempt to control. Heidegger offers the example of the farmer who tills and cultivates his field, who "takes care" of and maintains his crops. A taking care and its connection to *Umsicht*, a circumspect looking, was introduced in Chapter One in relation to Heidegger's hammer. The farmer who tills his field to feed his family sees the soil, the rain, the horse that pulls his plow, as the ground out of which his crop will emerge.

Juxtaposed to the solitary farmer, Heidegger holds up the mechanized food industry. The approach of today's industrialized farm factories is a "setting upon," an approach which moves away from technology as a means and arrives at technology *as an end in itself.* Where previously technology had been a way of effecting, of bringing forth, now it is about "driving on to the maximum yield at the minimum expense."[23] It is not much of a stretch to see in *Avatar* the pursuit of "unobtanium" as one such venture. Maximum yield here refers to extracting the largest possible ore deposit at minimum expense.

For the characters of Parker Selfridge and Colonel Quaritch and the RDA for whom they work, extracting the largest unobtanium deposit possible is a goal that obscures the enormous costs of their greed.

Whether Heidegger approaches a river, the chalice, or technology Alethe-ically, often what reveals itself is a bringing forth or an interconnectedness: the river, for example, can be seen as part of some larger ecosystem, supporting life, moving silt, smoothing stones, watering the vineyards that slope on the green hills of its shores, filling up with snowmelt from mountains and carrying it downriver to provide water for somebody's laundry, to offer up trout for someone's dinner, to turn a windmill to make power. Allowing the river to reveal itself, its interdependence is uncovered, a concept akin to the engaged Buddhism of Thich Nhat Hanh. Technology, too, can be seen in this Aletheic light, as a web or mesh, or perhaps, as Kevin Kelly, one of the founders of *Wired* magazine describes it, as an ecosystem or a super-organism.[24] Cameron makes this particularly visible in the biologically networked world of the Na'vi, examined more closely later on in this chapter.

Heidegger offers the Rhine as evidence of a movement from "bringing forth" to "setting upon." We may have once seen the river in the context of a landscape: bucolic and peaceful, an environment supporting fish and fowl, insect and plant life, a place in which to swim and alongside of which we might picnic. Heidegger then asks us to imagine the Rhine as the source of electricity: the mighty power of its waters harnessed to turn the turbines that create the current that the power station dispatches out across a network of cables. The Rhine now appears to be at our beck and call, providing for our energy needs. We don't *see* it any longer *as* simply river. Now dammed to increase its efficiency the river appears only as waterpower supplier.

At the ready, this revealing of technology is one that challenges. "Every-where everything is ordered to stand by, to be immediately on hand, ... so that it may be on call for a further ordering."[25] It is *people* who do this ordering which Heidegger refers to as *Gestell*, or enframing. And Heidegger, like McLuhan after him, thinks of the enframing, not the technology, as the supreme danger.

When technology reveals itself as enframing we tend to see the River Rhine, for example, not as a habitat for flora and fauna, but as something that provides a standing reserve for humanity. And when we are only able see the river enframed in that context, there is a tendency for us to exalt ourselves. And as such we lose sight of all that nature can be, seeing it exist only as a construct of humankind, something we regulate, command, and/or order. It is this ordering that covers over all other possible ways that technology or nature might reveal themselves and consequently pits them in the either/or relation that we have come to know all too well.

Technology Versus Nature

This black-and-white, either/or approach to technology doesn't serve us in either the short term or the long run. *Avatar* shows us this untenable oppositional approach in the guise of the forces of the RDA's military/industrial installation on Pandora. In the opening scenes of *Avatar* this conflict is laid bare in no uncertain terms with visual cues. We are first given the lush, green jungle of Jake Sully's VA hospital dreams, a premonition of what is to come. This scene in which he is soaring over a verdant landscape is immediately followed by one in which he is waking up encased in a coffinlike enclosure, emerging from his cryo-sleep. The cryogenic transport calls to mind a spiffed-up version of a scene from *The Matrix*, sterile silver pods as far as the eye can see. As the camera jumps to the outside of the spaceship that has ferried the cryo-pods and their inhabitants to Pandora, the spectator is clearly located in a future science-fiction scape in which technology figures prominently.

From the elegant cryo-ship, to the 3-D virtual instrument panel in the supersonic transport vehicle, to the mammoth excavation equipment on the surface of Pandora, there is no mistaking technology's role. It is a central figure to be reckoned with, spanning the arenas of travel, communications, war, surveillance, and the old school mechanical process of moving dirt from one place to another. The very fact that humans can function at all on Pandora is due to the technology of the "exo-packs" which filter the toxic Pandoran air.

The arrival scene on Pandora is set in steely gray; an industrial metallic sheen covers the tarmac, the AMP-suited soldier whose path Sully crosses in his wheelchair, the mechanical loaders, copters and ground vehicles in the background. We note, finally, in the brightly colored, iridescent arrows that have pierced the enormous tires of a company dump truck, something quite different, something alive, glowing, something that offers a counterpoint to all the monochromatic steel and iron, a visual hint adumbrating how the battle lines will be drawn as the film unfolds.

Where we begin to uncover the sort of enframing that results in Heidegger's standing reserve is in the scene where Grace Augustine is taking Parker Selfridge to task for simply substituting Jake for his trained and educated scientist of a twin brother.

The character of Grace herself embodies the fluxing of science and nature, and over the course of the narrative she moves from an "enframed" approach to an Aletheic one. Early on, Grace flat out rejects Jake because he is definitely not a scientist. She sees him as a jarhead flunky, useless to her scientific expedition because he hasn't been trained for this, because, in simplistic terms, he doesn't already know what he is up against. She rushes to berate Selfridge for what she perceives as a thoughtless choice, but he sets her straight. Holding up a small chunk of the sparkly unobtanium ore and waving it in Grace's face, Parker explains that they — the company, the expedition, the mercenaries — are only there to get their hot little hands on more of this "little rock." The unassuming chunk, about the size of Selfridge's palm, stands out against a ground of the eye-popping technology of his command center. All of these gadgets and screens and surveillance devices, colorful 3-D virtual replicas of the planet, demand, for the stockholders of Selfridge's company, this unassuming rock as a standing reserve. The discrepancy couldn't be more stark. A stone — a tangible, solid, "natural" piece of Pandora — on the one hand and the ethereal, virtual world of computer-driven imaging, replicating, discovering and destroying machines — "technology" at its finest — on the other.

But what Heidegger has made clear is that it isn't the excavation of the stone or the means of acquiring it that are dangerous. Nor is it the guns and the fighter copters and all the technology with which its excavation is made possible. "What is dangerous is not technology."[26] What is dangerous is the relationship that Selfridge has with that little rock. His enframing of the ore denies him a free relationship with the technology that enables him to excavate it, as well as with Grace, with Pandora, with the Na'vi, and ultimately with the world around him. He sees the technology — the big 3-D virtual model which reveals the mother lode of unobtanium situated beneath Home Tree, the mercenaries in their AMP suits, even the avatar project itself — as an instrument which will aid him in gaining control of the unobtanium, the scientific expedition, and the wealth he believes the company will amass when the valuable ore is sold. This enframed relationship with procuring the ore prevents him from seeing the essence of technology, from seeing the truth.

Heidegger's interrogation of technology continues beyond the simple dangers of enframing. But at the end of his essay — although we can imagine that his rigorous trek in pursuit of technology's essences may only be on pause — Heidegger suggests that because the *essence* of technology is not, in fact, something technological, it may be located in a realm "that is, on the one hand, akin to the essence of technology, and on the other, fundamentally different from it. Such a realm is art."[27]

It is within the realm of art that the nature of the essence of technology might be revealed.

Technology as a Narrative Foil

The figure of Cameron's *Avatar* emerges out of a ground of art that thinks technology. As Michel Foucault has suggested, it is not possible to see one's episteme clearly when still residing within it. It is only when we have moved forward in time that what was given to us to see in the past comes clearly into focus. McLuhan, too, reflected on the fact that a technological environment remains invisible when newly minted. It is only when a period of innovation has become old hat that it becomes clearly visible. He dubbed this the "rear-view-mirror" view of experience.[28] We know that when we stand too close to an image, our eyes blur and we lose the ability to see it clearly. Those of us of a certain age become practiced at extending our arms to their full reach in order to read menus in restaurants, ingredients on food labels. We require, in almost all cases, some amount of distance in which it becomes possible to see. The arts can function as our drugstore-variety reading glasses, bringing into focus that which we are too close to see.

Because reactions to technology have provoked debate over the centuries as to the extent of its dangers or its benefits, it has served the arts well as subject and as narrative foil. In this tension between what technology offers and what it takes away, we find the either/or reaction that Heidegger articulates and which ultimately prevents us from opening ourselves to a free relationship with technology. We are either carried away by the very force of technology or we resist it at all cost.[29] We label it good or bad, toxic or necessary to our survival, stultifying or enhancing. But no matter what we judge it to be, we are caught in an enframed relationship with it. And while this may prevent us from a more authentic way of being in the world, that very tension between these either/or approaches makes for good drama. This oppositional paradigm perpetuates a dualistic approach to technology that we may find at the heart of the genre of science fiction.[30] A comprehensive list of all the ways that technology has been represented either positively or negatively in the vast archive that is science fiction is beyond the scope of this chapter. But to flesh out Heidegger's observation of our either/or response to it, a brief, relatively random survey is in order.

There is no end of apocalyptic visions as technology is imagined and represented as running amok, giving credence to its intrinsic dangers and the wisdom of a stance of resistance. Technology is the muse that inspired a Frankenstein monster and all of his literary descendants. A fantasized technology brought us HAL, the recalcitrant and malevolent computer of *2001: A Space Odyssey*, *Star Trek*'s cybernetic Borg, *Blade Runner*'s Replicants, the rebellious Cylons from *Battlestar Galactica*, and the Terminators, to single out just a few examples. On the other hand, technology brought to life Jules Verne's fantasy of a world 20,000 leagues under the sea and carried us through time and into space in H.G. Wells' *The Time Machine* and in Dr. Who's Tardis. Technology has been the narrative pivot around which characters dance and philosophical, moral and ethical issues swirl. Fantasized technology has had the power to tempt many of us in a way that puts the Sirens to shame. As Heidegger has noted, "The approaching tide of technological revolution in the atomic age could so captivate, bewitch, dazzle and beguile man."[31] For many of us of a certain age, a *Star Trek* communicator was an object of lust, our fantasies realized with the onset of the flip phone. Have we not longed to step up to a replicator and, like Captain Picard, order, "Tea. Earl grey. Hot"?

If we look closely at science fiction and fantasy films and television series over the last several decades, we continue to see in the representations of technology a repetition of what was depicted in the ancient myth of Daedalus and Icarus: technology as a dual-edged sword offering hope and salvation or threatening our safety and liberty. And mirroring this split in representations we find those spectators who apparently take delight in technological innovations and those who are apt to give credence to the dangers that are portrayed.

Viewing audiences are enthralled with gadgets. Delightfully populating the spy genre, from serious to spoof, are the widgets of Bond, the shoe phone of Maxwell Smart. Those with more of a tolerance for the excesses of blood and bone have thrilled to the hospital drama, from the days of *Dr. Kildare* and *Ben Casey* when the plot was about the human drama of the kindly hospital doctor to those recently produced which reside in a swirl of biomedical technology like *ER*, *The Practice*, and *Gray's Anatomy*. Where decades ago television audiences were satisfied with a *Perry Mason* or *The Defenders*— good, solid courtroom dramas — there is now a passion for the forensic crime show. The heirs of the TV series *Quincy, M.E.*, a crime-fighting medical examiner, are *CSI* in Las Vegas, New York and Miami, *NCIS* in D.C. and L.A., and *Bones*.

In these popular high-tech whodunits, audiences are regaled with computer forensics, genome comparisons, mass spectrometers, as well as the surveillance technology that enables the unraveling of mysteries and, by proxy, the satisfying discovery and capture of the perpetrator. Even in the several series which rely more heavily on superior human sensitivity and intellect to catch the bad guys —*Criminal Minds*, *Numbers*, *The Mentalist*, and *Lie to Me*— the brilliance of the crime fighters is supported, extended and enhanced by computer networks providing immediate access to vast data banks or enhanced imaging technology that makes, for example in the show *Lie To Me*, the evaluation of micro-expressions possible. In these series we find technology as understood by McLuhan, as an extension of our human senses or our motor skills, similar to that found in the telescope, the microscope, in sound amplification, and so forth, if on a more sophisticated and complex level.

Within the popular *Star Trek* franchise spanning decades, technology was generally exalted. But in the cybernetic characters of Data and the Borg, we have representations of the ways in which technology can reveal nature, particularly the nature of humanity. Data, an android, is pure machine. Capable of lightning fast computations, his silver-toned skin, jerky motions, awkward speech and inability to understand humor endear him to audiences of the *Next Generation* series. In Data we have technology striving toward humanity and a poignant portrayal of longing. The Borg, on the other hand, grow out of a cybernetic hive mentality, moving toward an annihilation of individuality, to which "resistance is futile." In the Borg we have technology striving to destroy what inheres in humanity. Beloved Data and feared Borg — in these characterizations we find once more our knee-jerk responses to technology, our fears and our yearning, brought into high relief.

Shifting to the side of our equation where technology is ultimately represented as a threat to humanity, we find no dearth of examples of a future in which technology has brought ruination. *The Matrix*, *The Terminator* series, and Ronald Moore's *Battlestar Galactica*, for example, all graphically and dramatically present the dangers of technology taking a turn toward the despotic. These and countless other films situated in dystopian futures sit squarely in the lineage of Icarus, revealing the hubris of humankind and its dire consequences. Both *The Matrix* and *The Terminator* paint a picture of a post-apocalyptic future, the earth in flames and uninhabitable to humans, machines having rebelled and taken control, with a small, underground human resistance fighting away. *The Terminator* series will figure prominently in Chapter Seven, so here there is a look at the ways in which *The Matrix* thinks technology.

Like *Avatar*, *The Matrix* applied groundbreaking visual effects — Neo's uncanny ability to dodge bullets — in its inventive narrative treatment of technology. In a battle between humans and a race of machines loosely hinted at as emerging from the field of artificial intelligence, the humans "scorched the sky," believing this would destroy their mechanistic enemies, but it backfired. The machines didn't need nature to survive, but relied simply on the energy supplied by the humans, enslaved and imprisoned, horrifyingly becoming the battery power necessary for the machines to sustain themselves. The Matrix, then, in essence, is computer software programming that creates the illusion that these human battery cells are really living out their lives in a fleshed-out world. *The Matrix* blatantly trumpets the destruction of the world, and of life as we know it, as a result of technology.

Taking a page from Plato's "Allegory of the Cave," the Matrix is, in Morpheus' words, "the world that has been pulled over your eyes and blinded you to the truth." In the numerous references from *The Matrix* that map to Plato's parable, we find echoes of Heidegger as well, uncovering the ways the Matrix is the ultimate enframed perspective. When we are fooled by what we see, whether it is Plato's flickering shadows on the cave wall, the intricate programming of the Matrix, or our own circumscribed vision, it keeps us from experiencing the real or the truth.

The Matrix offers a mirror image of how we see our relation to technology made visible in *Avatar*. Just as Jake can't learn the ways of the Na'vi from the outside, Neo couldn't learn the truth from the inside. It was necessary for him to unplug, metonymically letting go of his enframed relation to technology, before he could experience the real or the true, before it could reveal itself to him. Morpheus tells Neo that no one can be told what the Matrix *is*. You have to see it for yourself. Like Jake, he had to have a firsthand experience. But unlike Jake, who experienced Pandora through his avatar's enlarged yellow eyes, Neo had to disconnect to realize that he had never even used his eyes at all.

The Matrix rests on a premise of the dangers of technology. But it does something else as well. As Neo begins to run the "training programs" as Morpheus works with him, the computer technology that comprises the illusionistic world from which he emerged starts to become visible to him. Slowly the Matrix reveals itself to Neo, and because he allows it to presence, more than any other character, Neo comes to understand its nature as well as to transcend its limits. The measure of freedom he gains comes from breaking out of his bounded understandings to see clearly the nature of the illusionistic world in which his battle for freedom is waged.

Like *The Matrix*, Ronald Moore's Syfy series *Battlestar Galactica* also rests on an apocalyptic premise. The opening episode of the series drops the viewer into the moment in which the planets inhabited by the human characters in this imagined universe are about to be incinerated. The Cylons, a robotic race invented decades earlier by these very same humans, have evolved, developed sentience, rebelled, and finally destroyed the human worlds from which they came. As the show moves forward from this point, it follows the humans' attempts to recover from this nuclear holocaust and the perpetual war with the Cylon race who are nothing if not technology embodied. The four-year-long, Emmy-award-winning series surfaced many post–9/11 issues related to war, racial profiling, abortion, relationships, religion, and more, but at the core, the show pitted the technological being against the "natural" being. In the final episodes of the series, the fearful, anti-technology perspective holds sway. Together what is left of the Cylons and their human allies eschew the technology that brought them all to the brink of annihilation, and together they embrace a kind of anti-technological stance, reminiscent of a late sixties — a hippie, back-to-the-land approach — which they are hopeful will keep them safe and keep them from repeating their missteps. Here, the resistance to technology that Heidegger warns is equally enframing as a whole-hearted embrace of its sweeping force is revealed.

Against a background of robotic destruction in *Battlestar Galactica*, humanity emerges. In the representation of this conflict between human and Cylon, it was often the Cylon who behaved with more compassion and the human who at times was rigidly mechanistic and inhumane. Against the ground of the technology of the Cylons, the figure of the essential nature of humanity revealed itself.

Fluxing of the Oppositional Stance

These black-and-white categories are, as Heidegger explained, useful for breaking up our experience into its constitutive parts so that we may see them more clearly and communicate each bit. But, in effect, experience is a much fuzzier thing, and the boundaries between our fear of and our attachment to technology are permeable. *Avatar* is neither the first nor the only film or series to flux this oppositional relationship to technology. We can see a melding of borders to a certain extent in all of the films touched on briefly above. Data and the Borg both inhabit the *Star Trek: The Next Generation* world, blending the ways that nature and technology are imbricated in one another. In *The Matrix*, Neo has to exit the nexus of the matrix to see nature as it exists in the sewers of this post-apocalyptic world. But he has to be plugged in, in order to gain the power to overcome the machine and transcend his "human nature." Over the course of the series, *Battlestar Galactica* confounds those viewers who seek the comfort of knowing who are the good guys and who are the bad. On numerous occasions Cylons sacrifice themselves for humans, exhibit compassion and great courage. In just as many cases the humans engage in cruel torture, betraying a frightening rationality, behaving much more like a machine.

But in *Avatar* we find technology actually residing in nature, and the natural embedded in the technology in a way that schmears the discrete edges we expect to find between technology and nature. *Avatar* demonstrates the figure of each emerging out of and hence revealing its other. Some critiques of the film have focused on the apparent hypocrisy of a film that uses inordinately expensive technology to promote a position that claims, "Technology is bad." Gary Westfahl approaches *Avatar* with a view that Heidegger might arguably see as *gestellen*. "Living off the land in a forest is good; living in a protective metallic shelter filled with scientific devices is bad. Killing animals with a bow and arrow is good; killing them with machine guns is bad. Riding through the air on the backs of pterodactyl-like creatures is good; riding through the air in futuristic helicopters is bad."[32] Westfahl misses the fact that Cameron is not in the least condemning technology, but rather our enframed approach to it.

The character of Selfridge is wedded to creating a standing reserve of his ore. His attachment to wealth and his detachment from the destruction he unleashes is a direct result of his constrained approach to the excavation project. Colonel Quaritch's blinkered determination to exterminate the Na'vi, the one-pointed perspective rooted in a power-over dominating gaze, was explored in Chapter One. Quaritch more than any other character personifies a frozen point of view in counterpoint to the fluidity that Jake grows into, resulting in shifting understandings and ultimately in the delight he takes in his new world.

When Quaritch first summons Sully to recruit him to secretly gather intelligence, we find the colonel pumping iron within a metal cage, the symbolism here transparent. Sully wheels his chair through the door—he is mobile, even if hampered by his disability—and enters Quaritch's space, framing his tight, metallic, immobile prison of a perspective.

In the early scenes of *Avatar*, Cameron familiarly juxtaposes nature and technology in an expected way: the technological, weapons-savvy approach of the corporate installation in opposition to the "natural," indigenous people. Cameron offers this as the opening gambit in a classical Hollywood narrative, as the equilibrium, which as the plot thickens will undergo a disturbance. When Jake experiences his first linkup into the avatar, the science/nature dichotomy is starkly exemplified.

Jake climbs into the linkup pod and, following Grace's instructions, lets his mind go blank. After a wormhole burst of computer graphics simulates his consciousness traveling along the imagined linkup into the body of the avatar, the camera point of view switches up. The spectator is now looking out of the avatar's body along with Jake for the very first time. As his vision comes into focus, we too are looking into the eyes of the medical team set to monitor his transition into the avatar. They begin their scan of him, as is characteristic of Cameron in this film, with the eyes, shining a bright light into them to gauge his pupil's reflexes and tracking ability. Jake is wired up, connected to all manner of medical recording devices and monitoring equipment. The technicians intend to measure his muscle tone and coordination, to run sensory motor reflex tests, to ascertain his level of functioning in the avatar, before letting him move around on his own steam.

Apparently this routine is familiar to Norm, who has practiced linking in to his avatar before. But Jake, thrilled to find himself with a pair of working limbs, has no patience for the protocol. He wiggles his toes, and once he determines that his feet are responding to his will, he tears out his leads and with complete disregard for the folks and the technology around him bursts out of the medical facility. As he runs along a garden path, digs his toes into the red clay of Pandora, and tastes the fruit Grace's avatar tosses him, he tests the workings of the technology of the avatar he inhabits. He can sense all he needs to through his avatar body, eschewing the more rigorous, constrained, and conventional approach that employs what would be considered medical technology. Not only is the tension between these antithetical approaches obvious, but Jake's independent spirit, which despite his training as a Marine informs his rebellious choices later on in the story, is established.

Moving Consciousness

A close look at the avatar project itself discloses a relationship with technology that resides in neither fear nor exaltation, but instead in the ways in which nature is interlaced within it.

The conceit of relocating a soul/consciousness/personality from one body to another can be traced, in recent fare, all the way back to a 1962 *Twilight Zone* episode entitled "The Trade-Ins." In this episode, Rod Serling recounts the tale of an elderly couple, very much in love, but trapped in their deteriorating bodies. Apprised of a radical new technology at the "New Life Corp.," they intend to purchase new, healthy, young bodies so that they may continue to live on, continue to love each other. Their plan is thwarted when they realize that they can only afford one of the youthful bodies they have seen on display. Since it is the husband who is the more physically debilitated by his pain, they decide he should go ahead and purchase the new body. The transfer of his being into the spiffy young athletic model occurs behind a set of closed doors. He goes in old and comes out rejuvenated in the body of one of the display models.

Within moments it becomes apparent to him and to his wife that his energy and exuberance are no match for his aged but devoted wife. He turns right around and goes back through that door, emerging again in his original, aged body. As the loving couple walks off hand in hand, Serling's voice-over quotes Kahlil Gibran and tells the television audience that this episode is a reminder from all the sentimentalists in the *Twilight Zone*.

The moral clearly indicates that love is enough and that we should strive to accept who we are; the desire for youth, strength, vitality, and immortality are all in vain. Yet the fantasy of evading our demise, of outrunning death, has a hold on even the sanest among us. Critic Gary Westfahl grants that it is this motif alone in *Avatar* that is not completely spent.[33] The notion that someday we might be able to assume not only a virtual alternative identity, but to inhabit an alternative physical body raises multiple issues that have been explored in fiction of the past and raised in the science of today, for example in the work of Ray Kurzweil.

In stories like *The Portrait of Dorian Gray*, by Oscar Wilde, in which a deal is struck with the devil, Gray remains young as his portrait ages. In the films *Heaven Can Wait*, *Switch*, and *Ghost* we find a soul who gets transferred from one body to another, at the hands of God or an angel or an incantation. It is only fairly recently that the pseudo-technological explanations of this turn of events have appeared in science fiction.

In the 1998 sci-fi novel *Circuit of Heaven*, author Dennis Danvers revisions Romeo and Juliet in a post-apocalyptic dystopia in which the surface of the earth is ravaged. Most humans have opted to upload their consciousness into a virtual world called the "Bin." Here they can live forever, be whoever they'd like to be, live wherever they'd like to live, in a virtual eternity. The only humans still existing on the actual surface of the planet are bands of roaming thugs and those whose religious beliefs prohibit them from abandoning their human bodies and entering the Bin. Visiting the Bin, Nemo, an outsider, meets Justine, a citizen of the Bin, and they fall in love. In order for them to be together they face a dilemma: Nemo must choose to discard his physical body to remain in the Bin forever with Justine, or she must find a way to leave the Bin — in someone else's body, because once you decide to enter the Bin permanently, your physical body is cremated. As Danvers comments on the dust jacket,

> As we set out to decipher consciousness and to create more perfect virtual realities, sooner or later these two ventures will cross paths, meet and wed. When that happens a virtual world won't just offer fun and games, but the far more seductive temptation of immortality.[34]

Released the year after *Circuit of Heaven*, *The Matrix* offered up a world not of mortality, but of utter virtuality. Human existence was portrayed as consisting entirely of a virtual life in which the corporeal function was simply to provide power to run the mammoth machine in a raw and startling graphic depiction of humans connected by means of electrical plugs and cables. Neo and his group of rebels "hack in" to the matrix and their virtual programs via telephone lines, while their bodies remain in a chair that has come to signify the linkup technology to a virtual world.

It is only a hop, skip and a jump from Danvers' Bin and *The Matrix* to the synthetic bodies of Jonathan Mostow's 2009 film *Surrogates*. Here we see Danvers' prophecy brought to life. Humans spend their waking lives in chairs that link to robotic doubles of themselves who never age and are tailor made. The film opens with a voice-over warning, "We are not meant to experience the world through a machine." A "mocumentary"-style montage follows the trajectory of the previous decades, outlining the use of surrogates first by the military and finally their adoption by the general population. The promise of safety, avoidance of disease and the "perfect looks" of synthetic bodies results in an inert population, traumatized by light and sound and unable to function in the real world. Ninety-eight percent of the world's population spends their days in their "stim chairs," equipped with headgear and goggles, surrounded by an array of infrared lights and a computer linkup that monitors their vitals.

The pseudoscience begins to get specific here — no more magical transformation behind closed doors as in the *Twilight Zone* episode. Before you can inhabit a "surri," it has to be coded to your neural signature. The "chair" as vehicle for consciousness transfer harkens back to the memory-implanting device of Paul Verhoeven's 1990 film, *Total Recall.* Surrounded by panels of flashing lights, Verhoeven's chair predates the hack-in chair of *The Matrix,* or the imprinting and wipe apparatus of Joss Whedon's 2009 television series *Dollhouse.*

In *The Matrix, Circuit of Heaven,* and *Surrogates,* the transfer of consciousness goes from the human brain into a virtual container: a program, the Bin, a synthetic robot. The opposition of the machine and the human are firmly locked into place. But the fully human actives of *Dollhouse* up the ante. Very real human subjects sign away years of their lives for any number of reasons — in lieu of a jail sentence, to erase a trauma or a psychosis — and during that time they agree to have their consciousness wiped and stored in a digital repository called a wedge. Topher Brink — the techno-wizard behind the "chair" in which the wiping and subsequent imprinting of engineered, composite personalities takes place — claims that these "actives," in their neutral state, "are a little bit bison," meaning a little bit like having not much more awareness or intelligence than a herding mammal. Topher's sci-fi fantasy technology, however, grows more sophisticated particularly in episodes where he expounds on his genius. Toward the end of the two-season series, however, issues centered on the ethics of "using" human subjects to feed the desires of the wealthy become usurped by the foreshadowed dystopian future in which the frightening dangers of "tech" come to be known. The series ends with an emphasis on the struggle between those who embrace the thrill of "tech," despite its dangers, and the choice of several other main characters to opt for a "back-to-nature" life, reminiscent of the choices at the end of *Battlestar Galactica.*

The company in *Surrogates* that advertised the "surris" for sale claims that with a transferred consciousness the advantage for humans is "Life, only better!" In *Dollhouse,* it is not the actives whose lives are enhanced, but the wealthy clients for whom the actives are programmed to fulfill a fantasy, a dream, or a desire. The technology of the transfer of consciousness in these relatively recent portrayals becomes more specific and enhanced with special effects and computer graphics depicting brain-imaging software. In *Surrogates*, the antipathy between those that inhabit a machine and those who don't is at the heart of the narrative and is resolved when the surrogates are brought down by a virus. In *Dollhouse* the machines are ancillary to the use/misuse of the human actives. But the underlying message in both seems clear: technology is dangerous and brings us to the brink of destruction, or if not, at least to a place where humans cease to live their "natural" human lives.

The Avatar Project

While the transfer technology represented in *Avatar* is certainly in the same ballpark as *Surrogates* and *Dollhouse*, in its treatment of relocating awareness it is doing something very different. While there are certainly ethical issues — how the Na'vi's genetic material was initially harvested to create the avatars is an obvious example; they didn't offer it up willingly — Jake's awareness is placed in neither a virtual environment, a machine, nor within the brain of an indentured human. The legal, imperialist, and ethical ramifications of how and why the avatars were created, who owns them, and who decides how they get "used" are only addressed in marginal ways in extra-diegetic texts like Pandorapedia. Within the context of the narrative, we are invited to accept that they are part of Grace's field project and as such are uniquely situated to straddle the relationship of the natural to the technological.

When Jake sees his avatar for the first time, during his introductory tour of the linkup center, it has not yet been "decanted." It is embalmed in a sea of something that resembles blue amniotic fluid. As his voice-over narration attests, these giant blue creatures are "grown" from a mixture of human genetic material and that of the indigenous Na'vi. The design of the avatar, a human-Na'vi hybrid, intrinsically fluxes the two races, even before they are inhabited by their drivers. In the large aqueous tanks in which they were grown, the avatars twitch reflexively, pointing to some autonomous nervous system already in place in the physicality of the thing. While they lack sentience, they *seem* alive. Embedded in the technology that was developed to grow these avatars, vivid reflections of human nature are visible: the creatures float in a womblike enclosure and are receiving their sustenance through enormous umbilical cords. The signification of some kind of impending birth is unmistakable.

The avatar signals both nature *and* technology. It is a piece of technology that humans inhabit, enabling their survival on the planet and ultimately facilitating their ability to conduct embedded science. It is *in and through* the avatar body that the Na'vis' world becomes accessible. The avatar is *in* and *of* the nature of Pandora and the Na'vi, but it is also a scientific vehicle, a technology for human exploration. Jake is of nature; he is not a machine. Yet his presence in the avatar is machinelike. He "steers" the avatar from a remote location in which he is enmeshed, with the help of "psionic amplification"[35] in the neural network of the linkup technology. Via some pseudoscientific version of mapping his brain functions to the brain of the "grown" avatar — his brain is "phase locked" to the brain of the avatar — Jake drives a natural creature. To set up a visual indication of this reciprocal reverberating link between Jake and his avatar, Cameron uses light and reflection.

Jake sits by the tank quietly contemplating the creature with an uncanny resemblance to himself. It floats in its beautiful, ethereal blue liquid, and Jake is tinged blue, bathed in its reflected light. When the camera slides behind Jake to show us his avatar from his point of view, a reflection of his human face can be seen superimposed on the avatar in its glass tank, pointing to the overlapping of their identities, the ways in which they are each technology to each other's nature.

That technology reigns in the bio-lab is a no-brainer. The avatars are being monitored in their tanks by the same kind of sophisticated screens and virtual readouts, 3-D imaging technology that was displayed earlier in Parker's control center and in all of the military vehicles. The linkup pods themselves are sheer technological brilliance which extend the chair metaphor to a full-body enclosure, and we simply must accept them as fact, suspending any reasonable disbelief. We are given little information about how, precisely, the linkup works other than inferences that conjure up virtual reality games. Only in this case the avatar exists not in some virtual space on a computer hard drive, but in the diegetically *real* world of Pandora. One lies inside the bed of linkup pod — which resembles sea-green memory foam — closes one's eyes, lets the mind go blank and voila! A blaze of color and light, an animated wormhole signaling what we might imagine occurs within the neural networks of the brain, helps us to make the leap to the body of the avatar.

But this technology differs in kind from that devoted to the excavation of the unobtanium. The whole purpose of Grace's avatar project is to promote access, to exchange information and understanding. The goal is to be within the object of investigation, to enter the world of the Na'vi completely, not to hoard a natural resource to create a standing reserve that remains at the ready no matter what.

Grace, who engineered and heads up the avatar project, was not predisposed to enframe her findings. She and Jake exemplify what comes closest to what Heidegger has described as being in a free relationship with technology. Heidegger's recipe for avoiding a circumscribed relation to technology looks something like this:

Wherever man [*sic*] opens his eyes and ears, unlocks his heart, and gives himself over to meditating and striving, shaping and working, entreating and thanking, he finds himself everywhere already brought into the unconcealed.[36]

Both Grace and Jake have open eyes and ears to see and learn about the Na'vi, without presuming to know them in advance. While Grace initially is prejudiced in her view of Jake — she wants nothing to do with a "jarhead flunky" — her passion for observation allows even that circumscribed view of him to soften and morph. She sees him succeed where others before him have failed. She perceives the changes he is capable of effecting and the changes he embodies through his apprenticeship with Neytiri. The transformation Jake undergoes under Neytiri's tutelage is plainly portrayed. The Jake who first runs from flower to flower hitting them to see what kind of reaction he will get — the childlike, impulsive, self-centered, flailing Jake — is a very different person from the Jake who at the film's end approaches Tsu'tey with dignity and deference, seeking his help in leading the Na'vi in their fight for survival. Jake manifests as self-contained, calm, respectful, and patient — this transformation is made visible even in the way he inhabits his avatar.

Grace is by definition a scientist, a botanist. Nature is what she studies. But she doesn't approach it by assuming in advance that she knows what it is. She strives and shapes and works and is rewarded in the end by what is revealed to her. Through her relationship with Jake, Grace also transforms, as does her understanding as a result of her discoveries. Grace's transformation is paler than Jake's, but through subtle visual cues, Cameron paints a picture of the character of Grace as one who embodies the fluxing of technology and nature.

The extra-textual running joke of her chain-smoking habit carried over from her role as scientist Ellen Ripley in *Aliens* notwithstanding, Grace likes plants better than people. And while the avatar project enables her to get data on the Na'vi, she is primarily interested in Pandoran plant life, which she discovers is comprised of a complicated root system, a network, if you will, through which the plants are able to communicate with one another and with the humanoid Na'vi. In the scene where Norm, Grace and Jake are first together exploring the jungle, Grace sticks a needle into the root of a tree. We can see immediately on the mini monitoring screen she carries around her neck that the root of the tree that was poked is communicating this information to the root system of an adjacent tree. Grace explains this *signal transduction* to Norm, but because in this scene the camera is trained on Jake's discoveries, the spectator is directed to follow his antics, while the audio levels of the scientific conversation behind him fades out into the background. But we are left with the delight of Grace's avatar's face at the speed with which this transduction occurs and the awe that Norm exhibits when he can see this occurring on the mini-monitor in front of him.

Here the technology of their portable monitor extends their ability to see beyond what is visible to them on the surface of the root system with the naked eye, but it doesn't prevent them from seeing what is in front of them, the way that Quaritch and Selfridge become blinded to all but what is revealed on their video and computer screens. For Grace, this technology reveals nature because she is able to approach it without assuming what Heidegger might describe as an enframed stance.

As the scene unfolds, Jake explores the jungle on his own. With no instruments to measure or sample, his experimentation is more spontaneous, less thoughtful. He reaches out to touch the vivid inverted parasol plants around him and is fascinated by their reaction. As his fingers extend toward these tubular umbrellas, they roll up and snap shut. After touching one or two plants, even the plants that Jake has not come anywhere near close up in advance of his touch. We see here a demonstration of Grace's signal transduction in action. We see the intelligence, the connection, the "technology," of the plant network. Jake observes this through the technology of the avatar he inhabits, the nature of Pandora revealed.

During Jake's apprenticeship to Neytiri, Cameron uses an alternating or parallel construction of montages, flipping back and forth between Jake's time in the avatar with Neytiri and his time in the linkup shack, where he eats and sleeps in an effort to sustain his human body so that it can continue to be able to drive the avatar. Here the natural and the technological sift back and forth like the sand in an oscillating hourglass. The sophisticated technology of the linkup pod supports the natural human body as it lies there. Jake's consciousness travels into his avatar which enables him to explore the natural world of Pandora through the technology of its sensory apparatus.

During one of these clips there is a close-up of Grace at her electron microscope. In this particular scene the Mobius strip of the natural and technological is vivid. Reflecting the eye motif central to the film, in this tight shot it appears that the light of the microscope is illuminating Grace's eye.

The microscope enhances, enlarges, sharpens what it might be possible for Grace to see. But the reflexive light is washing back on and igniting her golden iris, which now significantly seems to give off its own lustrous light. Grace's eye receives, her retina is stimulated and it sends a signal to her visual cortex. But it is the whole nature of Grace — her experience, her memories, her intelligence — that makes meaning out of, makes connections to, whatever it is that is revealed by the technology of the microscope. Here Cameron shows us Grace *seeing* in the way that the Na'vi *see*, even though she may be simply looking at a number of cells from a root system. In this shot Grace sees and technology reveals nature, in the way that Heidegger suggested it might. Grace's science, her free relationship to technology, stands in relief to that of Quaritch and Selfridge. They don't avail themselves of their image-enhancing technology in order to see more, better, deeper. Instead Quaritch and Selfridge close down what it is possible to see, limiting it only to one point of view: that of controlling and creating a standing reserve, no matter the cost.

The characters of Grace and Jake are not bound by *gestellen*, enframed preconceptions. When they first meet, Grace sees Jake as a detriment to her team. In return he views her as hard-assed, less than welcoming, and particularly unsympathetic to the loss of his brother. As the film progresses, however, they each grow quite fond the other. Grace takes on the role of mothering Jake, as he tends to neglect his human body in favor of the avatar he is driving. As the antagonism between Grace and Jake subsides, they come to "see" each other in much the way the Na'vi do. And in the end it is Jake who tries to save Grace's life when Quaritch shoots her escaping from the brig.

When Grace's life is threatened by the loss of blood from her gunshot wound, Jake appeals to Moat, the Na'vi shaman, for her help in saving Grace's life. He brings her weakened body to the Tree of Souls where Moat will try to transfer her soul, her consciousness, into the body of her avatar.

Jake carries Grace, barely conscious, to this sacred site. When she realizes that she is actually at the Tree of Souls, her scientist instinct kicks in, and she tells him that they really do have to get samples. The reflection of the Tree of Souls in the surface of Grace's exo-pak mask merges and blends with her face, reiterating the earlier reflection of Jake's face in the glass of the avatar's tank. These visual hints of overlapping connection are enlarged in the ceremony that follows. The ensuing scenes question what technology is and ultimately whether or not it inheres in the nature of Pandora.

As Grace is laid down near her lifeless avatar at the foot of the Tree of Souls, the very ground around them — its entire root system — begins to sprout fine, hairlike, iridescent tentacles, which enshroud Grace's human body and the body of her avatar. The Omaticaya clan encircles the Tree of Souls, each Na'vi connected to the root system through the links in their braids and to each other by their arms as they reach out to one another. The root system is illuminated with a phosphorescent glow, as are the weeping willow branches of the tree itself. The surface of the planet beneath them shimmers with luminescence, the light signifying life and a vast organic network that connects the ground, the Tree, and the Na'vi to Grace and above all to the goddess Eywa. The glowing tendrils that envelop Grace form an interwoven cable which attaches itself to the back of Grace's neck, plugging directly into her brainstem, an elegant echo of the way in which Neo and his comrades once connected to the Matrix.

As Moat leads the Omaticaya in a prayer to Eywa to allow Grace's consciousness to pass through the deity and reside permanently in the body of her avatar, the illumination of the root system and its connection becomes stronger. The people, the ground, and the surrounding trees pulse and breathe together like one giant organism, punctuated by a drumbeat that resembles that of a giant heart; the light intensifies and dims in unison with its rhythm.

Grace turns to Jake, the image of the Tree of Souls vivid in the reflection of her exo-pak mask, and she tells him that she is with Eywa — that Eywa is real. Ever the scientist, even on her deathbed, she is able to take in this empirical evidence of the existence of a goddess. As the camera point of view shifts to what Grace is seeing, we see the Tree of Souls behind a blurry Jake becoming more and more intense until, in a repetition of the wormhole computer graphics that signify the linkup to the avatar, Grace "links up" with the Tree of Souls, with Eywa, and simulating the proverbial white light that greets one at death, the psychedelic, pseudo-neural net image fades to white. In death, scientist Grace merges with nature. As the life leaves her body, the light ebbs from the root system and spreads a dark pall over the entire scene. This is a dramatic visualization of her spirit departing, of the life energy that Neytiri maintains is, after all, only borrowed, returning to its source. Neytiri removes the now unnecessary exo-pak from Grace's face, which she gently cups with her large blue hand.

There is much meaning that could be construed from this scene. Pertinent to an exploration of the fluxing of nature and technology, the natural technology of the Na'vi and of their world — the extensive network of connectivity, the signal transduction by which Grace was awed and which hints at the possibility of nearly instantaneous communication — points to the pervasive technology of our time. Again Sven Birkerts puts it elegantly: "We are, with that ever-amazing hi-tech effortlessness, threading ourselves to others in the great universe of signals."[37]

But the question Cameron poses is, if this biotechnology is embodied, does it blur the boundaries between what is technology and what is natural? Cameron offers a picture of technology — the essence of technology as Heidegger has thought it — as something that is able to make the natural clearly visible. In the powerful portrayal of Grace's death, the relationship of the Na'vi to their world, to their deity, and to each other is suggested not as circumscription, but instead as a free and open relationship to technology reminiscent of Heidegger's injunction to open one's eyes and ears, unlock one's heart, and give oneself over to meditating and striving, shaping and working, entreating and thanking so that we might be brought into the unconcealed.

Chapter Three

Thinking Technology: Technology of the Art

Technology as Performative: The Making Mirrors the Message

Having examined some of the ways in which the realm of the arts represents multiple views of technology, it is necessary to flip the picture and look at the ways in which technology supports the realm of art. Approaching technology as Heidegger has demonstrated, apprehending it as that which reveals or makes unconcealing possible, technology comes into view as a central architect of the arts. Whether we consider the various technologies that were gathered together — paper, ink, block letters, and a screw press — to enable the mass production of the printed page or those that enabled pigments to be suspended evenly in a medium of linseed oil or those that honed a chisel so that it might find a figure in a block of marble or those lenses, mirrors, emulsions, and projection systems which when organized appropriately yield the moving image, it is clear that technology has always been essential to the creative process. It has also functioned as a delimiting factor. While in myth, the character of Daedalus dreamed of flying and invented the necessary technology to realize his dreams, in reality it was millennia before the constitutive technologies would come together to make the flying machine a reality.

James Cameron famously tells the story of how in 1995, at the time that he conceived the script for *Avatar*, the technology just wasn't sophisticated enough to bring his vision to fruition. It would take another decade and specific technical innovations by Cameron himself to arrive at the point in time when he could make the movie he saw in his mind's eye. It was imperative to Cameron that the natural reside in the technological creation of the characters in *Avatar*. And until he could be assured of this he was not willing to risk making a movie that would ultimately fall short. When the time eventually came to make the film he envisioned, Cameron approached melding live-action capture and computer-generated animation in ways that have been touted as groundbreaking. This chapter explores the historical ground out of which this blend of cinema and animation emerged and looks at the specific choices that Cameron made in *Avatar* that were not only innovative but made clear his commitment to ensuring that what inheres in nature remained visible in and through the technology.

Animation and cinema might be seen as twin siblings born to the potential of the moving image. While stop-frame animation traditionally relied on the camera and a projection system and therefore post-dated cinema, there were other visual devices such as the zoetrope, which some trace as far back as China 2000 years ago, flip books, and the phenakistoscope disc, all which relied on the spinning or twirling or flipping of images to give the appearance of movement and which all pre-dated motion pictures. However, modern animation and modern cinema came of age concurrently toward the end of the 19th century and have fascinated audiences ever since. They have been held up as adversarial, as representing the polarities of what is possible to achieve with the force of the moving image. In an interesting way they flux the relationship between technology and nature. On the one hand, it is possible to see animation as natural because it relies on the human hand, the traditional pen and ink, brush and paper, colored pigments. To animation's natural, we can hold up a technological cinema: cameras and lenses, sprocketed celluloid treated with emulsion which is then cut and spliced, and projection systems. The cinematic machine, when juxtaposed with the hand-drawn animation, appears to weigh down the technological side of the scale. However, today most animation and film editing is done digitally by computers. By comparison, film now leans toward the natural end of the spectrum, where live action, that is, photographic images of real humans, animals, objects and places, are recorded and disseminated, as opposed to much of digital animation or computer-generated animation in which there is no human or animal, object or place that is being represented. While the digital might in some broad sense reference nature, it is all finally simulacra.

Thomas Lamarre takes this bifurcation one step further in looking at the dichotomy within animation itself. In his book *The Anime Machine: A Media Theory of Animation*, Lamarre investigates what he refers to as the "force of the moving image,"[1] locating it principally in Japanese anime. In taking the measure of the moving image, he draws some distinctions between the art side of cel animation — the literal craft in which the hand is engaged in the drawing, painting, and inking of the image — versus the technology side of animation. Lamarre bemoans this split, suggesting that it might not really be possible to separate out the yolk of poeisis from the white of teckne, that animation requires the whole egg. He worries that those who focus on the "art" of animation, that is, the rendering of image that evokes an art historical perspective, will miss the "underlying machine" of animation and therefore also lose a "sense of historical and technical specificity."[2]

In order to help make clear what the anime machine is, he draws a comparison between the *cinematic* as outlined by Paul Virilio and what Lamarre defines in contrast as the *animetic*. Cinema emphasizes moving into depth[3]: a train engine, chugging along the track coming toward the audience, a trail of smoke in its wake; Superman flying off into space after a super villain; or the quintessential image of Slim Pickens riding the atomic bomb like a cowboy at the rodeo in the final segment of *Dr. Strangelove*. In the animetic, Lamarre explains, the emphasis is not so much on moving into the depth of the picture plane, but on the gap that arises due to intrinsic qualities of the apparatus of animation, traditionally the animation stand.[4] Because the pre-computer generated animated image was created with overlapping layers of celluloid on which the characters and the background had been drawn, there is an inherent difficulty in penetrating that pictorial space. Between the animated figure and the depth of field portrayed by the layered scrims of landscape behind which the character moves we become aware of a spatial gap. In an animetic container, three-dimensional space is created not simply by flying into or out of it, but by the awareness of the gaps between layers.

Until recently, this was also true of nascent computer animation; it was difficult to move into the depth of field because the scale of the surrounding areas didn't change accordingly. Lamarre cites *Star Wars: The Phantom Menace*, 1999, in which much of the film was computer generated but, because of scalar limitations, to Lamarre's mind, resembles more of a tableau. In contrast to the animetism of *Phantom Menace*, there is the scene from the original *Star Wars, Episode IV: A New Hope*, in which Luke and his fellow pilots navigate the innards of the Death Star in order to destroy it from within. This sequence, released in the film originally in 1977, is one of a handful of early computer-generated animations embedded in a live-action film. Lamarre points to its "high-speed ballistic effects," more cinematic than animetic, within the computer-generated interior trench space into which Luke flew, suggesting the experience of the early computer games as well.[5]

By the time Cameron began production on *Avatar*, decades later, enormous changes had taken place in the technology of computer-generated animation, and in the ways in which animation and film have come to interact with one another, which hitherto could only have been imagined. *Avatar*, which was shot stereoscopically to create believable 3-D visual effects, gives new meaning to the animetic gap as it elicits a subtle but palpable three-dimensional experience, one in which the viewer is pulled into the cinematic world and can thus imagine that she could move around in this fantasy space, and can experience, as if first-hand, the distances between this palm frond, that stand of trees and the charging Thanator off in the distance.

Cameron's technological choices and inventions bring nature *into* the animetic machine. A cursory survey of the historical ground out of which Cameron's innovations have emerged reveal the ways in which cinema and animation have come to occupy an overlapping slice of the space of the moving image. Turning points in technological advances — the melding of animetic and cinematic spaces, the move from mechanical animatronics to the first completely computer-generated full-length film, early experiments with motion capture — become the trail of bread crumbs that led Cameron and his team of animators to the movie that *Avatar* becomes. The integration of what Cameron identifies as three new technologies — a stereoscopic camera system with which to create the subtle 3-D effects of the movie, a unique live-motion capture system that for the first time included a head rig that Cameron developed, and a virtual camera — was responsible for the ways in which, in *Avatar*, the medium *reflects* the message.

Animation in *Cinema*

While the joining of animation and cinema in the last 50 years has been heralded as revolutionary, in fact they had been integrated into one another, if simply, since their inception. *The Humorous Phases of Funny Faces,* by Stuart Blackton, was a short silent piece in which film and animation intermingled in 1906. The arm of an artist is the main character, chalk and chalkboard the supporting cast. A series of cartoon characters that, after being drawn, come to life, provide what little narrative structure there is. In 1922, Max Fleischer, creator of Betty Boop, Felix the Cat, and Koko the Clown, penned a short film, *Out of the Inkwell,* in which Koko clones himself, leaves the page, and with his army of cloned Kokos invades Fleischer's study, attacking and hogtying the cartoonist. While there are, no doubt, countless other examples of animation in film and film existing as container for animation, new-media theorist Lev Manovich has argued that cinema, for the most part, dwarfed and marginalized animation for the bulk of its first century.[6]

Cameron's seamless and elegant blending of live-action and computer-generated animation has its antecedents in some unlikely places. Generally, when many of us think animation, our minds race to Disney, Hanna-Barbera, Looney Tunes and even perhaps to Japanese anime. Classic Disney is about as far from what Cameron has accomplished with *Avatar* as one could imagine. Still, the unlikely precursor of *Mary Poppins* offers some insights into the historic roots of Cameron's achievement.

Released in 1964, Disney's *Mary Poppins* included a rather lengthy scene in which Julie Andrews' Mary, her young charges, and Dick van Dyke's Burt jump into a chalk sidewalk drawing, the gateway to an entirely animated countryside adventure. Predating today's green- and blue-screen technology for creating traveling mattes, Disney used a sodium vapor camera to create the matte around the live-action characters. They performed in front of a blank white screen that reflected sodium lights back into the camera. The camera is thus shooting onto two separate film carriers. One roll of film captures the live action. The other, being stimulated by the sodium lights returning to the camera and refracted through a prism, records everything *but* the live action[7]; this creates a perfect ground matte to the figures of Burt and Mary.

The shot footage of the live action finds its way to the animators who proceeded to design the countryside, carousel, foxhunt and dancing penguins around the filmed pantomimed gestures of the actors. Van Dyke, who began his comedic career as a mime, says this experience served him well during the animation clip. Animators, however, claim to have been challenged by the task of assuring that the troupe of penguins with which he danced the old soft-shoe didn't get trampled underfoot.[8]

One of the most difficult aspects of merging animated footage with live action is matching up the eye lines. Even using Cameron's uber-sophisticated technology, it only works if the animated characters and the live characters are making eye contact. *Who Framed Roger Rabbit*,[9] released in 1988, was a film in which "Toons" inhabited the filmic world. Animated completely by hand, this production included blue screen and the use of animatronics to create the realistic reverberations of the Toons stumbling through the physical world. As Roger scrambled across a desk, he would inevitably knock over the inkwell, crumple paper, and dislodge the blotter; this disarray was all accomplished mechanically or by puppeteers moving objects. In the case of the character of the baby who was always shown smoking a cigar, a robotic arm was created to hold the burning cigar and in the animation phase was then masked over by the animated arm of the baby.

In order to increase the accuracy of the eye lines, Toon-size dummies of the animated characters were used in rehearsal, enabling the actors to practice where to direct their gaze. Bob Hoskins also underwent mime training, learning well how to simulate the look of lifting the sheer weight of Roger when he pulled him up by the ears or threw him across the room. First blocking out the film using the actual rubber dummies, they would shoot a second time sans dummies but with eye lines established. Lastly, the animators would work with the daily guide track and draw in the animated characters.[10]

Director Robert Zemeckis discussed the challenges of having to make three "elaborate" movies in one: "a period film-noir live-action movie, a feature length animation movie, and a special effects movie."[11]

The advent of digital technology, however, altered this process considerably. The photographic image became malleable, could be tweaked, remodeled, stretched, and duplicated. As John Belton has suggested, digital technology has morphed the photographic image; it has literally become "plastic."[12] This turn to the digital has upended the hierarchy of the moving image. Where once film had pushed animation to the periphery, today, as Manovich has argued, cinema now has become subsumed by animation.[13] Oshii Mamoru, the Japanese director of the full-length animation film *Ghost in the Shell*, goes so far as to suggest, "All cinema is becoming animation."[14]

Issues of eye lines and weight bearing still plagued Cameron almost twenty years later, but computer-generated digital solutions combined with his specific improvements enabled *Avatar* to reach far beyond what had been possible in 1988.

The intervening decades saw the introduction of computer-generated characters, spaces and vehicles in movies as diverse as *The Young Sherlock Holmes*, which introduced the first fully computer-generated stained-glass creature, *Labyrinth, Flight of the Navigator, Willow*, and *Star Trek IV: The Voyage Home*, to name just a few.

Cameron's *The Abyss* in 1989 and *Terminator 2: Judgment Day* raised the stakes considerably for what could be accomplished digitally. Working with Industrial Light and Magic (ILM) visual effects supervisor Dennis Muren, Cameron created *The Abyss*'s watery alien creature in 1989, which was the first CG character to be able to show emotion. Even in these early stages Cameron was concerned with mapping onto computer-realized visions something that smacked of the human.[15] Working with ILM on *Terminator 2*, Cameron conceived of the new model of the Terminator, the "shape-shifting, liquid metal, T-1000,"[16] which was generated on the computer and adjusted with an early version of Photoshop to assure that its reflective surface would match the live action surroundings into which it was placed.

Walking the Walk

In the early nineties when director Steven Spielberg envisioned *Jurassic Park*, he imagined that they would be relying on large-scale animatronic creatures, but the expense of building these was astronomical and therefore prohibitive. They constructed small-scale models that were to be filmed in stop motion — or go motion, as the animators at ILM referred to this old-school animation process — but it wasn't until ILM's Muren suggested to Spielberg that they try to create the masses of creatures roaming the jungles and meadows of Jurassic Park by using CGI software that they then shifted to digital dinosaurs.[17]

Spielberg was skeptical at first, but the animation team, starting with simple skeletal versions of the dinosaurs to demonstrate the ways in which they would move, eventually won him over. Prior to this, CG "creatures" were just that, creatures that arose out of the imagination of their creators, creatures comprised of all-water or metallic surfaces, but not living, breathing animals. When Spielberg saw the first test scenes of skeletal dinosaurs running through their lush green habitat, he was struck by the fluidity of the motion. It was then clear that these computer-generated behemoths could replace the miniature stop-motion models that had preceded them.[18] When the fully fleshed-out versions of the dinosaurs appeared, the muscles moving beneath dinosaur hide could be seen vibrating with the weight of their feet pounding the earth — they had gone far beyond what was possible to achieve with go-motion animation.

In 1993, *Jurassic Park* was a pivotal point for those who had previously made careers out of puppetry, animatronics, and go-motion animation. They ended up advising the computer animators, and together they pooled their knowledge of movement in post-production to yield the amazingly lifelike CGI dinosaurs in the *Jurassic Park* series. Since the go-motion animators were used to a more hands-on approach, to physically manipulating their puppets or go-motion models to adjust their movements incrementally, they became flummoxed by the interface of the computer keyboard. To facilitate the translation of their sophisticated understanding of animal motion, they created a mechanical model wired up to a computer dubbed the "dinosaur input device."[19]

With this transformation of the input device, each subtle adjustment of the creature, which could now be made using the hands-on technique with which the go-motion animators were familiar, was recorded and downloaded into the computer and fed into the modeling software for the building of the gigantic, prehistoric, computer-generated critters.[20]

In the process of creating the over 50 scenes inhabited by CGI dinosaurs, the animators had to stretch their imaginations to conceive of how these animals might actually move. While they watched hours of footage of animal movement, the computer animators working for ILM were also invited to step away from their monitors and take mime workshops. They were encouraged to run around as if they were raptors and pay attention to the ways in

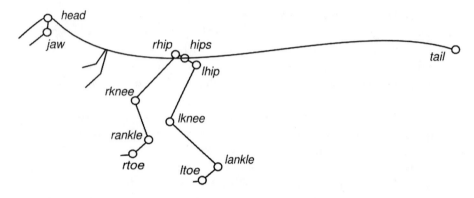

"Dinosaur input device" by Brian Kemp et al., in Proceedings of the 1995 ACM SIGCHI Conference on Human Factors in Computing Systems (CHI'95), pp. 304– 309 (© 2005 AMC, Inc.; reprinted by permission).

which they moved. In this way they explored their own body motion — the gait of their walk, the way their neck turned when they were looking, the way their weight shifted — to be able to more significantly inform the design of the raptors and T-rex's movement.

This imagined movement, while a significant milestone, was to be over-shadowed by the development of actual motion capture, which was not fully developed in 1995 when Cameron conceived of the idea for *Avatar*. The mechanical dinosaur input device was in some ways a precursor to the live-motion capture technology that evolved in the 1990s. Now sensors placed directly on living beings recorded their muscle movement and extracted that data so that it could be mapped to a computer-generated replica.

Dancer and choreographer Bill T. Jones pioneered this process working with digital artists Paul Kaiser and Shelley Eshkar in his 1999 piece, *Ghost-catching*. Jones performed a seven-minute piece covered in sensor dots, but the finished piece that was shown to the audience was a digitized version of his performance in which every gesture resulted in a mark on a virtual screen, as if there were a big chalk crayon attached to his limbs. These drawings remained visible long after the gesture, leaving a map or trace, if you will, of the dance. Kaiser and Eshkar edited Jones' movements in a variety of ways, including duplicating him so that Jones danced with a troupe of dancers made up entirely of his "others" and also by placing him in a wireframe box within which a skeletal version of Jones moved and strained.

Ann Dils, a dance historian commenting on Jones' performance, sug-gested that his "often fierce movement is performed by gutless animated line drawings."[21] She raises here the specter of the absence/presence dichotomy in the digitally animated performance,[22] not unlike the very experience of cin-

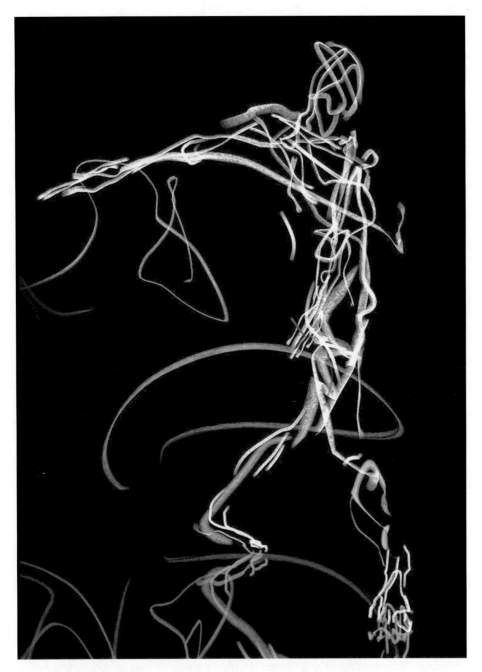

Still from *Ghostcatching* (1999) by Bill T. Jones with Paul Kaiser and Shelley Eshkar.

ema: we sit in the presence of a projection of something, someone, some place, that is not actually there before us. There is something intrinsically virtual about cinema.[23] The avatar itself might be thought of as coming to stand for this paradox and will be investigated in greater detail later on in this volume. But let it suffice to say that motion-capture technology accentuates the presence of what is absent. It literally captures and therefore is able to use and reproduce the organic movement of its source.

The nineties saw many advances in digital technology, including Pixar's *Toy Story* in 1995, the first feature-length film made entirely with CG; Cameron's *Titanic* in 1997, which incorporated CG as well as small model representations of the great ship's demise; and *The Matrix* in 1999, in which the Wachowski brothers utilized digital interpolation to create the effects that enabled Neo to famously dodge those bullets.[24] In *Star Wars, Episode I: The Phantom Menace*, George Lucas, working in conjunction with ILM in 1999, introduced the first CG film star, the first high-speed race through a digitally constructed landscape, and, again, the use of motion capture to move armies of characters across the screen,[25] their tableau-like stiffness that Lamarre notes above notwithstanding.[26]

This breakthrough, live-action, motion-capture technology combined with a photorealistic approach was incorporated in 2001 into the computer-generated film *Final Fantasy: The Spirits Within*, based on the popular video game. The film did not do well at the box office, and some have surmised that this was due to the "uncanny valley" phenomenon.

First observed by Japanese roboticist Masahiro Mori, the uncanny valley refers to the effect of robots or CG characters becoming *too* eerily human.[27] Mori observed that the more his robots approached a humanlike appearance, the more comfortable humans were — but only up to a point. At some point, people begin to experience a sort of cognitive dissonance, a "creepiness" in the extent to which the artificial being resembled a human. According to Peter Travers in *Rolling Stone*, "At first it's fun to watch the characters, [b]ut then you notice a coldness in the eyes, a mechanical quality in the movements."[28] It was this "dead eye" effect that Cameron was determined not to replicate.

The octopus-faced character of Davey Jones in the second and third installments of *Pirates of the Caribbean* was also a combination of image-based motion capture and computer generation. And *The Polar Express* was the first film in which all characters were created using live-action motion capture. But it was the creation by Peter Jackson in 2003 of the character of Gollum — a digitally created character in the live-action film, *The Lord of the Rings Trilogy* — that moved the possibilities for CG characters to new heights.

Jackson was committed to the creation of Gollum as a character that would be completely authentic, who would carry as much reality and emotional weight as the live action actors he was working with. "The character of Gollum is a completely digital creature, but I was determined that I wanted an actor to actually create the character, which in this case is Andy Serkis," says Jackson. The animators worked with four cameras that synchronously recorded his facial movements, which were then mapped to the gradient mesh of the digital character's face. His body and voice design was taken further into an animated world through the expertly combined motion-capture photography, computer-generated imagery and digital sound mixing. The resulting synthesis is a totally new visual effect. "Obviously, Andy creates the character through the voice," explains Jackson. "But also, we're doing a lot of Gollum as motion capture, which is when Andy wears a suit covered in these little dots, and he performs Gollum. He says the dialog, he plays the scenes out just as he would, and the computer is able to capture his movement and translate that to the digital version of Gollum."[29]

Serkis replicated the process of the multiple takes of *Roger Rabbit* days: he would act in a white suit with the live-action actors to establish eye lines and their relationship to him. His performance would then be erased. He'd repeat the action in a motion-capture suit in an empty gridded volume or on a minimal set resembling the terrain of the shot. Lastly the animators would work with the data collected from the motion sensors to fine-tune the digitally rendered character of Gollum.

Ready for Avatar

When Cameron saw the performances of Serkis as Gollum and Bill Nighy as Davey Jones, he knew that the time had arrived for the production of *Avatar* to begin.[30] Cameron had been clear from the get-go that he wasn't thinking about his actors simply standing at a lectern and doing the voices for animated characters.[31] He intended that they would "act," doing everything that the CG character would do. If the character runs, falls, jumps, leaps, straddles a banshee and takes off, smashes the video camera of an approaching bulldozer, these same actions are undertaken by the performer. Cameron had his performers enter a period of training for the film. Those that would ride direhorses were given equestrian lessons; those who needed to shoot a bow were trained in "Na'vi-style" archery, something Cameron invented in which the four-fingered Na'vi pulled back on the bow string with their hands facing outward. Worthington had extensive training by military specialists so he would be able to handle the automatic weapons like a polished marine.

Before even entering the volume to begin performance capture, Cameron flew the cast to the rain forest of Kauai. There the actors paraded around in their loincloths, carrying their bows and arrows, enacting the story of *Avatar*. It was Cameron's hope that when they returned to the studio, each actor and actress would have a body memory of what it felt like to step in the mud, to move a frond out of the way as they traipsed through the rain forest. At the same time, the trip informed Cameron's visual understanding of how light filters through the flora, of the sounds of the rain forest — all the important details that enhanced the "reality" of the rain forest on Pandora.[32]

The implementation of an image-based motion-capture system, *Avatar* producer Jon Landau comments, replaced prosthetics, animatronics, and hours and hours of makeup application for the actors.[33] The computers recorded whatever the actors and actresses did physically, every subtle gesture and expression. The audience is not engaged with a character imagined by a director in concert with an animator who speaks with the voice of an actor, but instead the audience sees a performance, an interpretation, as Sam Worthington, who plays the part of Jake Sully, notes. "It is my performance. This thing walks and talks and acts like me."[34] The ability to capture nuance, to literally capture "the intent of the actor,"[35] not just the arc of a movement, is what Cameron had in mind when he conceived of *Avatar* and what caused him to delay his production until the technology could provide this verisimilitude. Despite his love affair with technology as subject matter and as vehicle for bringing his vision to fruition, the deal breaker for Cameron was that the technology had to reveal the human nature of his characters, not obscure it.

Landau emphasizes the fact that in previous incarnations of CG characters, it wasn't possible to see the eyes of the character as windows to that character's soul. "In our movie," Landau asserts, "you need to make a connection for it to work."[36]

Very much like the motion capture of Serkis for Gollum and Nighy for Davey Jones, the actors and actresses in *Avatar* wore performance-capture suits with markers on them. Motion capture for the body movement was done conventionally, and Cameron had the actors do absolutely everything. Because the "volume" — the empty space in which the film was shot — was so extensive, Cameron could execute battle scenes and even run horses through it, circumventing the need to stitch pieces of scenes together.[37]

In order to create the viewing sensation that Jake and Neytiri were "flying" the banshees, that they were the ones initiating the movement, Cameron created life-sized soft models — a manually operated gimbal rig — of a large banshee-shaped thing that the actors and actresses literally hopped upon and rode. The rig banked and bucked like the ikran in the sky, and the actors had to learn how to stay on and give the appearance of initiating the flight.[38]

Once on their ersatz banshees, the actors view the virtual world of Pandora through which they are flying on computer monitors placed in front of them — somewhat like a spinning class in which you cover a virtual terrain of rolling hills. The actors were able to "see" and therefore imagine where, precisely, they were heading, and consequently their imaginations informed their performances.

The performers had to stay balanced upon these things —finding their centers of gravity, like a board sport where one's body responds to/and initiates movement all at once. This technological call and response — anticipating and mimicking the "bond" that supposedly existed once *sahelu* was made, resulting in the animal and the humanoid moving as one — increased the plausibility of the entire flying sequence.

The sensors on multiple cameras around the volume recorded the data of muscle movement and dumped it into a motion capture software program, generating a real-time skeletal model for each character. Dozens of cameras line this space, each capturing a fraction of the action. Turning the proverbial story of the blind men and the elephant on its head, in this case each piece of the larger puzzle is available to the animators when they are creating the computer-generated characters.

Despite the rigs and props, Cameron had reservations about the standard motion capture as it had been undertaken for Gollum and Davey Jones, feeling it was inadequate to the task of creating a more authentic, believable character.

"Gollum was a performance inspired by Andy Sirkus and Davey Jones was a performance inspired by Bill Nighy.... It is okay but what they are getting is a lower fidelity motion capture of the body.... It's an image-based system ... and then they are recreating the facial performance."[39] Cameron didn't want to give that much power to the animators; he didn't want a committee to be designing the characters "after the fact." He wanted the actors to act.

While Bob Zemeckis' work was also out in front of everyone else's, Cameron saw that, too, as somewhat flawed. For *The Polar Express*, Zemeckis used marker-based image capture. Like *Lord of the Rings*, *Pirates of the Caribbean*, and *Avatar*, the cameras were in a gridded volume, but they were too far away from the faces to actually capture any expression.[40] Cameron indicated that for him, what was most important was what occurs between the actors' eyebrows and their chin, and the cameras which were placed around the volume, as plentiful and high definition as they were, were too far from that expressive facial region to record that faithfully and in as much detail as is necessary to be convincing.

The Head Rig

Where Cameron radically diverged from his predecessors was in the development of the head rig designed to capture the actors' micro-expressions.

Cameron had proposed this head rig in 1995 when he first was inspired to write *Avatar*. He envisioned a headband with a boomed camera that would provide "100 percent capture 100 percent of the time, no matter where the actor turned, no matter what they did."[41] After the actor's performance, it would be possible to extract the data necessary through a process of image analysis. Digital Domain (founded by Cameron; Scott Ross, formerly of ILM, and Stan Winston); WETA Digital, an award-winning visual effects facility located in Wellington, New Zealand; and ILM all rejected his idea. These companies were engaged in their own variations of the theme of motion capture.

When the time finally came to design the computer versions of the Na'vi characters, the actors were initially placed within a well-lit geodesic sphere and their features mapped so that the animators could understand their facial structure inside and out, in three dimensions. Traditionally this scanning process is at the heart of facial performance capture, creating a more finite data set of the surface of their face, but Cameron felt this extensive scanning was a waste of time. "Scanning doesn't do what the actors are doing. What the actors do comes from the inside; it is informed by their emotions. They are firing off hundreds of facial muscles ... sometimes subtle or overt, the tongue with the teeth, to form phonemes."[42]

Taking a page from the book of phenomenological philosopher Maurice Merleau-Ponty, Cameron knew that what an actor was feeling is expressed in their bodily attitude, in what we can see happening in their expressions.[43] Merleau-Ponty refutes the idea that the only way we understand what others are feeling is by mapping our own internal feelings to that of the other. He reminds us that young children "understand" the anger, fear, and anxiety that they see expressed in their parents' faces well before they "understand" what these emotions are or have even experienced them. "Others are directly manifest to us as behavior."[44] In addition, it isn't just recognizing a set of behaviors or expressions, but we are able to recognize a set of behaviors or expressions that belong to a common structure of a particular individual. Therefore, it was imperative to have not just data of an expression of fear that would get mapped onto the CG character of Jake's avatar, but Sam Worthington's data, which would be consonant with his voice, his way of moving, his way of shrugging his shoulders. Merleau-Ponty's thinking suggests, and it seems likely that Cameron would agree, that the integrity of maintaining the inherent structure of each actor's expression by employing the intricate system of performance capture reveals not simply an understanding, but a being, which Merleau-Ponty insists is "thrown into the world and attached to it by a natural bond."[45]

To address the plethora of detail necessary to make what is going on inside the actors visible on the outside, Cameron designed a head rig in addition to the numbers of cameras surrounding the live-action volume. A small boom resembling a headset microphone is attached to the rig. At the end of it is placed a tiny camera that records every nuance of what is visible, every fleeting emotion that scurries across a face. Working with the head rig proved to be phenomenally successful, as evidenced by the extent to which we believe the Na'vi and avatar characters. But it was also a labor-intensive, dynamic process.

"The head rigs provide a visual stream that isn't something you can watch,"[46] Cameron explains. It produces a weird image because the camera is rigidly locked to the face. The background moves with the actor. In addition, the camera is so close to the actor's face that the lens is too wide-angle to create a reliable, realistic visual representation. Instead, the animators used the recordings of the facial performances to extract the data stream that in turn went into creating the mesh for the CG facial animation.

Once the data was gathered from the rig and applied to the CG character's face, Cameron and his team watched the results. In the early stages, Cameron tells, it was a big disappointment. Initially the characters would be stilted or just "wrong." But each time they watched the CG character, they would tweak it — the initial results informing the next set of adjustments — back and forth, viewing the expression over and over again, retweaking, until they had something that resonated, that revealed the "soul" of the actor originating the performance. This process was truly a collaboration between the natural expressions of the actors, the technology of the head rig coupled with the CG software and finally refined by the feedback of Cameron and his animators. Located in the software are hundreds and hundreds of sliders with which it is possible to adjust minute muscle movement — lift an eyebrow, dimple a cheek, twitch an ear — until each of the actor's faces has been approximated. This dynamic process of refinement occurred over the course of nine months to a year, at which point they had accumulated enough accurate data that, as Cameron explains, "they can slap a brand new piece of facial capture onto the model and boom! it comes out exactly what the actor did. Exactly."[47]

It is clear just how important it was to Cameron to avoid a mechanistic, robotic performance, or one that was anything less than "exactly" what the actors and actresses had performed. He was not interested in simulating an expression. He literally wanted to "capture" it as it had originated and reflect it back. In this case he was able to develop what Heidegger would call a free relationship with technology and called upon it in the service of creating a naturalistic representation of the dramatic interpretations — the feelings, motivations, intentions and intuitions — of the actors on the set, from the inside out. It would have been much easier, much less labor intensive, to approximate, using the animation software, a smile, a look of surprise, the tightness of fear. But that would have resulted in expressions not originating on the inside, not emanating from the performer, but instead being slapped on top of, covering over — what we might recognize as enframing. Cameron avoids Heidegger's "*gestellen*," avoids a circumscribed approach to performance by insisting on allowing the emotion to reveal itself through the performance of the actors. Just as Jake, in his avatar, serves as a bridge between his world and the Na'vi, the head rigs bridge and connect the dramatic interpretations of the actors and the computer-generated world they inhabit in *Avatar*.

Virtual Flight

If the development and implementation of the performance-capture system was all that was "new" about the way that *Avatar* was produced, it still would have been a groundbreaking experience. But there were two other technological innovations Cameron incorporated into the production of *Avatar*: the virtual camera and the SimulCam system.

Cameron developed a system ultimately dubbed the Fusion Camera that consisted of two Sony HD cameras used together to create the three-dimensional, stereoscopic 3-D effect achieved in *Avatar*. He eschews the old-school red/blue three dimensions, and with his partner Vince Pace he developed an intricate system in which these two cameras are synced to work together, shooting out of a single lens. The camera is 28 pounds, including computer elements that keep the cameras working synchronously, but still light enough that Cameron was able to use it to shoot almost all of the film's handheld scenes himself. This sophisticated juxtaposition of the camera lenses much more nearly replicates the ways in which we see, in three dimensions, even though the two lenses are not situated side by side, the way our eyes are.[48] Vince Pace describes what the cameras do as fusing "creativity and technology," but also as fusing the two simultaneous images they are recording.

The subtle ways in which Cameron employed this Fusion Camera system raised the bar significantly for 3-D and dramatically changed the quality of the viewing experience. No longer does the spectator feel like things are jumping out at us, poking us in the eye, or that the cinematic space created is unreal. The ballistic cinematism of Paul Virilio addressed earlier in this chapter, in which the train, the missile, or the speeding superhero penetrates the cinematic picture plane, is the counterpoint of the 3-D effect employed by Cameron. Instead of moving into depth, *Avatar* both moves out toward the spectator, but more importantly draws the spectator in.

Manohla Dargis described the experience most aptly in her *New York*

Times review, "A New Eden, Both Cosmic and Cinematic." "Mr. Cameron uses 3-D to amplify the immersive experience of spectacle cinema.... He uses 3-D seemingly to close the space between the audience and the screen. He brings the movie to you."[49]

Daniel Mendelsohn, writing for the *New York Review of Books*, remarked, "... (there are gratifyingly few shots of objects projecting into the audience's field; you just feel that you're sharing the same plane as the creatures in the movie)...."[50]

In an interview with NPR's Terry Gross, Cameron discussed what he felt was possible with 3-D that wasn't with conventional two-dimensional cinema. Cameron thinks of 3-D as "much more tactile. Like as simple as a shot in a snow storm ... the snow flakes would fall on you and around you.... Any time the medium of the air between you and the subject ... can be filled with something ... wrapping the audience in the experience of the movie."[51] These qualities, being wrapped, sharing the same plane, closing the space between the screen and the spectator, all speak to the notion of a shift in the paradigm of the cinematic apparatus, which will be discussed at length in Chapter Five.

For now let it suffice to notice that the choice to shoot in 3-D, and the particular brand of 3-D that Cameron tweaked technologically to achieve the results he had imagined, returned to most viewers the wonder intrinsic to cinema.

Cameron, like his predecessors, Bob Zemeckis shooting *Who Framed Roger Rabbit* and Peter Jackson shooting *Lord of the Rings*, was faced with the problem of having on the one hand 3-D footage shot of live-action actors, and on the other hand footage that was shot as performance capture and had been translated by the team of animators into the computer-generated world of Pandora, including the terrain, the wild creatures, and the Na'vi. Somehow these "two movies" had to be integrated, one into the other. Cameron's Simul-Cam system integrated the Fusion Camera system for shooting 3-D with the virtual camera system. "It overlaid a virtual capture environment on a live action set."[52] Cameron was working with the SimulCam as *if* it was a virtual camera allowing him to do "director-centric, real-time ... work flow on the production floor while working in the CG environment."[53]

The SimulCam/virtual camera was equipped with a monitor in which Cameron — while shooting the live-action performance capture of his actors — could literally see a low-resolution version of what had been generated on the computer up to this point. So while Cameron was shooting actors and actresses in motion-capture suits with their head rigs on, he was *seeing* them against a background of lush foliage and bioluminescent plant life.

For example, in the process of shooting the medical tech scene where

Jake experiences his first linkup to his avatar, they shot the gurney, the human technicians, and all their medical equipment in real-time live action. In this case the "set" was one of about 25 that were constructed in New Zealand and existed in the real world, but they had to feed in the CG of Jake's avatar to make the scene complete. As he is actually in the process of shooting this scene, Cameron sees a low-resolution, computer-generated version of Jake's nine-foot-tall avatar in the monitor of his virtual camera. Part of what contributes to making a film a *good* film is the composition of what lives within the frame of the screen. This system allowed Cameron to "see" the computer-generated characters and landscape at the exact time that he was filming the live actors in the volume, enabling him to thoughtfully and artistically compose each shot. Because Cameron was working with a real-time composite and a real-time track, each frame of *Avatar* is consistently beautifully shot. In fact, months after all the actors had finished their performances, Cameron was shooting, alone in the volume, composing the shots via the technology of the virtual camera.

During the time that Cameron was combining motion capture within the CG environment, he was able to share the blended footage, the live action combined with the CG, with the actors in order that they might also have a sense of what was going on. They can see Jake, flailing around in the medical tech facility, knocking things over with his tail. This also addresses the old problem of where, precisely, the animated character *is*, enabling the live-action actors to get the eyelines even more accurate.[54]

On the one hand you have the CG of Jake's avatar interacting with the live-action med-tech characters; on the other you have human characters interacting with 3-D computer-generated jungle, a fluxing of both the live-action environment and characters with the computer-generated characters and environment. One of the most stunning examples of this process at work, and incidentally one of Cameron's favorite scenes, rests in the segment of the film in which Jake and Neytiri are flying on their banshees.

Following the ways in which these scenes were put together gives one a sense of the complexity of this undertaking and the kind of thinking that goes into breaking down what has to occur to make the whole thing come together.

Initially, there has to be this place in the Hallelujah mountains where this all occurs. Designing these karsts that float in the clouds, spilling their waterfalls into space, is in and of itself quite a feat. But once we have this virtual location, it is necessary to create the ikran. If we think back to what Spielberg underwent to create his dinosaurs, we have a sense of what had to happen to create the banshees, who come directly out of Cameron's imagination but rely on many dragonlike creatures who came before them. Cameron worked for months with illustrators creating 2-D images of what these might look like.

Next he moved to the work of master sculptors who created 3-D lifelike mockettes of the creatures. With each iteration the details, the "bird of prey-ness" with which Cameron hoped to imbue each ikran, came into being. Eventually there are banshees, Na'vi, and floating mountains, all created in the virtual world on the computer.

To shoot the aerial scenes, the flight paths first had to be mapped out. They fashioned small wire models of the ikran and linked them with motion sensors so the computer would follow their movements, choreographing the flight patterns. Cameron and his team "flew" the model ikran — they literally moved them around the room, dipping and diving like kids playing with toy airplanes. The computer is recording a simulated flight plan based on the motions of the wire ikran models. And at the same time that they are flying their banshees around this empty space, they could see the computer-generated models flying through the skies of Pandora.[55]

Once the flight paths were set, it was time to bring in the actors. As mentioned above, they had balanced on ersatz ikran, and the trick was to time the way they were riding these to match up with the flight plans Cameron had created. So if Cameron had made his little model dive, its rider would have to adjust her body accordingly so it appeared that she was initiating the movement. It took a lot of rehearsing and "training" for the ikran riders to arrive at the seamless elegance and strength of the characters riding their creatures during this scene.[56]

When the flight paths are set and the riders are done riding, Cameron takes his virtual camera into the empty volume and begins to shoot the "film." Because he can see what was created by the CG through his monitor, as he moves his virtual camera through the empty volume he is establishing his director's point of view, placing himself in relationship to the flight patterns that are now already determined in the animated sequences. He can be shooting from a "virtual" helicopter alongside Neytiri, from the bottom of a water-fall looking up as they swoop down from above, from a piggybacking perspective on the soaring banshee. He "shoots" all these scenes by virtue of the fact that he can see where he is in the virtual world of Pandora that has just been created. In the video produced by Fox Movie Channel called *Making a Scene*, which details the making of *Avatar*, we can watch Cameron dancing around the empty volume with the virtual camera in his hand, shooting what appears to be nothing. Yet in the monitor in front of him he is seeing the world of Pandora; the diving, dipping, frolicking banshees; and the exhila-rating duet between Jake and Neytiri as they soar through the sky.[57]

This whole technical process brings to light the cinematic trope of absence/presence which we have lightly touched upon and will explore more fully later on in Chapter Five. But now this figure has become visible in the arena of production. Before the incorporation of the computer and its digital capabilities, we could imagine a single camera eye or perhaps several cameras shooting live actors on a set or on location. Not until that film was edited, distributed and finally projected on a screen in a theater did the spectator become aware of the absence intrinsic to all that was previously filmed. In integrating live-action performance capture with computer-generated characters and locations, the teeter-totter of absence/presence has asserted itself in the very making of the film. Particularly in a story in which characters leave their physical human bodies and travel into and through other humanoid bodies, reside in multiple spaces at once, or could be seen as absenting one body for a presence in another, it seems fitting that this paradox would surface in the site of the film's production as well.

Cameron looks at an empty room and sees flying banshees and a lush jungle. The actors "pretend" to interact with imaginary creatures who threaten their lives or fly them through floating mountains. As to the difficulty of working in an empty volume, pretending to be engaged with creatures and an environment that isn't there, Sigourney Weaver, who played Grace Augustine, explains, "People expected the actors to find [working this way] more difficult, but since we are always doing make believe anyway, pretending that nothing is everything, is second nature to us."[58] And Worthington underscores the ways in which this high-tech production environment gets closer to the nature of human emotion.

He shares the experience of acting under the watchful eye of 190 infrared, high-definition cameras all trained on his performance. "There is nowhere to hide, so every take you have to be truthful."[59] Paradoxically, upping the technological ante returns many of the actors to their theatrical roots. Joel David Moore, who played the part of the other avatar driver Norm, waxes nostalgic saying it took him back to his old theater days where all you might have had in your black box theater was a chair, and it was the actor's job was to imagine everything else.[60]

Avatar has as a leitmotif the notion that our relationship toward technology can obscure our ability to see. But if we can learn to approach technology without enframing it, without expecting it to be a certain way or provide a certain result, technology can, as Heidegger suggests, reveal nature to us, enhancing our ability to see.

The scope of the world of Pandora that had to be created down to the smallest detail — the flora and fauna, the military transports, the weapons, the linkup pods, the Tree of Souls — is mind boggling. One might recall Jake's response to Neytiri when she is teaching him how to track animals. She would force him to pay attention to the tiniest traces. This attention and care to detail in one's world or in one's filmmaking is only possible with an unenframed approach, with a soft and circumspect gaze. Ironically, the high-tech container in which the film was produced is infused with this motif, as is the experience of the actors and actresses. More sophisticated, more expensive, more complicated technology, instead of creating distance and dehumanizing, opens up truer, realer, more natural performances by the cast. Cameron insists that the technology that was created for *Avatar* was in the service of protecting and revealing the emotions behind the performances, was a vehicle making the heart of the movie visible.

CCH Pounder, the actress who plays Moat, Neytiri's mother and the shaman of the clan, embodies the wisdom of her character as she describes how it felt to work under these conditions. In the film Moat tells Jake that it is difficult to fill a cup that is already full, advocating an approach of openness, of embracing not-knowing. When she speaks about working on *Avatar*, she says that working under these unfamiliar conditions, she had to let go of all of the things that she thought were supposed to happen and just let go, just do it.[61]

Chapter Four

The Same Old Story

Play It Again

Anyone who has ever been a parent knows that children have a passion for repetition. Anyone who has ever been a babysitter, camp counselor, aunt or uncle, older sister or brother or grandparent knows that there is no such thing as watching *Mary Poppins* or reading *Goodnight Moon* too many times. "Again, mommy, again!" is the demanding mantra of the child who takes extraordinary delight in repetition. The thrill of knowing what comes next is almost too wonderful to bear.

Nor does this abate with age. During the sixties, Bill Cosby routines were recited verbatim over and over by many a teenager, not in the least diminished with the retellings. Children of the eighties came of age practicing pitch-perfect playback of Monty Python dialogs for hours on end. Perhaps because recitation has gone out of favor and there is little to no emphasis on rote memorization in today's classrooms, younger people find their own methods of exercising that particular node of the brain. The delight of getting it precisely right, in knowing exactly what comes next, remains evident. Out of this same joy the "sing-along" was born: midnight communal consumption of the cult classic *The Rocky Horror Picture Show* or family outings to *Mary Poppins*, *Grease*, and *The Sound of Music* sing-alongs. Costumed audiences, provided with props and karaoke-style words moving across the film screen, sing their gleeful hearts out.

There are other testaments to the fact that the pleasure of repetition is never completely outgrown. How else would we explain that at almost any hour of any day we can find repeat episodes of a myriad of *Law and Order* spin-offs playing somewhere on some cable TV station? Or that *Pretty Woman*, *Pirates of the Caribbean*, and *The Terminator* are regular offerings on TV movie channels? Or that the offerings of TCM, already viewed numerous times by most audiences, is as successful as it is? It is clear that if no one were watching these reruns, they would no longer be aired. Years worth of the *Star Trek* franchise, *Seinfeld*, and *Sex in the City* episodes and even ancient, by television standards, reairings of *The Twilight Zone* on the Sci-Fi Channel are consumed by audiences who look forward to the frisson of the familiar.

Not only are we inundated with television reruns but by a passel of remakes and adaptations. Where once it was fashionable to assign to each specific medium something at which it excelled, today the boundaries between television, comics, movies, novels, musical theater, ballet, opera, and video games are blurred and permeable. As Noël Carroll has argued in his essay debunking Rudolf Arnheim's specificity thesis, the world is far richer for having such diversity of narrative forms.[1] It is not too much of a stretch to assert that all of the arts draw from, are informed by, and react to what has gone before. Art historians outline the periods or styles in history against which artists reacted. The same appears to be true in music, literature, and dance. Creative people are influenced by work to which they have been exposed as well as by their own experience. It must be apparent as well that the producers of art products — those who invest their capital in such ventures — are intent on receiving a return on their investments. Something familiar, something proven, provides such security. The forces of artistic invention combined with a surefire money earner yield the remix culture with which we find ourselves besieged today.

Remediation has become the norm, or as New York–based filmmaker Kirby Ferguson argues in his four-part video, "Everything is a remix."[2] Seventy-four out of one hundred of the biggest blockbusters in the last ten years are either sequels, remakes of early films, or adaptations. Graphic novels, like Marjane Satrapi's *Persepolis*, become animated films. Animated films like DiMartino and Konietzko's *Avatar: The Last Airbender* (no relation to Cameron's *Avatar!*), which itself borrows shamelessly from Japanese anime, becomes the film *The Last Airbender*, an atypical box-office disappointment for M. Night Shyamalan. The *Transformers* series is based on a kid's toy. *Tron*, the *Lara Croft* series, and *Prince of Persia* are based on video games. The sprawling series of Batman, Superman, Spiderman, Hulk, Hellboy, and Ironman movies hail from classic comic books.

The move from stage to screen has become de rigueur, and the reverse is now also true. The musicals of Rodgers and Hammerstein achieved mass distribution when translated for the screen. Disney's animated *Lion King* and *Beauty and the Beast* became hits on Broadway. (Prior to this revitalization of the classic fairy tale, *Beauty and the Beast* also found its way into a television series set in New York in the late 1980s.) The 1964 Disney classic film *Mary Poppins* is a Broadway hit as of this writing. George Bernard Shaw's *Pygmalion* spawned Lerner and Loewe's musical *My Fair Lady*—first on stage and then adapted for screen—Garry Marshall's ubiquitous *Pretty Woman*, Robert Iscove's *She's All That*, and even the film adaptation of John Guare's play, *Six Degrees of Separation*.

The Shakespearean oeuvre has provided no end of material, Julie Taymor's *The Tempest* a case in point. *The Taming of the Shrew* was remixed as *Ten Things I Hate About You. Romeo and Juliet* was lushly transformed for the screen by Franco Zeffirelli, but there was also Jerome Robbins' musical *West Side Story*; Baz Luhrmann's *Romeo + Juliet*, a film which locates Shakespeare's dialog within a hip, contemporary mise-en-scene; Bartkowiak's martial arts version, *Romeo Must Die*; and the animated story of love among garden gnomes, *Gnomeo & Juliet.*

In short, films are based on other films, cinematographically, technologically, and narratively. Mark Sweeney, film critic for the *Boston Globe*, argues that films and other creative arts that emerge from within a tradition are richer than those that operate in a void. "There's nothing invidious in saying a movie is about other movies. It's like saying life on this planet is carbon based: It's just a fact."[3] The extra- and inter-textual has become almost a requirement.

When a story works, audiences are happy to be reminded of that fact and to experience it over and over again. We crave the familiar, but we also are entranced by the strange. We are allured by the prospect of a different telling, a new interpretation of the same old thing. Yet there have been those whose categorizations of the "story" of *Avatar*—the familiar in a strange new wrapper—have been particularly harsh. Daniel Mendelsohn, film critic for the *New York Review of Books*, called *Avatar's* plot "highly derivative, if not outright plagiaristic."[4] *Locus Online's* Gary Westfahl saw in *Avatar* "stale sentiments" and "threadbare themes."[5] And Salon.com's Scott Mendelsohn sees *Avatar* as "a mishmash of *Pocahontas, Dances with Wolves, The Battle for Terra,* and *FernGully: The Last Rainforest.*"[6] There is no argument here. *Avatar* resembles these and other narratives in obvious ways. But it is also much, much more. It is an anti-war film, a western, and a hero's quest, in Joseph Campbell's sense of the genre. One might ask, does the familiar story line diminish the experience or enrich it? Are complex plots reduced to pander to an audience whose attention span has dwindled or to enrich the meaning-making experience of the spectator by including the inter-textual? A tension exists between the strangeness of 3-D digital motion capture and the familiarity of the old-fashioned storyteller, between the euphoria induced by the lush, immersive visual experience and the disappointment engendered in some who expected something equally radical in the narrative's unfolding.

As Gérard Genette makes clear, the concept of storytelling embodies both the story and its telling.[7] This chapter focuses on the story Cameron was attempting to tell, the rich antecedents that inform its construction as a narrative, and the way in which the story was recounted.

The Story

In Genette's seminal work, *Narrative Discourse: An Essay on Method,* he embarks on a commonsense disentangling of the various strands of narrative. He may well have taken his cue from the *Poetics,* so closely do his discrete understandings of "narrative" resemble Aristotle's thought. Genette, like his ancient predecessor, gives us a three-pronged approach to what is narrative. First we have the object of mimesis or the "story" to be told. Secondly, we have the means or the medium in which the story is represented — the text, the speech, the opera, the screenplay, the film. The way in which this telling unfolds might be linked to what we colloquially consider "the plot." Genette refers to this signification of the story as the "narrative." And lastly, there is the telling or showing, the event in which there is the actual recounting of what had occurred, or what we might designate as the act of narrating.[8] Genette emphasizes that in any analysis of narrative, we are really engaged in an exploration of relationships — the relationship between what is being told and the way it is being told, the relationship between how the telling unfolds and how the story actually *happened.* The audience pieces together the story by responding to the cues afforded by the narrative, is privy to the narrative only if it is uttered. And while we separate these strands in order to better examine them, they are inscribed in one another.[9]

The strand of story that is *Avatar* is informed by the trace of the narrative's forbearers. Science-fiction writer and critic Gary Westfahl noted recurring narrative strains in *Avatar* and a cluster of sci-fi short stories, films, TV episodes, and novels. He suggested that this brought to mind an old Hollywood axiom: "Stealing from one source is plagiarism while stealing from several sources is research." Westfahl concluded that Cameron had, in fact, done his research![10]

Among those sources enumerated by Westfahl, a few merit mention. For example, Cameron's *sahelu—* the bond between Na'vi and banshee — resembles the relationships depicted between Dragonriders and their dragons in Anne McCaffrey's popular fantasy series, *The Dragonriders of Pern.* Westfahl, too, notes Cameron's adoption of the AMP suit, which brings to mind the Mecha or Gundam prevalent in Japanese anime. Yet the moments in *Avatar* of bonding with a flying dragon or hopping into a mechanical fighting suit do not, in and of themselves, sufficiently qualify, as Westfahl asserts, as plot "rip-offs."[11] They function rather as what might be designated "bound motifs." These themes add to the richness of the story and at the same time are intrinsic to its telling. The telepathy shared with the ikran and the direhorses offers a small indication of the extensive network of communication that exists between the Na'vi and their world. The AMP suit in which Colonel Quaritch spends much of his time becomes the perfect foil to Jake's existence in his avatar. Important motifs, yes, but not plot rip-offs by a long shot.

Westfahl locates in Ursula LeGuin's novella, *The Word for World Is Forest*, the story that he feels most closely resembles *Avatar*. However, aside from the broadest of plot outlines — a human invasion and consequent destruction of a planet inhabited by a race of peaceful aliens, a plot also loosely found in the animated film *The Battle for Terra* — there is little heft to this comparison, and here, as in his misinterpretation of Cameron's vision of science and technology,[12] Westfahl's critique falls short of the mark.

There is no question that the core story of *Avatar* exhibits similarities to films and stories that have preceded it. While it is not feasible to address each and every story that *Avatar* brings to mind — these may vary wildly depending on one's literary and cinematic tastes — a short list of the most salient tales with regard to *Avatar* and which also happened to be the ones most frequently mentioned in critical reviews will be referred to as "source stories" and considered in the pages that follow.

These source stories include, in no particular order, *Dances with Wolves*, *The Last Samurai*, *Pocahontas*, *FernGully*, *Broken Arrow*, *Dune*, *District 9*, *Lawrence of Arabia*, *A Man Called Horse*, "Desertion," and *The Wizard of Oz*, known to be one of Cameron's favorite films and the one that critic Daniel Mendelsohn of the *New York Review of Books* asserts "haunts *Avatar*."[13] Some of the stories most nearly resemble *Avatar* by evoking what David Brooks has labeled the white messiah complex,[14] notably *Dances with Wolves*, *The Last Samurai*, *Dune*, *Lawrence of Arabia*, and *A Man Called Horse*. Others in the group echo the pro-environmental ethos of *Avatar*, like *Pocahontas*, *FernGully* and *Dances with Wolves*. Some speak to the literal physical transformation of a protagonist, for example *FernGully*, "Desertion," *Dune*, and *District 9*, while just about all of the stories chosen emphasize an anti-imperialist slant except for *A Man Called Horse* and *The Wizard of Oz*. While all of the stories grouped here are dissimilar from *Avatar* and one another in at least some regards, a content analysis of this grouping reveals a narrative core consisting of an archetypal tale that also informs the heart of *Avatar*.

The Story of Avatar

If the 3-D motion capture, computer-generated characters, futuristic science-fiction wrapper, consciousness-swapping apparatus, and luscious oceanic world of Pandora are stripped away, with what are we left? Scott Mendelsohn of Salon.com asserts that *Avatar* is "at its core, a relatively obvious parable of the European settlers in North America and their subjugation of the Native Americans who were here first."[15] The extent to which *Avatar* is indeed obvious will be explored in the context of examining its structure as a classical Hollywood narrative later on in this chapter. While there is ample evidence that the story of decimation of Native American peoples and their way of life is strongly evoked in *Avatar*, it is merely one of several subsets of motifs. In an interview with NPR's Terry Gross, Cameron admits that any references to Iraq, to Vietnam, to Western colonialism in general are in the film by design. "At a very generalized level, it's saying our attitude about indigenous people and our entitlement about what is rightfully theirs is the same sense of entitlement that lets us bulldoze a forest and not blink an eye."[16]

So yes, *Avatar* elicits our national guilt with regard to the treatment of native peoples, our incursions in Southeast Asia and the Middle East. Yes, *Avatar* is an anti-war film. It is also an anti-imperialist film. *Avatar* is a love story, an adventure story, a sci-fi story. *Avatar* is a story about taking care of our environment. And *Avatar* is a story about relationships: our relationship to technology, to ourselves, to each other, to our planet. In the pages that follow these story arcs will be traversed. Yet each of these narrative threads emerges first and foremost from a primal and pithy archetype. If *Avatar* is considered at its heart to be a parable — or perhaps more accurately an archetypal myth — then we must consider at what universal truths or lessons it is pointing.

Applying Genette's idea of story as the events that transpired and are thus made visible in the act of a narration, the bare bones story of *Avatar* might look something like this: Jake is recruited to drive an avatar. He is shipped miles away from his home. He is given an alien body to inhabit which transforms his disabled human body into something whole and in some ways "super-human." In his new body, he is dispatched to the Pandoran jungle by Grace and Colonel Quaritch. He meets Neytiri, and her parents set the terms of his task: he must learn the ways of the Na'vi and then he will be judged. He is guided in this task by Grace's coaching and Neytiri's instruction. He falls in love and consummates a relationship with Neytiri. He faces the opposition of Quaritch and his minions, the anger and mistrust of Neytiri and the rest of the Na'vi. He escapes from jail, bonds with the giant banshee and becomes Toruk Makto. He fights alongside the Na'vi in battle and defeats Quaritch. He becomes transformed and in an ultimate sense is reborn.

One might, at first glance, recognize amid this stripped-down synopsis the morphology that Russian formalist Vladimir Propp was able to extract from the hundreds of folk tales that he surveyed. Propp concluded from his research that there is a common structure to all narratives that relies, in part, on the functions and interactions among the seven character types that he identified and which are certainly evident even in the skeletal outline of *Avatar*.

The villain: Quaritch/Selfridge.

The donor: Grace, who provides the avatar.

The helper: This role is shared by several characters in *Avatar*. We might imagine Grace again as helper, but a more likely candidate is Moat, Neytiri's mother and the clan's shaman. She suggests that Jake become an apprentice to Neytiri, and she frees him toward the end, when he is bound and Quaritch is attacking. She tries to save Grace's life and oversees Jake's transformation at the end of the film.

The princess and her father: These characters set the hero on his journey, or tell the hero what it is necessary for him to know. In this case, it is clear that this description most nearly fits Neytiri and Eytukan, her father.

The dispatcher: Here we could see Grace, or Selfridge or even Quaritch, since in some ways they all sent Jake to the Na'vi.

The hero: Jake

The false hero: Up to a point, Tsu'tey might be considered as the false hero, in the ways in which he rejects Jake's presence and is jealous of his relationship with Neytiri, to whom he is promised. He then becomes yet another helper.

Propp looked not simply at the character types inherent in the folktale and the ways in which their interactions move the story forward, but the overarching shape the tale takes as well. He articulated four spheres: in the first we meet the characters, in the second we enter into the heart of the story, in the third the hero locates what he might need to succeed on his journey, and in the fourth he returns home. This can be easily mapped to the unfolding story in *Avatar*. Cameron, a consummate storyteller, takes his time introducing the characters, setting the scene. When Jake takes on the three-month apprenticeship, we can see that as Propp's heart of the story. The giant Leonopteryx is what Jake figures he needs to succeed on his journey, especially since bonding with it returns him to Neytiri, to the Na'vi, and wins him the respect and brotherhood of Tsu'tey. Jake's return involves his transmutation and returns him to the self that embodying the avatar allows him to be.

Propp's simplistic and overly broad outline adumbrates the more intricate structure of the mythic archetype of the "hero's quest" made popular by the writings of Joseph Campbell, which built on the thinking of Carl Jung. (It is not simply that films resemble other films. But theories and paradigms resemble other theories and paradigms.) The synopsis of *Avatar* sketched out above fits neatly into the loosely delineated structure of the hero's quest below.

1. *The hero, a regular schmoe, is pulled out of his ordinary life by extraordinary circumstances.* Jake is recruited by the RDA Company to drive an avatar. He is shipped light-years away from home to an alien land.

2. *In an unknown land, he is offered a supernatural aid or talisman or power.* He is given a new body to inhabit that transforms his disability into something whole and in some ways "super-human."

3. *He crosses a threshold and enters the unknown.* In his new body he is able to travel to the Pandoran jungle and undertake his adventure.

4. *He is in the "belly of a whale," swallowed and on a road of trials, impossible tasks, and insurmountable obstacles.* Neytiri's father sets the terms of his task: he must learn the ways of the Na'vi, and then he will be judged worthy or not. He must ride a direhorse, fly an ikran, and kill a hexapede.

5. *The hero is guided.* He is aided in this task by Grace's coaching and Neytiri's instruction, providing him with a new set of skills.

6. *The hero joins in a mystical marriage with the "queen/goddess."* Jake and Neytiri choose one another after he is initiated.

7. *The hero faces a battle with the monster.* Jake meets the opposition of Quaritch and his minions, the anger and mistrust of Neytiri and the rest of the Na'vi.

8. *He becomes free of his fear.* He becomes clear about the nature of his task.

9. *He attains "godlike stature."* He escapes from jail, bonds with a giant Leonopteryx and becomes Toruk Makto.

10. *The supreme ordeal.* He, Neytiri, and Tsu'tey lead the Na'vi in battle and defeat Quaritch.

11. *Separation or transformation or his return occurs.* He becomes transformed and reborn as a Na'vi.[17]

Myth in general orders the everyday experience and communicates this order through a formal structure, a story.[18] This monomyth, a word Campbell borrowed from James Joyce to designate the hero's passage,[19] continues to touch audiences because it speaks to the challenges individuals face in their less-than-dramatic lives, but which nonetheless become our personal quests. Whether or not we embrace the more esoteric notion of a collective unconscious that responds to intra-psychic tropes, when the inspiring actions of the hero are writ spectacularly large as in film, the universality of the journey resonates across and beyond specific story lines, cultures and time. Campbell saw this action as reciprocal: individuals striving to live creatively influence our world in much the same way as the stories of the mythic quest affect the individual. Clarissa Pinkola Estes, author of *Women Who Run with the Wolves*, characterizes Campbell's understanding of this reciprocity in her introduction to the 2004 edition of *The Hero with a Thousand Faces*. "By restating this primordial understanding, Campbell offers hope that the consciousness of the individual can prompt, prick, and prod the whole of humankind into more evolution."[20] It was not enough for Cameron to make just an entertaining movie. He wanted to affect the actions of his audiences. In the "Capturing *Avatar*" video that accompanies the three-disc Extended Collector's Edition of *Avatar*, Cameron says, "One can hope that people feel that little twinge of conscience, of responsibility.... I'll settle for a small change." Cameron's aspiration is clearly visible in Jake's own quest.

The Wounded Warrior

In the opening voice-over of the film Jake alludes to the fact that he'd had a hole blown through the middle of his life. He comes to us damaged, as do a long line of mythic heroes, their quests often aimed at repairing their fractured souls. But as in Campbell's paradigm where the healing that transpires internally affects what occurs in the outside world, Jake's transformation affects more than simply his bereft soul. The journey he undertakes encompasses what is known in the Jewish tradition as *Tikkun Olam*, a healing of the soul of the world. If the bulldozing and scorching of the Tree of Souls signifies the shattering of the Pandoran soul, Jake and the Na'vi are fighting to preserve its wholeness, to set — or in Jake's case reset — the world aright.

The damaged protagonist who finds him- or herself on some sort of transformational journey, whether consciously chosen or not, populates not only the bulk of the source stories listed above, but extends outward to countless myths and narratives, from the ur-hero's quest of *Ulysses*, to the contemporary journeys of Luke Skywalker in the *Star Wars* epic and Neo in *The Matrix*.

In each case, the more wounded we find our hero, the more powerful is his or her redemption. Kevin Costner's *Dances with Wolves*, 1990, and Edward Zwick's *The Last Samurai*, 2003, each depict the hurting hero who quite inadvertently finds himself not only immersed in an alien culture but privy to the spiritual teachings of a mentor who ultimately steers his transformation. In the opening scenes of *Dances with Wolves*, Lieutenant Dunbar, sick to death of the Civil War, canters off on a suicidal ride into enemy fire. Nathan Algren, disenchanted with his less-than-illustrious military career in which he was instrumental in the defeat and decimation of the Cheyenne tribe, is portrayed as a drunken hawker during the opening scenes of *The Last Samurai*. In David Lean's 1962 *Lawrence of Arabia* and Delmer Daves' 1950 *Broken Arrow*, we encounter the marginalized hero. Both Lieutenant Lawrence of the British army and Tom Jeffords, the man who purportedly brokered a peace treaty between the Apache chief Cochise and the U.S. government, fell outside the proscribed parameters for their ilk. Lawrence was a scholar, a bit of a buffoon, a mapmaker, a clown. None in his regiment took him seriously as a soldier. Jeffords, like Dunbar and Algren, but not quite as downtrodden, was frustrated with the lack of civility between the settlers of the west and the Native tribes inhabiting that part of the then territorial United States. Unlike his compatriots, he had an encounter in which he saved the life of a young Apache boy and came to see these native people as "human." Lawrence saw beyond what his fellow soldiers could conceive and imagined an end to the warring among Bedouin tribes. Both Lawrence and Jeffords put themselves in harm's way in order to remedy situations for which they could envision a more just solution. Both were ridiculed and ostracized by their peers.

In Neill Blomkamp's 2009 sci-fi/anti-apartheid film, *District 9*, we have an unlikely protagonist in Wikus van de Merwe. An ineffectual bureaucrat Wikus finds himself heading up the relocation of an alien population detained in a ghetto outside Johannesburg. Having been assigned this task by his father-in-law for whom he works, Wikus is played as a pawn in the relocation of the dangerous "prawns," and his lack of agency may be precisely why he was chosen to execute the unpleasant task of confronting a hostile alien population and informing them of their impending need to pack up and move.

Lastly in this string of wounded warriors is the short fiction story "Desertion," one of a grouped series in a book by Clifford Simac entitled *City*. Taken together these stories recount the fall of human civilization and the beginnings of a canine world. "Desertion" introduces us to Kent Fowler, a military man, head of his division on the planet Jupiter. Racked with guilt over the loss of several men he sent out to explore the surface of what was perceived as a hostile planet, Fowler can bear to lose no more soldiers to the "keening gale." He opts instead to go off to explore the planet himself. While this short story on the whole resembles the trajectory of *Avatar* in only very small ways, there is one significant similarity. When his troops — and one dog — venture out to explore the planet, they do so inserted into the bodies of the Lopers, the native inhabitants of Jupiter.[21]

Similar to the way that Jake's perceptions were enhanced and intensified by the physical body through which they came, when Fowler and his dog Towser embody the Lopers, their perceptual experience was transformed.

What appeared to their human and canine senses as a howling, gaseous, toxic planet was now received as beautiful, musical, energizing, and seductive — so much so that they were loathe to return to their original forms. Inhabiting the Lopers also enabled the dog Towser and the man Fowler to communicate directly with one another for the very first time.[22]

The two protagonists of Disney's 1995 version of *Pocahontas* and Bill Kroyer's 1992 animated feature *FernGully: The Last Rainforest* are less damaged than simply unsettled and falling somewhat outside the bounds of what is expected of them. Their transformation has to do more with righting their course, with stepping into the communal roles expected of them. Pocahontas struggles with a symbol from a dream that she can't decipher and is frustrated that perhaps she won't be able to find her destined path. In *FernGully*, the fairy Crysta, an unwilling apprentice to Magi, the aging but powerful source of all creativity, hasn't the patience to practice her magic and hence can't gain access to her birthright, the creative force. Dorothy, in Victor Fleming's 1939 *The Wizard of Oz*, like Pocahontas and Crysta, was in the throes of an adolescent angst, feeling misunderstood and betrayed by her aunt and uncle who yielded to Miss Gulch's demand to destroy her dog Toto.

In the case of Eliot Silverstein's 1970 *A Man Called Horse*, the character of John Morgan — a wealthy, privileged Englishman who travels the world shooting grouse and other game birds — is bemoaning the emptiness and purposelessness of his life of leisure just prior to his capture by the Sioux.

The Hero's Transformation

We are told how destroyed Jake was in the opening voice-over in which he describes the "hole blown in the middle of his life."[23] But it is in the details of several minutes of deleted scenes that we are shown the breadth of his physical and intra-psychic damage. In these cut scenes of *Avatar*, Cameron locates us on a dystopian earth reminiscent of classic *Blade Runner* in which a disgruntled, wheelchair-bound Jake makes his way to a bar amid a sea of masked faces. The obvious conclusion is that Earth's atmosphere has been polluted beyond what is now safe to breathe. Once inside the bar, Jake throws back a couple of shots to the raucous cheers of onlookers and proceeds to get himself into a brawl — the aftermath of an attempt to intervene when a young woman is being slapped around by her boyfriend. A self-destructive, drunken, yet chivalrous Jake reveals his deep desire to find "something worth fighting for."[24] When he is tossed into an alley behind the bar, the symbolism is starkly blatant. Lying on his back in the rain, arms extended and feet crossed at the ankles, the allusion to Christ is clear. The pink and blue pastels of the city lights ripple in the watery pool in which Jake lies, a powerful portent of the bioluminescence of the Pandoran world yet to come.[25] Finally, the viewer can't help but notice that emblazoned across Jake's T-shirt is the Harley David-son logo, bracketed by its extended pair of soaring wings. The logo buffets us both back to Jake's dream of flying and foreshadows his piloting the ikran. The signification here points to the wounded warrior, but also to the possi-bility of redemption.

The transformation of the protagonist is an essential element of the mon-omyth. A cursory scan of the selected source stories evidences the range of transformative motifs. Lawrence's passion for justice and his belief in what he unabashedly refers to as his own "extraordinariness" enables him to break barriers, to accomplish the impossible task of crossing the impassable Nefud desert and to lead the warring Bedouin tribes in their revolt against the Turks. When his invincibility is challenged by unendurable torture at the hands of a brutal Turkish official, Lawrence loses his confidence and transforms himself yet again, from a uniter of the feuding Arab tribes to a humble Englishman who wants nothing more than to return to his home.

Under the wise and generous tutelage of his Samurai master, Katsumoto, Nathan Algren finally sobers, begins to meditate, and masters the martial arts of the Samurai. He earns the admiration of the practitioners of the dying art, the respect of the young Japanese emperor. When his army is defeated and his master is killed in the fray, Algren returns to the Samurai village to live out his days in peace. *Dances with Wolves'* John Dunbar learns the language and customs of the Sioux through his developing relationship with Kicking Bird, a Sioux warrior.

Through his time among the Apache and his relationship with Cochise, Tom Jeffords is able to act on his newly developed awareness that native peo-ples too are humans, and in the end he helps to broker a government-man-dated peace treaty. John Morgan, in *A Man Called Horse*, goes from being a wealthy disinterested British aristocrat in search of the ideal grouse hunting ground to releasing his inner savage and discovering, through his association with the Sioux, a justification for a disturbing brutality. In different ways and to different degrees, each of these men fills a lack in his life, and finds, in the culture of an indigenous people with whom he lives, a meaning that resonates where once there was none.

Through her experience of loving John Smith and the terror of the ensu-ing war between the British Virginia Company and her people, Pocahontas finds the courage to step up to take her place as tribal leader, gaining the key to divine the meaning of her dreams. Crysta, the fairy protagonist in *Fern-Gully*, leaves her frivolous impulsiveness behind, matures and embraces her destiny as the creative force and protector of the forest. Dorothy's transformation in *The Wizard of Oz* also takes the form of maturing into and becoming aware of the knowledge she intuitively has and in accepting the poignancy of her ordinary lot in life. In keeping with the structure of the monomyth, these three protagonists, though changed, "return" to their roles, to their lives as they have been living them, to their families, to their "destinies."

In *Dune* (the film based on the Frank Herbert saga), *District 9* and finally in *Avatar*, the transformations the heroes undergo become progressively more radical. *Dune*'s Paul Atreides leaves his home after the assassination of his father and relocates to Arrakis, the planet on which the highly valued and much fought over "spice" is harvested. Paul leads the downtrodden Fremen in their revolt and rides the giant sandworms, ultimately fulfilling the Fremen's messianic prophecy. Paul's transformation builds on his childhood training at the hands of his mother, a priestess, and ultimately includes the physical alteration of his eyes that turn the intense electric blue of the spice-consuming Fremen.

In the process of commandeering the relocation of the alien population ghettoized in District 9, Wikus van de Merwe accidently comes into contact with an alien substance. Reacting to the contact with the extraterrestrial ooze, Wikus begins to mutate. The metamorphosis is external at first, loosening his fingernails, altering his arm and hand, but soon he also develops a fondness for canned cat food, a delicacy among the aliens. His hybridity keeps him from returning home to his wife, to his job, to the life he once knew. He has become the shunned other and suffers the same injustices as the colony of aliens that he had come to relocate.

His physical transformation, while endowing him with special abilities — his transfigured arm is now able to shoot the advanced weaponry of the aliens — distinguishes him in other ways. The corporation that has been running genetic experiments on the aliens now takes an avid interest in Wikus, who narrowly escapes their efforts to turn him into a vivisection subject. But Wikus' transformation is not simply morphological. Wikus also develops a conscience.[26] As he embodies a visible, external difference, an extreme and frightening otherness, his wife rejects him, and he is hunted like an animal. Wikus sees now the ways in which the "prawns" have been demeaned and begins to understand the objectification, ghettoization, and persecution he had been involved in perpetrating. Wikus helps Christopher — an alien who understands the technology necessary to restart the aliens' main spaceship — to head for home, if only selfishly because he believes that Christopher will return and restore Wikus to his human form. The film ends, the audience assumes based on documentary-style interviews, with Wikus living the life of a "prawn" in the new alien home, District 10. He longs to reunite with his wife and is shown fashioning a little metallic flower to remind her that he is still out there.

In each of the source stories the protagonist embarks on a journey — actual, figurative, and/or psychological — and finds him- or herself in a new "place" at the stories' end. Jake is no exception to this paradigm, and his transformation occurs on multiple levels, the most obvious being that of his physical body. When he is within his avatar, he is whole and able bodied; his senses are enhanced, he is able to link to the creatures of Pandora, and to hear the voices of the Na'vi ancestors at the Tree of Souls. He began his journey as a broken soldier with the hope of being of use to Colonel Quaritch, gathering intelligence for the impending genocide. But through his experience in the avatar and his relationships with Neytiri, Grace, and Pandora, he comes to embrace Neytiri's "tree-hugger crap." His transformation is political as well. Jake begins to fill the hole in his life with meaning. He becomes, in his own words, a "warrior for peace."

When Jake's video blogs expose his conviction that the humans have nothing to offer the Na'vi that would induce them to move — not blue jeans, nor lite beer — they reveal his deepened understanding of capitalist imperialism as well. He explains it all, albeit reductively, to Grace. He tells her that when people are sitting on shit you want, you go ahead and make them your enemy. Then, he explains, you have a justification for taking it.

In the scenes preceding this one, where Jake realizes the damage his video-blog self has caused, he is profoundly disturbed. When Neytiri realizes his duplicity, his remorse is redoubled. He tries to explain to her the ways in which he has changed by professing his love — of the forest, of the Omaticaya, and above all of Neytiri. Love as transformative power is as clichéd as it gets, yet runs as true. Through his apprenticeship to Neytiri, Jake saw the Pandoran world as she saw it, understood what she understood, came to know what she knew. The Jake who stands with Neytiri under the dangling iridescent strands of the Tree of Voices is a changed Jake. He is not the impulsive Jake, who, like a child, couldn't keep his hands from slapping at the nearest plant or flying insect just to see what would happen.

At the Tree of Voices, just before choosing Neytiri as his mate, Jake stands in a respectful, contained, almost reverent manner, as all around him electrifying creatures swirl in the air. Instead of swatting at them to get a reaction, he takes them in with his eyes, appreciates them with a quiet acceptance.

Jake was always brave, but now his courage is corralled in the service of others. When Grace is mortally wounded, he knows he must find a way back into the good graces of Neytiri and the Na'vi. In his avatar he returns to the scorched and burned Home Tree covered in ash. This scene is strikingly constructed without any of the lush color we have come to associate with Pandora. Like a Phoenix rising out of the ashes, Jake is reborn here as Toruk Makto, the rider of the great Leonopteryx. When he swoops down on the Na'vi gathered in prayer around the Tree of Souls, the full fiery color of the giant banshee and the cool greenness of the Pandoran forest is restored.

The new Jake, still impulsive in his claim on the giant banshee, approaches Neytiri and Tsu'tey with a respectful reverence. He is there for Grace first, to save Pandora second, and, lastly, when he has succeeded in restoring the peace and the humans have been sent home to their Earth, he is saved by the transfer of his consciousness into his avatar body. The permanent morphological metamorphosis follows his political, spiritual, and personal transmutations.

Avatar and the Western

Earlier in this chapter Cameron's aspirations to create a film that transcended simple entertainment were underscored as were his hopes that *Avatar* would, if only in small ways, move audiences to act: to act in small ways in our individual lives and in large ways, to change how we live together on this planet. One can only imagine that the author who experiences the transformation of his or her protagonist also undergoes a bit of that change him- or herself. When we are personally transformed, we use that transmutation as source material for the creation of art. As was noted above, the process by which we are changed and change others through myth and through individual actions in our lives is a reciprocal one.

In his essay, "The Structure of Myth/The Structure of the Western Film," Will Wright sees the structure of the western as similar to that of myth, a "symbolically simple but remarkably deep conceptualization of American social beliefs."[27] Wright is interested the social meaning that inheres in myth, and he explores the "interaction between symbolic structures and the possibility of human action."[28] He highlights the hope of an author that a narrative might move a spectator to social action, but he insists that this can only happen if we understand what the characters *do*.

Building on the structuralism of Claude Lévi-Strauss, Wright posits that simply being able to recognize oppositions inherent in myth is not sufficient to distill meaning. So while a spectator might discern the antithetical poles of good/evil, familiar/strange, nature/technology, war/peace, and alien/indigenous prevalent in *Avatar*, it isn't until we come to terms with the story, "the progression of events and the resolution of conflicts,"[29] that we can put these together to more fully understand the social meaning the myth imparts.

Wright offers a method of narrative analysis that focuses on what he has observed as the shared functions across the structure of the western film. Not surprisingly, these *functions*, which Wright defines as either actions or character attributes, are appropriate to *Avatar* and a significant number of the source stories herein. The functions undergird the second-level meanings signified by the narrative that will soon be examined. It is clear that *Avatar,* while not a western, metaphorically evokes the western genre and with it America's collective guilt at the mistreatment of Native peoples. *The Last Samurai, Dances with Wolves, Broken Arrow, A Man Called Horse,* and *Pocahontas* are all quite literally stories about the lives and treatment of Native American tribes at the hands of white men. But *Avatar* and the source stories also evoke the Western because they appropriate its narrative structure. Not unlike Propp's morphology of folktales or Campbell's interpretation of the monomyth, Wright's narrative structure for the western film prescribes a list of the hero's actions and qualities that in most instances fit snugly into the stories we have been examining.

1. The hero enters a social group.
2. The hero is unknown to the society.
3. The hero is revealed to have an exceptional ability.
4. The society recognizes a difference between themselves and the hero; the hero is given a special status.
5. The society does not completely accept the hero.
6. There is a conflict of interest between the villains and the society.
7. The villains are stronger than the society; the society is weak.
8. There is a strong friendship or respect between the hero and a villain.
9. The villains threaten the society.
10. The hero avoids involvement in the conflict.
11. The villains endanger a friend of the hero.
12. The hero fights the villains.
13. The hero defeats the villains.
14. The society is safe.
15. The society accepts the hero.
16. The hero loses or gives up his special status.[30]

The reader will have no trouble mapping Jake to the hero, the Na'vi to society and Quaritch and his men to the villains. We might imagine that Grace is Jake's endangered friend and Jake's special status as the first warrior avatar. The weakest links in understanding the structure of *Avatar* as a western arise within number eight above, regarding the friendship/respect between hero and villain. A case could be made for the respect Jake and Quaritch have for each other early on in *Avatar* when Jake is successfully providing Quaritch with reliable intelligence. Or, if Tsu'tey is understood as a villain, by the film's end they not only respect one another but call each other "brother." However, Tsu'tey does not threaten the society and so doesn't precisely fit that aspect of Wright's western narrative structure.

Wright suggests that the western revolves around the three types of characters — hero, villain and society — who in their relationships with one another enact three basic encoded oppositional structures: inside/outside, good/bad, and strong/weak.[31] The consumer of western films will recognize these relatively obvious archetypal antagonisms and perhaps grasp the ways in which they structure a number of the source stories cited. Crysta is good and Hexxus bad. Wikus was an insider who became an outsider. Algren was spiritually weak but became strong. The Samurai swordsmen were weak in the face of gun power, but strong in their resolve and practice. Like critical flicker fusion — the essential process of cinema by which our eyes blur the discreet flicker of the frames into one continuous motion — these discreet oppositions tend to blur. *Avatar* then could be seen as a post-structuralist myth, one in which the binaries are visible not as discrete entities but as oscillations between poles along a continuum. Within the narrative of *Avatar,* the western is elicited and re-formed all at once.

Jake is encoded as outside almost from the earliest scenes of *Avatar.* He is "othered" by his disability. In the early deleted scenes of him in the bar, he is marked as outsider, even as he is cheered by onlookers while he balances a shot of tequila on his forehead doing wheelies in his chair. When he arrives at the base at Hell's Gate, a mercenary refers to him as "meals on wheels." Although he espouses the belief that one never becomes an ex-marine, he is clearly on the outside. When he makes his way to the linkup pod, he is again ostracized: for being a marine, for being untrained, for not being his brother. He is not like Norm or the other scientists or avatar drivers.

Jake's entry into his avatar begins the shift toward the inside for him. It allows him access to Pandora and to the Na'vi. He remains, to the Na'vi, alien, the outsider. But in the eyes of his human compatriots he has gotten inside. Inside the avatar, inside Home Tree, and ultimately, inside Neytiri's heart. Jake straddles inside and out.

Spectators will notice the blurring of discrete boundaries between good/bad, strong/weak as well in *Avatar.* (In Chapter Two this fluxing of technology/nature across the good/bad axis was visited in some depth.) When the audience arrives at Hell's Gate, we are given in no uncertain terms the badness of the Na'vi, which we accept at face value along with the requisite safe/unsafe and dead/alive dichotomies that logically follow. Quaritch sees Jake's worth as a marine and offers to get him the surgery he needs in exchange for Jake's assistance. While the spectator can't help but be suspicious of Quaritch's denigration of the "limp-dick" science being done, his goodness in his offer to Jake is plain, as plain as his growing badness that results in his just desserts at the film's end. The Na'vi undo their characterization as bad almost immediately, except for Tsu'tey, who retains a certain level of badness, in the best and worst senses of the word.

The strong/weak binary stretches across the text of *Avatar* like the connective tissue of the Pandoran root system. Selfridge is in charge, so strongly powerful, but weak in his capitulation to Quaritch, in his bondage to his corporate shareholders, and is seen that way by Grace and Jake. Selfridge perceives the strength of Grace's convictions and the Na'vi's strong connection to the sacred as some kind of weaknesses. Grace and Norm perceive Jake's lack of training as a weakness, in spite of the strength of his resolve and spirit. The Na'vi see the Sky Walkers as weak to the point of insanity. And they are in turn perceived as bow-and-arrow toting savages, and therefore weak in the face of the vast artillery at the disposal of the RDA. Yet the strength of their faith, their resolve, and their perseverance triumphs.

The structural polarities of *Avatar* and the accompanying source stories make visible a core motif of difference. Because binaries are almost never neutral, Jacques Derrida has argued,[32] they reveal the intrinsic ideological power dynamic encoded within all narrative. There is more intrinsic power typically associated with being inside rather than out, white than black, human than alien, European than African, male rather than female, and so on. What meaning these structural pairs together offer inheres not simply in these crude polar oppositions, but in their capacity to uncover what is not always obvious. It is their fluidity, their shades of gray as given in the narrative of *Avatar* and several of the source stories above, that offers up the possibility of revealing, deconstructing, and transforming embedded and entrenched paradigms.

The Tree and the Spirit

The mythic story at the center of *Avatar* and the other source stories — whether we see them as a hero's quest or a version of the western — is what Roland Barthes might refer to as the first level of meaning. It is essentially denotative. It describes the most important events as they transpired. But it doesn't tell us what the movie was *about*. It is within this second level of meaning that signification occurs, that the spectator responds to narrative cues not simply by constructing a narrative, but by determining what meaning inheres.[33]

Within this second-order level of meaning it will become clear where there is overlap of signification in the source stories and to what extent there might be anything original at all in *Avatar*. For example, *Pocahontas*, *FernGully*, *Avatar*, and to a certain extent *The Last Samurai* and *Dances with Wolves* are films that point to the value innate in the natural, the threat of the exploitation of resources, and the potential dangers of technology, particularly technologies of war. Encoded in *Dune*, *District 9*, *Pocahontas*, *Avatar*, *Lawrence of Arabia*, *Broken Arrow*, and *Dances with Wolves* are the evils of imperialism. In *Lawrence of Arabia*, *Broken Arrow*, *Dances with Wolves*, *District 9*, *Pocahontas*, *Avatar*, and *A Man Called Horse*, otherness is brought into focus and transcended through love and friendship. *Dune*, *Avatar*, *The Last Samurai*, *Dances with Wolves*, *Pocahontas*, and *Lawrence of Arabia* vividly render the ravages of war. *Last Samurai*, *Dances with Wolves*, *Lawrence of Arabia*, *The Wizard of Oz*, and *Broken Arrow* could be categorized as "buddy films," in which the force of friendship is front and center, and *Broken Arrow*, *Last Samurai*, *Dances with Wolves*, *Pocahontas*, *Avatar*, *FernGully*, and *Dune* as love stories. Ascribing meaning to film watching in these broad strokes takes on a rhyzomatic aspect with multiple entries and points of purchase.

According to Graeme Turner, author of the book *Film as a Social Practice*, "The audience [watches] any one film within a context of other films, both those they have personally seen and those they have heard about or seen represented in other media outlets."[34] We watch *Avatar* mediated by the trace of the source stories in whose midst it sits. Each movie, short story, or animated film that comprises the list of source stories enlivens and deepens the experience of audiences consuming *Avatar*. Even neo-conservative columnist John Podhoretz, who energetically panned the film, citing its "undigested mass of ... standard-issue counterculture clichés," gets this part right when he asserts that "Cameron has simply used these familiar bromides as shorthand."[35] This chapter has underscored what Shakespeare so eloquently expressed in his sonnet 59 and what Ecclesiastes claimed even earlier: "There is no new thing under the sun." In this post-modern remix of a world in which we find ourselves, the extra- and inter-textual marks the text *and* the interpreter equally. So when Podhoretz alludes to the Keebler elves in the process of ridiculing the notion of the Na'vi living in a tree, it tells us more about Podhoretz than about Cameron's use of the venerable old sign.[36]

There are several well-worn significators in *Avatar* and in the source stories from which it comes. Because they have such richly used histories and indeed do function as a kind of shorthand, they allow the spectator to understand them both broadly and deeply, in their function as concatenating signs. The tree is one such motif.

In recent times the tree has come to be synonymous for the pro-environmental, in Jake's own words, for that "tree-hugging crap." Loving trees has come to stand for loving our environment, tying oneself to a tree is the near-clichéd equivalent of taking an environmental stand. Planting a tree in a loved one's honor has become commonplace practice, a memorial that also supports the environment by reforesting. The bond between trees and humans is thick with connective tissues. We even find trees that act human — talk and walk like humans — in the beloved *Wizard of Oz*. In *The Lord of the Ring Trilogy* we welcome the treelike Ents when they come to the aid of the humans and elves in their battle against the evil Saruman.

The tree is as ancient as the biblical Tree of Knowledge and links us to the mystical Kabbalah. The Bodhi Tree under which the Buddha became enlightened is oft used as a symbol of meditation. This symbolic steeping of the tree layers Pandora's Tree of Voices or a Tree of Souls with meaning. The power of the tree — rooted, branching outward, and in the case of the Na'vi's Home Tree, incorporating the emblematic spiral — is redoubled by the extent of the perceived horror and loss when Quaritch and his men reduce it to flaming, splintered shards. In the scenes following the behemoth's felling, its exposed roots are silhouetted against a fiery sky, unearthed, vulnerable, disconnected.

Trees figure prominently in the pro-environment animation *FernGully: The Last Rainforest*. The fairies are really "tree sprites" who, like the Na'vi, dwell in the trees. The tension in the film erupts initially because a demolition crew is out cutting down old trees and inadvertently destroys a tree in which an evil spirit, Hexxus, had been imprisoned. Visually, the scale of the sprites in relation to the trees in which they live maps consistently to the scale of the Na'vi in relation to their Home Tree. Cameron and co-producer Jon Landau were well aware of *FernGully* and in fact made note of it in the video "Capturing *Avatar*." Landau explains that they worried during an early preview that the scene where the seeds from the Tree of Souls cover Jake's body might be "too FernGully."[37] *FernGully*, then, has come to stand for the close-up lush world of the rain forest, the notions of interconnection and luminosity as well as the inner spiral world of the tree in which the tree sprites live. You can't watch one without seeing the other.

The tree is central, too, in *Pocahontas* as a symbol of wisdom and guidance. The young woman goes to the "Mother Willow" to speak with and be guided by the ancient tree spirit who inhabits it. Mother Willow helps Pocahontas to interpret her dream and warns her about the impending danger of the approaching British. That there is a living, communicating spirit within the old willow tree in a child's animated feature can be easily accepted, or if necessary, overlooked. But when Cameron's adult blockbuster suggests in the root system of the trees an interconnected network of living organisms and spirit — or in his words, "energy" — we run into trouble.

Ridiculing the entire idea as Podhoretz does with his Keebler analogy is a facile tactic. Along with an unwillingness to suspend disbelief, Podhoretz distances himself from the deeper meaning that resides in even a possibly clichéd presentation. In Pocahontas' popular but sappy song, "The Colors of the Wind," we find the same pro-environment, anti-imperialist sentiments as those expressed by Jake toward the end of *Avatar*. In her song, Pocahontas asks of Smith, Who really is the savage here, who is the one with the rifle, who is the one destroying the trees, exploding the earth in search of gold? She disabuses him of the notions that he and his kind "own" whichever shore they touch down upon, that "the earth is just a dead thing that you can claim."[38] In response to Slavoj Žižek's review that saw "brutal racist motifs" underlying "politically correct themes,"[39] blogger Max Ajl envisioned instead a fluxing of the savage/civilized dichotomy.

> Moreover, *Avatar* re-codes typical imperialist memes. It is the natives who have an advanced society, and they who civilize the invader, who can only fight with the invaded, for their land, after becoming one of them. This is not so much against the typical pattern as the creation of a totally new one.[40]

An intelligent and thoughtful exposition of these ideas which surface throughout *Avatar* can be found in Ken Hillis' essay, "From Capital to Karma: James Cameron's *Avatar*."[41] Hillis notes a trend in which there is an "under acknowledged yet widespread" resurgence of Neoplatonism.[42] The idea of the "demiurge" which can be found in Plato's *Timaeus*, written around 360 B.C.E., looks not all that dissimilar to the kind of pantheism or animism that might be imagined belonging to the hodgepodge of native cultures Cameron has appropriated for the Na'vi. Plato posits that there is "a single visible living entity containing all other living entities, which by their nature are all related,"[43] and the fantasy of Pandora, of Eywa, exemplifies such a world.

Hillis points out that what *Avatar* uniquely does is to blur the boundary between the kind of "hive mind" normally associated with a networked existence — take for example *Star Trek*'s Borg — and a more atomistic, individualistic one. The "carbon based wet-ware"[44] of the Na'vi is allegorical, Hillis claims, but it raises the specter of the possible. What distinguishes *Avatar*'s representation of the Neoplatonic from other networked intelligences is that the Na'vi retain their distinct individuality while at the same time they are connected to one another and to the whole of Pandora through their goddess Eywa. This imbrication of the networked and the spiritual, offers Hillis, is "a hybrid of Neoplatonism's World Soul and of Cartesianism's mind-body dualism."[45] Hillis believes that this "fuzzy ... pantheism" is one of the reasons the film resonates so strongly with audiences who understand themselves to be individuals yet at the same time part of a vast, ubiquitous, networked existence.[46]

Avatar, and to a certain degree most of the source stories listed above, risks touching on the overtly spiritual and, as such, opening themselves to the kind of easy ridicule — like the Podhoretz analogy — that is a knee-jerk response for those who find this subject matter troublesome, too new agey, threadbare, and/or over-the-top fantastical.

The White Messiah Fable

David Brooks' *New York Times* piece about *Avatar* entitled "The Messiah Complex" is one such reaction that has gotten enormous play.[47] Because the film draws on what Brooks has dubbed "The White Messiah Fable," he categorizes *Avatar* as some kind of benevolent romanticism, as "escapism," and ultimately as simply offensive.[48]

Since Brooks' arguments seem on the surface to be rational and cogent, if slightly snide in tone, it is worth taking a closer look at the conflations, elisions, and distortions on which he relies to make his point. The White Messiah Fable is comprised of the racially offensive stereotype that people of color need white heroes to come and rescue them, to lead them in their revolts. Brooks lumps together in his short list of examples of this familiarly encoded story line *A Man Called Horse*, *Dances with Wolves*, *The Last Samurai*, and for children, *Pocahontas* and *FernGully*. We may grant Brooks that his white messiah genre, if it might be called that, bears closer scrutiny in order to ascertain to what extent racial fantasies and stereotypes are in evidence, and Chapter Six will take this chore to heart.

It has been made abundantly clear that the story of *Avatar* resembles many other stories, and the ways in which this fact both strengthens and weakens *Avatar* has been explored above. Yet it must also be noted that Brooks glibly skims *Avatar* without bothering to allow what resides beneath the surface to bubble up. Yes, the computer-generated Na'vi characters are tall, thin and athletic, strong and spiritual. But when Brooks asserts that they are pretty good singers and dancers, one has to wonder what film he has seen and why he chooses to mention that when the Na'vi never dance and barely sing in the theatrical release of the film.

Brooks allows for the fact that because *Avatar* is even "a little socially conscious," "environmentally sensitive" and "multiculturally aware," this fact has increased its popularity.[49] No argument there. It is the overarching assumption that his list of messiah fables includes stories depicting "nonwhites need[ing] the white messiah to lead their crusades"[50] that strikes one as a gross and inaccurate generalization and makes you wonder if Brooks actually watched the films that he lumps together with *Avatar*. What does appear to connect the few films Brooks mentions is the immersion of a white/European/human hero into the midst of an indigenous/extraterrestrial culture.

Immersing oneself in, adopting or experimenting with the trappings of an other's cultural milieu is distinct from emerging as its leader. Transcultural sampling extends beyond its ubiquity in the creative arts to those seekers who find a sense of home in a place or within a culture other than that of their origin. There have always been explorers, converts and ex-patriots. And there have always been those for whom these changes have been perceived as a threat. While Brooks doesn't include *Lawrence of Arabia* in his list, Lawrence's peers worried over the thought that the lieutenant had "gone native" when he returned from his first desert excursion wearing Bedouin robes and a head-dress. The connotations of this characterization emerged out of an imperialist legacy and sadly evidenced the beliefs that indigenous peoples were largely presumed to be "savage" or "barbarian," and that colonizers ran the grave risk of contamination. Famously sketched in the character of Kurtz in Joseph Conrad's *Heart of Darkness* and reimagined in Francis Ford Coppola's *Apocalypse Now,* the hero who turns against his own kind, who "goes native," serves the function of simultaneously showing the imagined dangers of succumbing to the ways of the savage and highlighting the horrors of the actions of the colonizers. Perhaps extreme romanticizing and/or exoticizing of indigenous cultures as solely spiritual or peaceful could be viewed as a flipside to their demonization, an attempt through the use of a kind of representational hyperbole to make visible the injustices of European and American colonization. In the song of Pocahontas and in Jake's tirade against the RDA, it is easy to hear the echoes of Conrad's Marlowe. "The conquest of the earth, which mostly means the taking it away from those who have a different complexion or slightly flatter noses than ourselves, is not a pretty thing when you look into it too much."[51]

It is Marlowe's narrative that infuses and informs *Avatar* and its source stories, not the white messiah fable, and looking closely, which Brooks was reluctant to do, reveals as much.

Beginning with the "children's" versions Brooks cited, in neither *Pocahontas* nor *FernGully* would the protagonist be considered the white men who inadvertently wandered into the worlds of Pocahontas and the fairy Crysta. An adventure-seeking John Smith comes upon Pocahontas in the woods. She educates him with regard to her people's relationship with nature, with the earth, and together they attempt to interrupt the warring that is about to erupt. When Smith is wounded, he is sent back to England, and Pocahontas remains with her people. He does not lead the native peoples to victory against his shipmates.

In *FernGully,* Crysta inadvertently shrinks Zak, a white male logger, and he and Crysta explore her world together. When the evil spirit Hexxus escapes, Zak comes to the aid of the fairies and helps them in fighting against Hexxus by climbing up into the tree leveler and disabling the machine, depriving Hexxus of the energy upon which he had been feeding. It is the old fairy Magi who sacrifices herself and in the end Crysta who destroys Hexxus from the inside out by exploding him with her creative energy. Zak is restored to his human size and bids Crysta farewell. Again, there is no triumphant ride into the sunset with Zak at the helm.

In *A Man Called Horse*, John Morgan is captured by a band of Sioux, humiliated and treated like an animal. He is "owned" by an old woman, and although she has him tethered and treats him like a workhorse, over time he comes to understand/appreciate the ways of his captors. Eventually he is granted status in the community and he marries. He endures unimaginable torture as the men of the tribe initiate him. He proves himself worthy as a warrior, finding and accepting his "inner savage"—shades of Robert Bly!—and as the film ends he gets his long-desired wish to lead a war party, which at first he imagined would be his ticket out. He is neither the chief nor the leader of the tribe but of a small band of men. In this film, instead of an emphasis on the purity or spiritually elevated nature of the native peoples, Morgan's bloodthirstiness is underscored, and within the world in which he has been relocated, this violence is not only tolerated but exalted. There is no hint of him leading them or rescuing the Sioux from the white man's genocide. In *A Man Called Horse* the dangers are from a warring tribe, and it is off to fight them that Horse goes with a small band of warriors at the film's close.

In *Dances with Wolves*, Dunbar finds a home with the Sioux when he relocates to an abandoned Civil War post in the western United States. He comes to live with and learn the language and rituals of these people. He does join with them in fighting against an army regiment. But the film ends when Dunbar leaves the tribe in order to keep them safe from the regiment's pursuit of him in order to gain retribution for what they perceive as his treasonous acts. Again, he doesn't lead the Sioux into battle, he doesn't become their leader. He does develop an enduring bond with the character of Kicking Bird; he does fall in love with and marries Stands with Fist, a white woman who had been raised by the Sioux. Together they ride off into the snowy wilderness at the end of the movie. Again, there is no white messiah to be seen here.

Similarly, Nathan Algren in *The Last Samurai* is captured by a raiding party of Samurai warriors and is spared a terrible death because Katsumoto, their leader, has had a vision foretelling Algren's arrival. Badly wounded, Algren is taken to their village in the mountains and nursed back to health. He becomes Katsumoto's pupil and teacher. They learn from one another about each other's strangeness. Algren joins with Katsumoto in a last stand against the Japanese troops who have been fortified with guns and trained by American soldiers, the job Algren was originally hired to do. Katsumoto's army of Samurai is no match for the guns and cannons of his enemies, and they are badly defeated. Katsumoto is killed and Algren seriously wounded. Again, there is no white knight leading his Asian brethren to victory.

Finally in *Avatar* we have Jake, the wounded, grieving warrior, who through the technology of the avatar is given a second chance. Through his experience perceiving, understanding, and moving in his avatar's body, Jake grows and changes. Even Brooks grants that Jake has his consciousness raised, although one might infer from the tone of Brooks' critique that the observation is meant sarcastically. Perhaps Brooks, like Robert Bly before him, has a problem with the "soft male."[52] But it is important to note that even before Jake arrives on Pandora, the Na'vi have long been retaliating. When the RDA comes to strip-mine the homes of the Na'vi, contrary to what Brooks implies, they don't wait around for any kind of messiah. In one of the film's earliest scenes, we learn how dangerous the Na'vi are, how deadly their arrow's dipped in neurotoxins are, how likely it is that the mercenaries who are working for the RDA aren't going to survive the incursion. The Na'vi don't wait for Jake when their Tree of Voices is bulldozed. They declare a war party from which Jake attempts to dissuade them. When Quaritch pulls the plug on Jake and Grace, and their avatars fall where they stand, the Na'vi don't wait around aimlessly. They jump on their direhorses and ikran and attack. In a deleted scene, we see the damage they inflict, the lives they have taken, which is the proverbial straw that breaks the camel's back and sends Quaritch into action.

Brooks' claim that there is offense to be taken in the supposition that indigenous people *need* the white man to lead them to victory is of course valid; it is just not the way this movie unfolds. Jake doesn't save the Na'vi. On the contrary, Jake is the one who is saved. The Na'vi, Grace, and Trudy save Jake. They save him metaphorically, by teaching him to alter his stance in the world from one of domination, greed, and perceiving the other as an enemy to be colonized, to one of "seeing" the other as the Na'vi see, with respect, openness and curiosity.

But they also literally save his ass. Moat saves him when she releases him from his bindings during the destruction of Home Tree. Trudy rescues him from the brig and flies him to safety. Yes, he wows the Na'vi by making a grand entrance, flying in as Toruk Makto. It is perhaps this scene that is most messianically colored. When Jake dismounts from the giant banshee, the Na'vi tremble in awe, bow to him, back away and seem to want to reach out and touch him, all at once. But it is only with the help of Tsu'tey and Neytiri that Jake is able to marshal the aid of the clans in the fight. The three of them together fly out in front of the legions of their ikran army to meet Quaritch's warships.

When the colonel is merely seconds away from ending Jake's life, Neytiri is the one who saves him. She has saved him by staying her bow, by seeing him, by teaching him, by loving him. But when she frees herself from the weight of the ferocious Thanator, she literally saves Jake first by depositing two giant poisoned arrows into Quaritch's heart and then by racing into the linkup shack to get him the exo-pack so that he will not suffocate in the toxic Pandoran atmosphere. The unlikely possibility that all of the beasts of Pandora might come to the aid of the Na'vi stretches credulity but within the diegetic world that Cameron created, Jake and the Na'vi win their battle because they are ultimately saved by the grace of Eywa.

In the films *Lawrence of Arabia* and *Dune*, we at least do have a protagonist who is followed by a constituency that is "other." Lawrence is not a Bedouin nor is Paul Atreides a Fremen. Brooks' messiah theory might have held more water had he chosen these films as exemplars. In *The Last Samurai* and *Dune*, the protagonists benefit from some messianic prophecy or omen that would strengthen Brooks' argument. And there is no mistaking the scene in which Jake is covered in iridescent wood sprites as anything but an anointing. Each of these scenes points to the stage in Campbell's dissection of the hero's quest in which the hero "attains god-like stature."[53]

At the same time if Brooks had allowed for the details and inconsistencies in these films, he would not have been able to tie them all up so neatly in the white messiah package. Still, there is something that Brooks finds disturbing in the films he *did* lump together and ultimately with *Avatar*. Since the case he has made for it is a flimsy reductionist one, we are left to guess what, precisely, he finds so objectionable. Daniel Mendelsohn of the *New York Review of Books* suggests that we not dismiss Brooks' criticisms out of hand.[54] But he also notes that it is striking how many critiques, including Brooks,'

> go out of their way to elide or belittle the movie's overwhelming successes as a work of cinema — its enormous visual power, the thrilling imaginative originality, the excitingly effective use of the 3-D technology that seems bound to change permanently the nature of cinematic experience henceforth — as if to acknowledge how dazzling it is would be an admission of critical weakness.[55]

In fact Brooks assiduously avoids any mention of dazzle, which with a film like *Avatar* requires a serious effort. Perhaps if he yielded on any point, Brooks may have feared his nice little package would begin to unravel. Perhaps he didn't trust the merit of the valid points his did raise to stand on their own without the aid of his reductive belittlement. There *are* stereotypical assignments that Brooks underscores: the depiction of all native peoples as spiritual and peace loving and way cooler than the "greedy corporate tools and the bloodthirsty U.S. military types."[56]Although this kind of gross encoding — black/white, good/evil, us/them — often functions as the DNA of filmic entertainment, *Avatar* goes far in suggesting the possibility of an alternative narrative archetype which encompasses a blurring of traditional binaries. In each of the films that Brooks has included as messiah fables, the heroes undergo change, moving from one antithetical pole to the other. He or she gains an awareness of their connection to nature, to spirit, to themselves and to those who have been heretofore seen and kept at arm's length as "other."

In the scene where Neytiri brings Jake back from the brink of death, she cradles him in her enormous arms and cups his head in her capable hands. She sees Jake not as human or Na'vi but in that moment as small, differently abled, weakened, gasping for breath, alien: as he truly is. And she loves him. Sappy, sentimental, yes, but moving and potent nonetheless.

If one is predisposed to lumping these source stories together, there are many other overlapping themes from which to choose other than the spottily inconsistent, though alluring, white messiah fable. As trite as it may sound, what also links this group of narratives is the alteration in perspective that love affords. Crysta loves Zak. Pocahontas loves Smith. Algren loves Katsumoto. Dunbar loves Kicking Bird and Stands with Fist. Paul Atreides falls in love with the Fremen, Chani, and the Fremen way of life. Lawrence loves the desert. Wikus loves his wife and comes to love cat food. Dorothy loves the Scarecrow, Tin Man, and Lion. Tom Jeffords loves Cochise and Morningstar. And Jake, as he tells Neytiri when she discovers he had known all along that the humans intended to destroy Home Tree, loves Pandora, the Na'vi and especially Neytiri. Love is the vehicle that leaps over the abyss of difference that keeps us locked in an us/them stance. It is what transforms our seeing from one of circumscription to circumspection. *Avatar* offers a fantasy that illuminates a shift from the familiar power-over paradigm of separation to one in which the possibility of the transcendence of difference and the hope of connection is made visible.

The Telling

The prismatic nature of the structure of *Avatar* affords it many points of entry. It can be viewed through the lens of the monomyth, categorized as a sci-fi flick, an anti-war film, a love story, and/or a pro-environmental film. Having explored what the story was about — alienation, difference, love, transformation — and the deep structural binaries that create narrative tension — self/other, nature/technology, strange/familiar, dreaming/awake — we can shift our focus to Genette's second meaning of narrative, reflecting on the relationship between the story, the events as they occurred and the structure of the telling. In an interview with NPR's Terry Gross, Cameron himself commented on the fact that although the technology changes — for example in Cameron's filmmaking there is no longer film or painting on glass to create illusory backdrops — "the basics of storytelling don't change."[57]

Cameron is, above all, a storytelling artist; cinema is his canvas and palette. Even though, as he pointed out, he is employing some pretty spiffy new brushes — 3-D, computer-generated characters, performance capture — at the core he is painting us a narrative picture. As Manohla Dargis notes, "Mr. Cameron might be a visionary of a type, but he's an old-fashioned (and canny) storyteller and he locks you in tightly."[58] In this way the spectator has the experience of the familiar and the strange all at once. Cameron's technological innovations are in the end subsumed by story, as they should be. As Dargis points out, Cameron utilizes his directorial discretion — including camera placement, point of view, editing, the vast pro-filmic touched on earlier in this volume — in order to direct the viewer's attention. As critic Scott Mendelsohn of Salon.com agrees, "While the film does not portend to be the most original story ever told, it makes up for it by telling it in high style."[59]

A Classical Hollywood Narrative

In attempting to pigeonhole *Avatar* as a particular kind of narrative, however, one runs into a problem. This chapter has laid out the myriad tales it tells. Not to beat the proverbial dead direhorse, but it *is* a love story, it *is* an anti-war film, a pro-environmental film, an example of myth, and so on.

In our post-modern, remediated world, however, it is tempting to disregard substance and pay attention only to surface. David Harvey has categorized post-modernity as privileging exterior over interior, "collage rather than in-depth work."[60] On the surface *Avatar* presents spectacularly as a science-fiction story. It takes place in the future. It has aliens; space travel; fantastical flora and fauna; new planets and moons; snazzy technology which includes 3-D simulations, cloning, and computer imaging that slips from screen to tablet and back to screens; awesomely terrible weaponry; and the ability by which one can inhabit new, blue, agile, giant beings. *Avatar* sits more than comfortably within the parameters of a definition of science fiction outlined by Robert Heinlein: realistic speculation about possible future events, based solidly on adequate knowledge of the real world, past and present, and on a thorough understanding of the nature and significance of the scientific method.[61]

Avatar rests solidly on knowledge of our early 21st-century world, our ubiquitous linking to networks, devices, and each other, a frightening disregard for living sustainably and for addressing global climate change. One has simply to look at the powerful 2009 documentary *Crude*, which recounts the struggle of thousands of indigenous Ecuadorans in their fight against Chevron, to recognize the plight of our present being extrapolated into an imagined future.

Cameron's concern for weapons and transport vehicles that not only look cool but actually could mechanically work, his dedication to rendering flora, fauna and the Na'vi in a way that gives credence to the story line, speaks to his ability to grab on to the science of today and douse it with his fanciful imagination, offering the essence of speculative fiction. In the process, Cameron surfaces the philosophical and ethical conundrums this book has been investigating.

Yet, all the flash in the world, including futuristic sci-fi gloss, cannot conceal that at its root *Avatar* is a classical Hollywood narrative. David Bordwell has outlined criteria for the canonical narrative that overlays neatly with the story arc of *Avatar*. Classical Hollywood film can be articulated as being divided into sections: the undisturbed stage, the disturbance, the struggle, and the elimination of the disturbance.[62] The reader will have no trouble mapping these stages of plot evolution to the way that *Avatar* unfolds. The narrative proceeds forward in a linear fashion with only one small flashback to Jake's brother's cremation. In the uncut version, however, the cremation sits in the forward momentum of the film.

Avatar, as it has been made clear above in the examination of the monomyth, hero's quest, and structure of the western film, is Jake's story. The classical Hollywood narrative is identified by "psychologically defined individuals"[63] who solve the clear-cut problem that upends the undisturbed initial stage. While attempting to set things right, the protagonist struggles with other characters or with forces beyond his or her control. In the end, there is a clear-cut resolution. The ending may be happy or sad, a victory or a defeat, but there is no ambiguity. The spectator is provided with a sense of closure. *Avatar* ends definitively yet with expectation. We know that Jake's transfer into his avatar has worked, and we suspect that the story will continue with a sequel. Our anticipation of what might come next is simply the natural conclusion of what Bordwell outlines as the chain of causality intrinsic to the classical Hollywood narrative. Underlying any meaning the spectator may discern is the force of the forward motion of the *syuzhet*, the Russian formalists term that denotes the construction of the plot.[64] The classical Hollywood cinema is structured with two related plots. The first, as mentioned above, entails a disruption, a problem to be solved, a goal to be achieved, a story line that resides in the public sphere: a war, a struggle over natural resources, an imperialistic company destroying an alien planet. The second story line revolves around a romantic entanglement that also has to overcome its impediments: difference across class, race, species, the intrusions of betrothals, and distance.

One of the salient features of the classical Hollywood cinema, according to Bordwell, is that it is an "an excessively obvious cinema."[65] Yet the obvious in cinema is paradoxical. As Rosalind Galt points out in her essay "The Obviousness of Cinema," the question of the obvious in film mirrors all iconoclasm. The image deceives because it is surface, because it is easy, accessible, and it deceives because it masks and removes the truth. The image widens the philosophical gap between reality and appearance, and as such it is not to be trusted.[66] Galt suggests that classical Hollywood cinema is particularly suspect because it *appears* so simplistic that "its systematic transparency [is] so effective that nobody realizes how complex it actually is."[67] It is this obviousness that makes a series of flickering frames into a seamless narrative, and, as Galt offers, makes it "the source of cinema's meaning and structure.[68] While this is true in the assembling of any cinematic narrative — the illusion of any continuity of time or space or relationship between characters only *appears* obvious — nowhere is this more apparent that in the making of *Avatar*. The enormity of the production processes that are constitutive of obviousness in *Avatar* is unparalleled.

Cameron handles cinematic storytelling deftly and in a way that parallels the process he employs during the making of the film. Any creative artist will recognize the iterative and layered approach that Cameron embarked on to bring to life the pro-filmic world that heretofore had only existed in his imagination. In the video "Capturing *Avatar*" which accompanies the three–DVD extended version of *Avatar*, the spectator is privy to the art of the collaborative Cameron. The process of researching, designing and building the computer-generated characters of the Na'vi detailed in "Capturing *Avatar*" reveals a layering approach that moves from two dimensions to three, becoming incrementally fleshed out. We are first shown the dozens of full-color images drawn by multiple artists that brought to life the Na'vi that Cameron had in mind. Similar to a brainstorming session, the artists lengthened and shortened necks, moved the locations of the eyes, coming closer to and then moving farther away from a humanoid type. When Cameron zeroed in on a prototype that felt right, sculptors took these 2-D renderings and fleshed them out in clay maquettes.

When the animators had sufficient performance-capture data from the actors, they repeated this process within the character-generating software. Sometimes taking months for each actor or actress, the animators refined the computer-generated character until they had a low-resolution version of the role as well as of the flora and fauna of Pandora. This cubistic low-res version resembles a low-end video game, but also smacks of an under-painting an artist may lay down — broad strokes, areas of color as placeholder, a structural layer on top of which each tiny detail would ultimately be refined. Through each iteration the image becomes more and more fleshed out, more three dimensional, more real.

Cameron's storytelling follows a similar trajectory. He literally builds his story slowly, in causal steps, one scene following the next, adding texture, meaning, backstory, and complexity until the audience is fully engaged in the layered dramatic tension of the world of *Avatar*.

Cameron takes his time telling the story of *Avatar*. Scott Mendelsohn[69] notes the restraint Cameron exerts by slowly introducing each syuzhet segment and advancing the causal progression.[70] Alternating between telling and showing, between using words and images to narrate — which Christian Metz reminds us is "one of the most obvious characteristics of film"[71] — Cameron initiates his tale with Jake's voice-over. In both the theatrical release and the extended version, we are given his circumstances, a touch of backstory, and his dream, in the confined space of the cryo-ship or the back alley of a bar. Jake is talking to us, sharing his story directly with us. We are already linked to his character and to his point of view as we move forward to Pandora.

Painstakingly, Cameron layers on plot element after plot element. We are shown Hell's Gate, given a hint of both the military environment and the savageness of the Na'vi in Quaritch's welcome speech, and an entrance into the technology-rich world of the command center and the linkup room. Alternating Jake's voice-over with a third-person omniscient point of view, Cameron adds piece after piece of the *Avatar* puzzle. We meet Selfridge and Grace, each character introduced in a spacious enough way that the spectator is led carefully forward and at the same time is able to integrate each new puzzle piece.

Jake's video log, discussed at length in chapters Two and Five, functions as a narrative device. His voice-overs slowly decrease in frequency as we are shown more and more of what he is experiencing. Cameron leads us in ever-widening circles, moving outward from Jake's experience in the avatar in a confined environment into the Pandoran jungle with a focus on the glories and dangers that lie in wait there. By the time we meet Neytiri and the Na'vi, we are fully engaged and invested in Jake, in the success of his mission, and the development of his relationship with Neytiri.

Mendelsohn suggests that by embracing a slow entry into *Avatar*, by taking the time to develop place and character and by not "jumping headlong into spectacle, the film allows us to become used to each fantastical element before introducing more, helping to sell the illusion."[72]

Since Cameron has done such a good job of laying a solid narrative foundation, he needs to rely less and less on the telling. As the story deepens in complexity, so does the visuality of its diegetic unfolding. Cameron's low camera angles speak to the strength and size of the direhorse that Jake is learning to ride, giving the spectator the horse's multiple exhaling nostrils, her muscular legs and her dilating eyes from the ground up.

As the film progresses, Cameron relies more and more on the narrative syntagma, for example to compress the time of Jake's three month apprenticeship to Neytiri. Here he alternates showing Jake's experience in his avatar with the in-between times back in the linkup shack. The same narrative device is used to juxtapose the preparations for war undertaken by both the Na'vi and Quaritch and his troops. Cameron uses temporal manipulations, an exaggerated computer-generated slo-mo, to bracket the intensity of the moments surrounding the felling of Home Tree; the deaths of Eytukan, Trudy, and Tsu'tey; and the final destruction of the bomb intended for the Tree of Souls. In these scenes even the sound is distorted by its retardation, magnifying the sorrow and enormity of those moments.

Cameron's thoughtful use of sound throughout the film undergirds the visual extravaganza for the viewer. In his words, Cameron wanted the music to "accent" the emotional response to the film, but not force it upon viewers.[73] The score for the film, written by James Horner, travels from indigenous sound to cinematic score, incorporating aboriginal instruments, vocal chanting, compelling drumbeats, full-scale choral arrangements and orchestration. Working with an ethnomusicologist and Paul Fromen, the man responsible for the development of the Na'vi language, Horner sampled sounds and in true mash-up fashion, digitally remixed them to achieve a spectral or otherworldly sound.[74] The musical motifs for individual places and characters — the flying ikrans, for example — subtly underscore the emotional power of *Avatar* with its own narrative arc.

In thinking about the overarching structure of narrative in *Avatar*, one assumes a big-screen, 3-D experience. But it is also true that this film has been watched on laptops and cinema displays, on plasma screens in living rooms, on iPhones. As Manohla Dargis so rightly observes, it is because of its "narrative strategies and visual style [that] it carries the deep imprint of cinema.... Like a video game designer, Mr. Cameron seems to want to invite you into the digital world he has created even if, like a film director, he wants to determine your route."[75]

In evoking the deep imprint of cinema, Cameron summons the kind of cinema that Sontag bemoans the loss of in her essay, "The Decay of Cinema"[76] — the kind of cinema we might call tipping-point cinema, the kind of cinema born of wonder, which Sontag describes as "the wonder that reality can be transcribed with such immediacy." This is exemplified in the moment

Sontag reminds us of when, a century ago, the Lumière Brothers screened *The Arrival of a Train at La Ciotat Station* and people ducked as the locomotive appeared to move toward them,[77] or the wonder of the moment memorialized in *Singin' in the Rain*, when a group of Hollywood partiers were shown their first talkie and searched for the man behind the curtain, or the eye-popping instant in *The Wizard of Oz* when Dorothy emerges from her house in Munchkinland to the shimmering, Technicolor world of Oz.

What Sontag rued is the fact that we no longer submerge ourselves in film the way cinephiles once did. We no longer embrace the experience of surrender, or as she put it "of being transported by, what was on the screen."[78] A polysemous *Avatar* has once again transported viewers and, paradoxically, has brought them home again to the wonder of cinema.

Chapter Five

The Apparatus of *Avatar*

"This passion for seeing ... the foundation of the whole edifice...."
— Christian Metz[1]

Much has been made so far in this volume of seeing. In Chapter One, attention was paid to the ways in which *Avatar* contrasted a monocular, constrained gaze, handed down from its coalescence during the Renaissance, with a "fluxual," embodied perspective imbued with movement. The circumscribed vision exemplified by the characters of Selfridge, Quaritch, and their minions was at least partially culpable for their ultimate failures. This is the kind of *enframing* which, as the investigation of Heidegger's thinking on technology revealed in Chapter Two, inhibits a free relationship with that which has been reified.

Paradoxically, the *frame* itself remains a central fact of our engagement with cinema in general and with *Avatar* specifically, which pushes against the edges of the cinematic frame but still resides within it.

The frame[2] has been imbricated in our ways of seeing since frescoes left the safety of the walls on which they were painted and became mobile pieces of art. Before pictures came to stand on easels and could therefore travel — from one room to another, in one palazzo or another — the prevalent tools of perspective were complicit in constructing an immobile totalizing viewer. This spectator stood in a prescribed location in front of the canvas, co-inhabiting the spot on which the artist stood and first gazed upon what was ultimately to become the painting. Much has been written about perspective, its conflation with the thinking of Descartes centuries later, and the teleological force of its headlong rush toward the development of photography and ultimately toward the moving image.[3]

Erwin Panofsky saw perspective not as a science but as a symbolic form. The specified relationships between orthogonals, vanishing points and horizon

lines offer up a conventional way of seeing to which those of us who reside
in the West have become accustomed. We have become adept at making meaning out of what are essentially flat splotches of color and shape, shadows and
light falling on two-dimensional surfaces. The extent to which this way of
seeing has seeped into every aspect of our scopic regime cannot be ignored.
Its pervasiveness extends to the all-knowing, all-seeing stance exemplified by
Colonel Quaritch and Parker Selfridge explored earlier in this volume.

The spectator of cinema is not immune to this paradigm. She has been
configured much like the viewer of Renaissance painting, in a fixed position
that insists on a type of one-pointed, totalizing perspective — except that her
gaze is trained on a series of moving images bounded on all sides by a frame.
This tension between fixity and movement that shapes the viewer's experience of cinematic space has fascinated and challenged film theorists of the
twentieth century.[4] Implicit in this discourse is the role of the viewer in a
meaning-making process. When Stephen Heath sums up in his essay "Narrative Space," he offers us the paradoxical, "What moves in film, finally, is the
spectator immobile in front of the screen."[5] We can guess that he is referring
to the fact that meaning making resides in the spectator. It is the visual apparatus of the viewer — the phi effect or what is commonly referred to as persistence of vision — that turns an array of still images flickering on a lighted
screen before us in a darkened chamber into moving pictures.

In the earliest moments of *Avatar*, we are given Jake's narration of his
dream of flying. We see out of his dreamer's eyes as we, too, soar over the
Pandoran jungle. Jake is our entry into the film. Through the melding of an
omniscient, third-person point of view — Cameron's cameras' eyes — and Jake's
first-person point of view — his voice-over and subsequent video logs — the
spectator constructs the story, feels the feelings, has the experience, and makes
the meaning of *Avatar*. Film theorists ask how, from a series of fragmentary,
still photographs, flashing in sequence in front of us, do we understand the
story the director wants to tell? According to Maurice Merleau-Ponty, our
perception allows us to skim from the surface of cinema a meaning. "A movie
is not thought; it is perceived."[6]

In the 1970s, proponents of apparatus theory looked toward the technical
components of cinema for an explanation of how it is that we see film in the
way that we see it. A psychoanalytic frame supports this approach that has
been tarnished, if not completely rusted out and in most cases abandoned,
for its lack of historicity and attention to the gendered spectator, and for its
perceived technological determinism.[7] Nonetheless, essays by Jean-Louis
Baudry, Christian Metz, and Stephen Heath, to name a few central theorists,
remain canonical in the study of cinema. These thinkers together investigate
the relationship of an immobile viewer's eye to the camera lens, to the screen,

to the point of view of the characters being portrayed, and to the dominant scopic regime that they trace back to that of Quattrocento perspective.[8]

The spectatorial complicity in constructing a narrative by overlaying unity and continuity on top of fragmentary images is also examined by suture theorists and by David Bordwell's narrative theory. In each case what surfaces are inherent dichotomies, including what is still and what moves, what is inside and what is out, what is present and what is absent, what is visible and what is not. Seeing through a particular ocular apparatus affects how and what we are able to see. And even though the average contemporary moviegoer is not literally looking *through* anything — except recently and on occasion 3-D glasses — the fact of the viewer's identification with the eye of the director and/or the point of view of any number of characters places them in a virtual space and alters their perception.

This chapter takes as its premise the point of view of the spectator as a complicated paradoxical thing that itself can be looked at from many angles, each theoretical lens restructuring what can be revealed about how we see and understand cinema. Apparatus theory, although seriously flawed, seems an apt armature on which to build an interrogation, asking to what extent have the changes that Cameron has made to the cinematic apparatus transformed the viewing subject. One might also investigate the extent to which the shift to a digital paradigm breaks apart Tom Gunning's three levels of narrative discourse: the pro-filmic, the enframed image, and the process of editing.[9]

In addition, the diegetic apparatus of the avatar itself merits a closer look. It serves as a theoretical double the way it torques at the axes of mobile/fixed, present/absent, inside/out, and introjection/projection that inhere in cinematic apparatus theory.

Back to the Quattrocento

The idea that the spectator of modern cinema has descended from the rational objectifying subject prevalent during the Renaissance has been the source of much debate. Yet the immobile centralized gaze engendered by the systems of perspective, as they were articulated by Alberti and others, remains a touchstone for film studies. Conjured up by Bordwell, Metz, Baudry, and Heath to lay the foundation for both apparatus and narrative theories of cinema, perspective merits a cursory reexamination here.

In Chapter One, we touched on the deeply entrenched connection in the Western tradition between seeing and knowing. This link has been problematized over the centuries beginning with Plato's distrust of our sense perception. The tension between what we see and how it informs what we know has been epitomized in the historical polarization of the empiricists, who emphasized knowledge gained through experience, and the rationalists, who highlighted the role of reason. It has been disparaged by many post-modern thinkers, including Jacques Lacan who insists that, "in this matter of the visible, everything is a trap."[10] And yet the link persists.

At one end of the spectrum we have *seeing as believing* and at the other end, traced back to the biblical injunction to make no graven images, *seeing as a dangerous business* that threatens our believing. History seesaws back and forth between times when images were revered, times when they were feared, and times in which both were true. While the link between our seeing and knowing is established and, ironically, at the same time tenuous, when we look at the notion of perspective, we must also at least glance at the meaning of perspective that is tangled up in that web of knowing. If we have a perspective, a point of view, it emerges out of that which we believe we already know. And if we approach a practice of looking assuming that we already know, then what we will see and ultimately understand will be diminished. Or as Nietzsche maintained, when we allow ourselves to be "deceived" by what we think we know, we are "deeply immersed in illusions and in dream images; ... [our] eyes merely glide over the surface of things and see forms."[11] To experience "perspective" in all its multi-faceted glory, it may be necessary to tiptoe up to it with an attitude similar to that of the early Renaissance cleric and philosopher Nicolaus Cusanus, an attitude of "learned ignorance."[12] Nietzsche suggested a similar stance in his parable "On Truth and Lie in an Extra-Moral Sense," and Wittgenstein observed in his *Philosophical Investigations* that in order to properly philosophize, one must adopt the stance, "I do not know my way about."[13] Hegel encourages us to be mindful of what we *think* we know: "When engaged in the process of knowing, it is the commonest form of self-deception, and a deception of other people as well, to assume something to be familiar, and to let it pass [*gefallen zu lassen*] on that very account."[14]

Cusanus not only advocated an approach of a learned ignorance, which maps to the "not-knowing" stance exemplified by Neytiri and the other Na'vi and discussed in earlier chapters, but he also promulgated other ideas that might be seen as embodying a rather radical perspective for his time.

While Copernicus and Kepler after him posited a heliocentric solar system rather than a geocentric one, they both perceived a center out there in the cosmos. Cusanus, on the other hand, suggested that our center resides within us. His notion of a center was that it was simply a perspectival illusion, a human projection. "Our life world has its center established by the accident of our body's location." But Cusanus realized that he could imagine any number of places he might occupy.[15] If we can imagine ourselves on the sun, on Mars, or traveling between, then we become aware of shifting perspectives and consequently of a "shifting" reality.[16]

This re- and sometimes de-centering of the spectator has also been the focus of a group of cinema theorists, including Jean-Louis Baudry, who hold to the notion that the technical cinematic apparatus determines the "setting up of the subject as the active center and origin of meaning."[17]

We sit in a darkened theater and from lights and shadows flickering on a screen in front of us, we create a planet with a lush moon populated with tall blue humanoids sporting tails. Yet even within this mind-stretching notion, we are confronted with a dualism embedded in our understanding of perception. There is *an* observer. And there is *an* object observed. Or in the case of cinema, there is the representation of an object that was once observed by the director or by the person whose eye peered through the lens of her camera. Or in the case of Cameron's digital realm, there is his imagined world, the drawings and maquettes, the software and computers that in concert bring this world to fruition so that then it can be observed, marked, and shot. But in either case the chain of what is seen, what is invented, and what is represented ends with the viewer's perspective.

The Story of Perspective

As any student of art learns, "perspective," the "scientific" system of rendering a flat, two-dimensional surface in such a way that it appears to have three-dimensional depth, was one of the "great advances" of the Renaissance.

As presented by Alberti in his treatise on painting, this new science brought together mathematics and representation. Alberti's system provided painters with a mathematical approach to creating convincing three-dimensional space. It was Alberti's intent that this system would enable painters to "master illusion." Putting into practice a mathematical theory of representation did not simply serve a quest for truth or for reality but, instead, a quest for control.[18] And while the immediate results of these illusions were for the eyes of the Renaissance quite magical, the long-term effects of the implementation of this "science" resulted in an artificiality of vision and a monolithic point of view. At the cost of attempting to control representation, the experience of apprehension was lost.

The system of perspective as it is understood today created an ideal viewer, a beholder whose eye was the apex of a pyramid of vision, a point in front of the canvas to which everything there was to see returned. John Berger compared the way this viewer is constructed to a beam from a lighthouse, only instead of light emanating from the beacon outward, everything that appears travels inward to the eye of the spectator. This eye mirrors a vanishing point on the picture plane into which everything recedes. "The visible world is arranged for the spectator as the universe was once thought to be arranged for God."[19] Berger is suggesting too, that this viewer is not complicit in arranging what she sees. It is all arranged for him beforehand. The viewer sees what she is directed to see. She has no option of seeing differently than the next viewer might.

The discourse surrounding perspective was as fraught during its heyday as is the resultant debate today as to whether or not we have a centralized, monocular spectator of the cinema. Leonardo da Vinci described perspective as the "rein and rudder of painting."[20] At the same time, however, Hubert Damisch finds in Leonardo's *Treatise on Painting* an unsettling conviction that utilizing one-point perspective "reduces the viewing subject to a kind of Cyclops, and obliges the eye to remain at one, fixed, indivisible point."[21]

This one-pointed Cyclops is completely antithetical to our "natural" way of seeing. Early, primitive understandings of how human vision operated included various models, one in which the objects of our sight shot out little versions of themselves that were introjected into our eyes and enabled us to see them. There was also the camera obscura model in which rays of light enter the eye and invert the objective image so that it appears whole, intact, but reversed and upside down on the retina, exactly like the image on the surface of the wall in the camera obscura.

What we now know shades these early models quaint yet richly metaphorical. In fact there is no inverted image painted on our retina but a series of receptor cells that get stimulated as the light enters our eyes. These cells are sensitive to different things in different parts of the retina, and it is necessary, in order to construct a complete image of what is before us, to scan our environs repeatedly. This ceaseless scanning motion, called *saccades*, is easily observable, and in the absence of it, we no longer see. We have all had the experience of staring off into space when we literally stop seeing what is right in front of us. This constrained approach to seeing, which has been associated with the viewer that perspective intrinsically has constituted, looks a lot like Heidegger's *gestell*. It looks like enframed perception. In the natural flickering and scanning of our visual apparatus, we find a close match to an Aletheic perception, the inherent motion building up information, multi-layered and rich.

When we pay attention to the innate way our eyes dart and scan, incessantly moving, we have to wonder how a practice that stills or restrains our vision, literally and metaphorically, affects us. Aldous Huxley noted that when our eye's natural motility is constrained, it no longer functions correctly; what we see becomes distorted, and our vision deteriorates. The impetus to fix a moment in time, notably deployed by Kodak's marketing campaign in their "Kodak Moments," is seen by Huxley as a "greedy anxiety" to "do the greatest possible amount of good seeing in the shortest possible time."[22] Paradoxically, as a result of the fixity imposed by the use of optical apparatuses such as lenses, the "starer neglects the only means whereby this end can be achieved."[23]

Paul Virilio asks the following question regarding the ways in which our vision changed with the advent of optical extenders like the telescope or the microscope: "But what does one see when one's eyes, depending on sighting instruments, are reduced to a state of rigid and practically invariable structural immobility? One can only see instantaneous sections seized by the Cyclops eye of the lens."[24]

Here again we find echoes of Leonardo's Cyclops, metonymic of a kind of shortsighted, limited kind of vision. But Leonardo was not the only artist to critique the prevalent system of perspective. Many modern artists have, at the core of their work, commented on perspective, either by patently refusing to employ it like Cézanne[25]; fragmenting it, like cubists Picasso, Braque and Gris; or by playing with it, like surrealists Dalí and Escher. David Hockney's photo collages, which break a scene into hundreds of "points of view," exemplify a non-perspectival, saccadic picture plane. But these relatively recent artists and others have had the time and space history affords to give them their perspective on perspective.

Dürer's Point of View

Albrecht Dürer, however, was able to represent the practices that were compelling to artists in the 16th century and, at the same time, embed his thinking on these practices as commentary in his art.

The etching entitled *Artist Drawing a Nude in Perspective* was used in Chapter Two (see page 33) to demonstrate the ways in which the artist comments on the technology that helped to make his art possible. Dürer was able, in the way he represented this phenomenon, to annotate the practice of employing perspective in his work.

In this horizontally constructed image, the picture plane is divided into almost equal halves, a nod in the direction of our bifurcated world. This division is not just spatial but aesthetic and contextual as well. The right side of the image is drawn with an emphasis on its horizontal and vertical elements, echoed in the *Lucinda*, the gridded window before the artist. Everything about this "right" side of the image has right angles, is geometric and orderly. The eye of our artist is fixed on the pointed obelisk in front of him. His posture is erect, and there is a restrained stillness about his demeanor. It is clear that he sees the grid, sees the guide for his eyes, sees his technique, but we are left to wonder whether Dürer's artist, so intent on the science of representing this model, actually sees her at all.

On the left side of the image we are confronted with the model. Her breasts and abdomen, the pillows cushioning her head, her flowing hair, and drapery, couldn't be more antithetical to the geometrically mapped world opposing her. She presses up against a space that appears as if it can't possibly contain her, as if she is being squeezed to fit the tiny cells of the artist's grid. Her knees buckle up against the grid as she strains against the confines of this constructed space. By contrast our artist, safely ensconced in his opposite quadrant has all the space in the world. He is seated far back from the Lucinda, a distance that underscores his distanced perspective, his scientific, rational approach to his subject matter, but one at which Dürer is perhaps hinting that misses the essence of this living, breathing model. Again, we can find in this etching examples of the one-pointed monocular gaze on the right, and an Aletheic reality on the left. The narrative embedded in Dürer's image undoes the prevalent historical construction that we had been striving happily head-long from the system of perspective toward the more and more accurate and objective representations that are photography and cinema. There is something more, Dürer is telling us, *than enframed accuracy in art.*

Dürer is suggesting that a particular kind of one-pointed seeing makes it difficult, if not impossible, to inhabit experience fully. In his portrayal of this particular immobile artist, Dürer gives us the impression of a rational subject who stands outside — "over and above" — the world.[26] He is pointing to the lack of movement without which an Aletheic practice of looking is unavailable to us.

Mobility Versus Fixity

Apparatus theory takes as one of its central tenets the relationship between the eye of the spectator and that of the monocular lens of the camera. Our examination of the perspectival eye — one-pointed and fixed — has opened up the limitations of a spectator whose vision is constrained. And yet the question as to whether or not the cinematic subject's eye is mobile or fixed — or perhaps even mobile *and* fixed, as Stephen Heath would have it — has been a pivot around which much of cinema theory has turned. Apparatus theory, as presented by Jean-Louis Baudry, looks at the structures, spaces, and mechanisms that shape the cinematic spectator's experience and elicit a particular response.

In order to follow Baudry's thinking we must accept certain of his assumptions. First, Baudry asserts that the rectangular screen models its shape, aspect ratio, and resultant perspectival space on the paintings and photographs that historically preceded it, drawing on the teleological force of Renaissance perspective to impact the cinematic spectator. Second, the spectator watching the film enters a relatively regressed state — like that of a dreamer or akin to that described by the Lacanian "mirror stage" — and consequently has what might be described as a hyper- or ultra-real experience. The emotional or narrative content of the film being watched notwithstanding — and this is certainly one of the weaker links of apparatus theory — Baudry asserts that this regressive state and hyper-real experience are the result of being an immobilized viewer in a darkened chamber viewing moving images on a screen and alternately engaging in an identification with the lens of the camera and with the characters before him. When we see through the point of view of an actress on the screen, that point of view joins us to the person, object, or space that is being seen; it inserts us into the cinematic space. The camera shows us what the character sees so that we may see *like* the character. We have no choice but to identify, according to Christian Metz, with this camera, which is revealing to us what it has seen before us. We may consider, then, that there are two cameras: a subjective camera that places us *in* the film, *in* the eyes of an actor, and an objective camera which constructs us more as an external viewer or, as Stephen Heath explains, as an "immaterial 'voyeur' of the pro-filmic pseudo-reality."[27]

Jean-Louis Comolli suggested that it is to the camera that we should look for indications of how the apparatus perpetuates a particular code of representation and its concomitant ideology.[28] In much the same way that the centralized, cycloptic gaze of perspective returned an objectifying stance, the cinematic apparatus, too, is not without its hegemonic ideological power. In initially describing the effect of the cinematic apparatus, Baudry zeroed in on how the literal arrangement of immobilized viewer — darkened chamber, framed screen, and light-spilling projector — joined forces to contribute to the extent to which the spectator was unconsciously "more" receptive to the images before him.[29] This receptivity, in turn, intensifies the viewer's willingness, perhaps even need, to identify with the all-seeing eye of the camera lens.

So let us look first at this camera to see how it sees and what it shows us, before investigating the underlying philosophical and psychoanalytical tenets which Baudry, Metz, Heath, and others maintain predispose the viewer to identify with it so completely. The subtle differences effected by the production of *Avatar* raise important questions here — about the relevance for apparatus theory when production relies heavily on a digital context, on the use of multiple cameras in a layered procession of shoots, on a pro-filmic environment that is captured in pixels instead of on emulsion — which will be addressed later on in this chapter.

Cinema is a process of transformation that is essentially opaque to the viewer. Given only the film in its final form, the spectator doesn't see the pro-filmic world established by the director, the individual camera shots and scenes, the editing process, or the inspiration of the initial "objective reality" that becomes the film. The movie camera, unlike the regular still camera, collects from that objective reality "instants of time" but, Baudry insists, from a reality that has already been "looked upon, elaborated and selected."[30] In the case of the making of *Avatar*, there was no pre-existent, objective reality that was selected or elaborated on in advance. Instead, the entire pro-filmic world was created and refined digitally, in most cases before Cameron shot it with his virtual camera and SimulCam system. For *Avatar*, Cameron had to first imagine the selection he might make from the fantasized world of Pandora, work with his animators to actually create it and, finally, only after it had been imagined, designed and programmed into existence, did the camera come to work its magic by selecting and fixing the images.

But writing in 1970, Baudry would have the camera sitting squarely between the raw material and the final edited film in which this original reality is "mutated" rather than translated or transcribed.[31] The mutation, in this case, consists of the slicing up of a particular reality into fixed fragments, interrupting the flow of movement. What once was wind blowing through leaves becomes a series of still photographs, each one differing in a minuscule way from the one that precedes it and the one that follows. And between each of these frames, there is a quick slip of black. Here the camera has dissected the intrinsic motion of the wind into tiny temporal chunks, breaking and disrupting the fluidity of the movement in the original scene. As the French critic Emile Vuillermoz has observed, "The eye that carves up space and fixes inimitable tableaux in time, that renders eternal the fleeting moment in which nature reveals its genius ... is the eye of the lens."[32]

This slicing and fixing of the moment is addressed as well by director Jacques Tourneur who remarked, "In Hollywood I soon learned that the camera never sees everything. I could see everything, but the camera only sees sections."[33] The camera's job, then, according to Baudry, is to mark these sections, to indicate the differences between the discrete frames each separated from the other by a sliver of black.

The camera breaks apart some kind of reality into sequential images, and the ensuing editing and projection of these serried frames restores movement to what had been stilled. In the darkened theater, the duo of screen and projector together return light and motion to the original occurrence of the wind blowing through the leaves. The screen reflects back to the eye of a viewer—fixedly gazing at the screen—24 flashing images per second, neither the individuality nor the separateness of which the eye can discern.[34] It is this inability to see each unique image, to distinguish the infinitesimal differences that each frame holds that creates the persistence of vision, hence the illusion of movement. The paradoxical mechanism insists on motion being disrupted and broken into pieces, and then, significantly, precisely because these pieces are invisible to the spectator, the initial movement is reinstated. The camera fractures what it shoots, and then, via its proxy the projection apparatus, heals the fracturing and returns motion to its rightful place.

But if we were to assume that the camera's function is simply to freeze and interrupt what moves, we would be mistaken. The cinematographic camera also wanders. Unlike the photographic camera, which at times may be bolted to a tripod and to which even the slightest tremor may cause the image to blur, the movie camera moves. It tilts and pans; it tracks or rides along on a dolly. And the spectator, without moving his head, tracks the movement that the camera offers.

The movie camera changes its point of view, offering a multiplicity of perspectives. This eye which can move every which way, up/down, left/right, in/out, is not, as Baudry would have it, "fettered to a body,"[35] and therefore is in a sense limitless, can go anywhere, see anything, and offers the viewer that same unlimited perspective. We have then a series of discontinuous still images, which may include a range of originating perspectives, a range of focal lengths, a range of framing mechanisms, from long shots to extreme close-ups, from aerial points of view to shoots through a car window.

The reconstituting of all this motion, all these points of view, the transformation of individual frames into some sort of continuity, some meaningful narrative, resides in the *eye of the subject*, bringing us full circle to Heath's immobile viewer in whom motion inheres. French film theorist Jean Mitry explains, "In the cinema I am simultaneously in this action and outside it, in this space and out of this space. Having the power of ubiquity, I am everywhere and nowhere."[36] It is this omnipresent viewer who, by virtue of the fact that she cannot perceive the image fragments, enjoys the illusion of full movement and identifies with the eye of the camera as it traces the movement that it follows. As Baudry poetically emphasizes, "To seize movement is to become movement, to follow a trajectory is to become trajectory."[37]

Think Fly

The first flight of Jake and his ikran is an apt example of movement seized, of trajectories followed. Movement inhabits the narrative action within the film as Jake, Neytiri, and their respective banshees soar, glide, dip, and dive through the floating mountains. In this montage of flying creatures plunging into the air beneath the gravity-defying peeks, the movement of the camera reflects the trajectory of the flight. At first, Jake is struggling to control his ikran, twirling and clambering up the side of a cliff or flung out wide, trailing the banshee as it fights to get away. The camera assaults this struggle by emphasizing the chaos. First it is beneath Jake as he dives into the camera lens. Then, in a very tight shot, the camera brings the viewer in close to the spiraling and wriggling of the winged thing. The camera moves from above to below, zooms in tight and pulls back, until finally it hovers above in an aerial view as the banshee dives, trying to shake Jake loose in the process. A steady ominous drumbeat and the sound of the frightened banshee's wings flapping intensify the pitching and the danger that the erratic camera reveals. When in frustration Jake yells to his ikran to shut up and fly straight, the birdlike creature levels out its massive wings and glides. The drumming ceases, and the camera pulls back for a long shot and steadies. Everything colludes to float the spectator along with Jake as he finally gets a handle on flying the ikran.

As Jake first tackles his banshee, Neytiri urges him to seal the sahelu bond with a first flight. She yells to him to "think fly." In this terse command we find the encapsulation of the mechanics of making this ambitious and exhilarating section of the film. Cameron could not simply take his crew on location to some remote banshee rookery and film B roll to make the scene realistic. He had to "think fly." He and his team of animators and camera folks had to "think fly." They had to imagine first what these banshees would look like: what colors they would be, the shape and relationship and the significance of their doubled eyes, how the scalloped aspects of their wings would flap in the wind, how their jaws would snap in anger, and how their talons would grab the bark of a tree to land. All of this and more had to be imagined. In a pre–computer-generated film, the director, working off of a screenplay or storyboard, might go on location or, failing that feasibility, might create a set on which to film. But there was some "objective reality" out there that could then be recorded in some manner and edited to produce the final product. Ultimately in the theater a story would unfold. But because there were so many more layers, so many more steps to undergo in order to arrive at the world of Pandora, the unfolding of the production apparatus of *Avatar* is more like a paper fan, unfolding and unfolding and unfolding again.

In the "First Flight" montage there is a short scene between Jake and Neytiri which takes us to the meta-level, a scene that stands in for Cameron's process of designing the flight paths. Jake and Neytiri share their experiences of flying with one another, miming the turns and banks, the feel of the wind. Using their arms, they imitate the motion of the ikran diving through the sky. On the classical narrative level, we may take this as just another episode in their developing flirtation. The entire flight scene plays as a dance between Jake and Neytiri, flirting like adolescents. Jake flies close enough to Neytiri to flap her with the wing of his ikran, and she retaliates. There is a physicality, an animalistic texture in this seduction; their bodies are one with their banshees. One could interpret this brief interlude of debriefing the flight simply as demonstrating the "human" need to verbalize after a wondrous experience. There is an intense urgency to their conversation that matches that of the energy of their flight.

On the meta-level, however, this small scene gives us the intricacies of scene creation — the planning, the rehashing, the stepping outside of the diegetic world to revisit what had occurred. More importantly, it gives us what Mitry noted above. Jake and Neytiri are in the action *and* outside of it commenting on it; they are in the space of flying as well as outside of it looking in. They are, like the cinematic spectator, in the flying and perceiving it, feeling the wind and then describing, noticing, and naming what the wind felt like. Even though the event of the first flight had just transpired, they are recollecting. In the process of remembering, they detach themselves from the present moment. They are absenting that beautiful moment where the moons are rising in the Pandoran sky behind them to return to their exhilarating flight. Henri Bergson compares this process to the focusing of a lens: "In order to replace ourselves, first, in the past, in general, then in a certain region of the past, — a work of adjustment, something like the focusing of a camera. But our recollection still remains virtual."[38] As they zoom in on the past, they are neither in the present moment nor in the past. They are in a virtual space, in between a now and a then.

In Chapter Two, a great deal of attention was paid to the filming of this particular scene, the plotting of the flight trajectories, the algorithms which were input into the computers and translated into virtual flight paths. The conversion from the little wire-hanger mock-ups of the ikran dotted with sensors that were flown about the empty space of the volume like toy airplanes to the awesome majestic soaring beasts the spectator sees flying through a phantasmagoric sky speaks to the transformative power of the cinematic process.

But it is ultimately the viewer who not only follows the trajectories but who "sees" flight. It is the viewer who, when confronted with the montage of whirling, banking, diving ikran and their riders, overlays upon this hodgepodge of images a unity, a continuity, a story. Through a process of virtually identifying with the eye of the camera as it seizes this monumental movement, the immobile viewer also "thinks fly."

Where Are We?

A close look at the camera has revealed the way it moves and, at the same time, undoes motion. The immobile spectator of the cinema appropriates the eye of the moving camera, seeing as it sees. But how does this identification happen? What are the conditions that increase the possibility that it might? Where are we when we watch film? Or, as Christian Metz asks, where is the ego during the cinema showing, "Where is that someone who is capable of self-recognition when need be?"[39]

Anne Friedberg answers this question in a series of layered responses, looking at the way different theoretical approaches might locate the spectator.[40] For example, apparatus theorists emphasize the relationship of the components of the apparatus — the projector, the screen, the arrangement of the spectator with her back to the thrown light, the darkened room — while a phenomeno-logical approach to the question takes as its center the immediacy of the image and the way cinema invites an engagement with one's senses.[41] A more literal answer might have been at one time that we are *in a theater* and might have described this space as architect Frederick Kiesler did, stressing the power of an auditorium to concentrate our attention.[42] Although today we may watch movies on an iPhone or BlackBerry, in our living rooms, on airplanes, or in a minimized window in a corner of a flat screen while we are doing our taxes on our computer desktop, we still enter a spectatorial space that transports us to some virtual elsewhere. Even Keisler, in describing a literal architectural site, offers a nod in the direction of the viewer inhabiting some kind of altered virtual space when watching movies. Keisler sees our involvement with the cinematic medium as overriding any sense of confinement we might have, and he describes a "reflex which the film creates in the psyche of the spectator [that] must make it possible for him to lose himself in imaginary, endless space, to feel himself alone in universal space."[43]

Baudry and other apparatus theorists make a strong psychoanalytic case for why it is that when we are inserted into the cinematic apparatus we are more apt to experience this "reflex" and find ourselves susceptible to a regressive state in which we tend to identify with "what makes the spectacle possible" or with the apparatus itself.[44]

The darkened space of the theater, the projected light situated behind the immobile viewer, and images reflecting off of the screen reproduce "in a striking way, the mise-en-scene of Plato's cave."[45] Baudry locates in Plato's allegory the signification of a desire that looms large in the invention of cinema and haunts its history.[46] Historians, looking to justify an intrinsic yearning for the illusion of the moving image, dredge up a line of precursors to the cinema, including the praxinoscope, the magic lantern, or the camera obscura. Plato's parable holds such fascination precisely because it so acutely resembles the apparatus of today's cinema. This famous allegory might seem almost pre-scient, until or unless one understands that Plato was not predicting a time when we might fulfill an instinctual desire to fix our experiences on strips of emulsion, but instead was attempting to illuminate the illusions under which the common person may suffer while not having access to the world of ideal forms.[47]

A more pervasive underpinning of the effect of the darkened room and immobile spectator draws on the psychoanalytic theories of Jacques Lacan — particularly his *mirror stage*— riddled with notions of lack and desire.

Lacan's mirror stage is a psychological phase that occurs between the ages of six and eighteen months. At this time, the pre-verbal child ostensibly becomes aware, through discovering his or her reflection in a mirror, that they are not connected to or a permanent part of the mother, that the arms that hold the child are not an extension of him or herself. When the baby sees this image in the mirror, they imagine themselves as whole instead of fragmented with undefined boundaries conflated with the mother. The imagined perfection of the idealized self in the mirror intensifies, according to Lacan, the infant's sense of her or his own imperfection. The child becomes aware that he or she is separate, other. So he or she has the first sketchy sense of being an "I" and at the same instant experiences alienation. The infant feels the lack of his or her own incompleteness.[48] The child sees herself in the mirror, and she sees herself looking at herself. This orchestration of looks makes visible the Lacanian model in which the self that forms during this mirror stage presents as a divided entity; it is intertwined with, it *desires,* that which is other than itself.[49] Baudry and other apparatus theorists suggest that this desire for the other, for that which we intrinsically lack, can find its expression in looks between actors on screen and between the audience and the screen.[50]

The circumstances of the mirror stage, the "immature powers of mobility and a precocious maturation of visual organization,"[51] are viewed by Baudry and others as being repeated during the projection of a movie and thus restimulating the lack or incompleteness that the infant had once experienced. This induces the spectator to identify with an *other*— in this case the characters in the film and/or the omnipresent eye of the camera. The spectator of cinema, like the infant, is in a "sub-motor and hyper-perceptive state" and, accordingly, is likely to engage in two levels of identification: one derived from the characters portrayed and one in which the spectator identifies with what makes the spectacle visible, that is, the apparatus itself.[52] The camera does the work of seeing *for* us. Identifying with the projector/camera stand-in, we allow it to pan and track without needing to swivel our neck or turn our head. The screen, like the primordial mirror, reflects characters, objects and places. However, due to the fact that our egos have long since formed, we no longer need to literally see ourselves reflected back. We are able to recognize the people and places reflected even though we ourselves are "absent" from the screen.[53]

Mirror, Mirror

Feminist and post-structuralist thinkers like Hélène Cixous and Luce Irigaray have taken issue with this Lacanian primordial scene, finding it securely rooted, as is much of Freudian and Lacanian psychoanalysis, in a *phallogocentric* paradigm that marginalizes the experience and the point of view of women. In order for the scene of the mirror stage to make sense, there are some underlying phallocentric assumptions that must be uncovered. We must assume that this infant somehow inherently values independence and separateness over connection and attachment. We must assume that the infant's desire to be whole is equated with disassociating from the mother, from her breast, from her arms. Somehow, this tiny being already knows that to form a sense of him/herself, of being an "I" who stands on his/her own, s/he must abandon, literally and metaphorically, his/her connection with the mother. This rejection of the mother, what Lacan calls the "real," translates into a wholesale rejection of the female body and the subjectivity that surrounds it.

Lacan's primordial scene denies the value of the feminine, of connection, by necessity. In order to enter the "symbolic," what Lacan denotes as the realm where the infant accesses language and becomes part of the "social," the child must put aside any unmediated perceptions of her environment. To enter the symbolic, she replaces that which she perceived directly with the relevant signification. This is yet another reason Lacan's paradigm is imbued with loss. When we enter the arena of the social and gain language, we theoretically leave behind our embodied engagement with our world. As mentioned earlier, language serves our knowledge development, but its enframing effect distances us from an Aletheic experience of the immediate.

The fictional apparatus of the avatar link closely resembles and comes to stand for the cinematic apparatus. But the apparatus of the avatar link leads away from a reinforcement of the symbolic and toward a return to the kind of embodied seeing alluded to in Chapter One. The avatar linkup is cast not in the shadow of the Lacanian mirror in which there is loss and lack of connection but, instead, in the light of a reflection in which we leave incompleteness behind and discover connection.

When we encounter the character of Jake, he embodies nothing so much as loss. He has lost his twin brother, he has lost the use of his legs, and this disability has lost him his privileged status as a man and a warrior. It is clear early on in the film, when the RDA-employed soldiers greeting the new recruits refer to him as "meals on wheels," that he is diminished in their eyes. We see him as they see him, as less than whole.

The avatar linkup provides for Jake an uncanny parallel to the imaginary that is perceived by the infant gazing into the mirror and to the cinematic spectator entranced by the flicker of images on the screen in front of her. Jake, the infant, and the moviegoer are all stationary. Jake is laid into his casket-like container. The lid is shut, and he is placed completely in the dark, much like the spectator. His body sinks into something akin to memory foam, and a metal cage comes over his rib cage, keeping his body inert. Following Baudry's requirements for a repeat of the mirror-stage event, Jake and the audience find themselves in a "sub-motor and hyper-perceptive state."

But while Jake's eyes are closed and his body is constrained in his linkup pod, his consciousness inhabits his avatar and he virtually enters a more nearly perfect version of himself. His wizened legs become but a memory as he races out of the med-tech tent and into the Pandoran fields. Like the viewer of cinema, for Jake everything seems more vivid, more pronounced in this new, more perfect body. His experience, like that of the theoretical viewer, is hyper-real. He is, like the camera before him, like the cinema viewer, mobile and inert, running and utterly still, awake and asleep, in the dark and in the sunlight, here and there, all at once.

We have asked where we are, where is the ego when the subject is viewing cinema, and we have suggested that we reside in some virtual space, some other space than that of our everyday existence. Surely Jake, inhabiting his avatar, is in some other kind of space, one in which it is most difficult for us to even conceive. His body is still, entombed in the avatar apparatus. His consciousness has traveled elsewhere. And while we might, if we stretch, imagine a situation like entering an online environment, either a game-scape or a *Second Life* sort of world peopled with "avatars," in those cases we are still using our imaginations to project us rather than having an embodied experience of inhabiting an "other."

We have in the apparatus of the avatar the perfect other and desire satisfied. Jake is not imagining this better, stronger, able-bodied other; he is living in it. And yet, all the while, he remains without—lying in the linkup pod. He is running away from the wild Thanator, and he is safe in the mechanism; he is leaping across tree branches, and he is prone, in some sort of altered reality, in his pod. Like the cinematic spectator, he is within and without. He leaves the real to experience a *really* real. When his consciousness returns to his disabled human body, he is thrown back into his lack, his incompleteness.

Absence and Presence

Jake balances on a teeter-totter of absence and presence, much like the cinematic spectator and, even ultimately, like cinema itself. As Christian Metz points out in his seminal article, "The Imaginary Signifier," what we see when we watch film is not there. The camera that at some moment in the past shot some objective reality is not there. The story that unfolds in front of our eyes may or may not be a fictional narrative, but the unfolding itself is fictive.[54] Unlike the theater or opera or ballet where the performers, the sets, and the orchestra are present in the auditorium with the spectator, nothing of what we may see in the movies is actually there. Metz posits that it is not that the cinema purports to represent something imaginary — for example, a far-off moon inhabited by very tall blue humanoids — but that it itself *is* imaginary. It is absence masquerading as presence.

Metz asks us to consider — and again we are brought up short by the radical changes in the film industry in just a few decades — the film canister: "a little rolled-up perforated strip which 'contains' vast landscapes, fixed battles, the melting of the ice on the River Neva, and whole lifetimes, and yet can be enclosed in the familiar round metal tin, of modest dimensions, clear proof that it does not really contain all that."[55] If we are now to consider the bits and bytes which comprise the world of the Na'vi, the ikran, and the lush tropical jungle of Pandora, we realize the even greater tension of the pull between what is present to us on the screen as we watch *Avatar* and an undeniable and ultimate absence.

Cinema is intrinsically not there, just as the cinema spectator is also absent from the screen and, yet, essentially present to its unfolding. As Metz declares, we are a great perceiver, an eye and ear without which there is no one to perceive the perceived. "It is I who make the film."[56] We are by necessity present to the screen and absent from it. We are necessary to its presence and the recipient of its absence, all at once.

Jake, like cinema and the cinematic viewer, balances between his absence and presence. We might ask, in the same manner in which we have inquired of the spectator, where is Jake when he is in the apparatus of the avatar? Is he present in his human body or does he leave his body when he is present in the avatar? And if he is not in his biological body, then does it remain alive and his? When he is present to the world available to him through the perceptions of his avatar, is his brain, which resides in his own body, perceiving? When he absents his avatar, we assume it becomes lifeless, a shell. But when he absents his own body, what keeps him alive? Is the avatar linkup like a life-support system? And when we say "he" absents his body, what precisely do we mean? His soul? His mind? His consciousness? His ego? When his avatar speaks and the voice of Jake Sully comes out, who is speaking? All we can be sure of is that some construction of memories, perceptions, and identity that we recognize as the character Jake moves back and forth, present in one body and absent in the other until the film's end.

The avatar linkup apparatus could be perceived as wedding the antithetical perceptual models of Descartes' *cogito* and Merleau-Ponty's embodied subjectivity. Cameron makes a point of showing the viewer close-ups of Jake in the linkup pod, his eyes closed but darting, typical of the REM movements that have long been associated with a dream state. This image seems to reinforce a cognitivist paradigm, one in which we understand that while Jake is linked to his avatar, his brain is hard at work back in his human body. At the same time, for the most part, whenever Jake inhabits his avatar, Cameron tracks his actions from the outside, as if we were meant to assume Jake is, in fact, present in the avatar, experiencing the world of Pandora through its intensified sense organs and therefore having an embodied experience of the world around him.[57] We have, then, in the apparatus of the avatar, a mind that is separate from its body in that it travels to a new location, and an embodied mind, located within the body of the avatar and perceiving in and through it.

Perhaps looking at Metz's notion of vision as encompassing a double movement can help us in understanding here. Metz bisects vision into the projective and the introjective. We first look, perhaps with the "sweeping searchlight" motion that Metz describes: our eyes scour things, they send out a sort of visual stream. We might recognize this metaphor from Berger's lighthouse, briefly touched on earlier in this chapter. But then, as in Berger's analogy to perspectival vision, the lighthouse beam is inverted, and what was seen returns to us, strikes our consciousness in the form of a perception that, as Metz might have it, is no longer emitting but receiving like an impression made in soft wax.[58] And while Metz is quick to label this fantasy notion of how vision works "banal," it serves his purpose in likening this process to the apparatus of the cinematic spectator.

The camera, as it shoots its subject matter, is projecting; what is recorded, whether on film, on tape, or on disk, is the object introjected. If we look at the language used to describe the acts of the camera, they contain both the projective and introjective attributes. The verb "to shoot" certainly yields up a projectile sense. On the other hand, when we "take" a picture, are we not introjecting? Jake, in the avatar linkup pod, is projected into the avatar, his perceptual experience in the avatar introjected into the part of Jake that perceives. The viewer, too, is part of this apparatus. As the audience watches the screen, our vision scans, much like that metaphoric searchlight and, Metz adds, at the same time duplicating the function of the projector, which in turn is standing in for the camera. As the viewer takes in what she sees, as she introjects, she resembles the reflective surface of the movie screen, which in turn is standing in for the strip of film, videotape, or DVD on which the images have been recorded. Metz would have it that the spectator is projector and screen, the camera that points yet also records.[59]

The Double

We don't really perceive the object of cinema but a shadow of it, a "phantom, its double, its replica."[60] This theme of doubling is pervasive in Metz's writings: the projector doubles for the camera, the surface of the screen for the emulsion of the film. The viewer stands in for projector, screen and camera. Metz underscores this chain of reduplication and reminds us that this mirroring or chain of mirrors in which the subject is constituted resembles the technical innards of the mechanisms. "The apparatuses too contains series of mirrors, lenses, apertures, and shutters, ground glasses, through which the cone of light passes: a further reduplication in which the equipment becomes a metaphor ... for the mental process instituted."[61] The light that penetrates the aperture and bounces from mirror to emulsion or to light-sensitive microchip yields the quality of play, fluxes the discreteness of the seer and what is seen. We have then the shore and strand of which Merleau-Ponty spoke,[62] the washing back and forth of light and image from projector to screen to subject and back again.

Metz calls this fluxing the "play of the imaginary" and articulates the need of each side of the seesaw for the other. The child can't construct his ego identity without the "fabulous figure" he perceives in the mirror.[63] Presence requires absence; projection depends on introjection. Metz enacts this self-reflexive play in his essay when he steps outside of his narrative to note the fact that he was adding to this passel of reduplications. "Am I not looking at myself looking at the film?... Am I not still the voyeur I was in front of the screen, now that it is this voyeur who is being seen thus postulating a second voyeur, the one writing at present, myself again?"[64]

Unlike the cinema, the diegetic world Jake visits in his avatar is no less real than the one he has left behind. It is not a shadow or a replica or a simulacrum. But in linking to the avatar, Jake doubles himself, and this doubling is a central motif traceable throughout the film, is even apparent in its production.

Jake links into his avatar, which was initially the avatar of his twin, his biological double. When he inhabits his avatar, he is reduplicating his existence in another vessel. This reduplicating becomes a chain during the times in which Jake establishes a bond with the ikran or the direhorse creatures. When the Na'vi make "sahelu," they are simply extending their consciousness, joining it with the creatures, blurring the lines of where one starts and the other stops. In Jake's case, it can again be likened to the folded paper fan; his consciousness moves from the linkup pod into the avatar, from the avatar into the creature — the doubling of the double.

Jake's dissembling may also be interpreted as a sort of doubling. Initially, he is covertly gathering intelligence for Colonel Quaritch, keeping this mission secret from Grace. Once he becomes convinced of the value in the Pandoran way of life, his pretense is for the colonel. Jake doubles as an agent of the RDA and an ally of the Omaticaya. It is this doubling which is his undoing and, in the end, is used against him by Quaritch. The inadvertent discovery of his duplicitousness by Neytiri damages their relationship as well as the trust he had worked so hard to build with the Na'vi.

There are also visual doubles that underscore the reduplication motif. Virtual models of the Pandoran jungle created by the sophisticated computer technology abound. Surveillance technology often places the spectator within the diegetic container whenever he or she looks at or through the visual apparatus in the film. We see through windshields of helicopters and transport vehicles, through the sensor and radar screens in their instrument panels. When Jake destroys the "eyes" of the bulldozers, we experience another chain of doubles. Jake, lying in his linkup pod, moves in the body of his avatar to destroy the bulldozer's video cameras that facilitate their being piloted by drivers at a remote location. We watch Jake's destructive actions through the remote driver's monitor. We are witness to it a second time, once removed, when Quaritch is researching the tape to discover who it was that attacked the bulldozers, and a third time when he uses the tape to nail Jake.

As discussed earlier, Colonel Quaritch is doubled himself by his mechanical suit. His small motions are enlarged and strengthened by the AMP suit in which he sits. He flails his human arms, and his huge mechanical arms wreak havoc. The final battle with Neytiri on the back of a Thanator, Jake in his avatar, and Quaritch in his AMP suit is a dance of doubles. The colonel's attack on Jake at this point offers him twice the number of usual targets; he can go directly for the avatar, or he can try to undermine Jake by attacking him in his linkup pod, doubling his opportunities for inflicting harm.

The Suturing of Avatar

The video log that Jake maintains throughout the film serves as an important narrative device as well as yet another form of doubling. Stepping back from his experience in the avatar, as any good scientist must, Jake documents his observations. As he does so, he is recorded by the digital camera; his words and his image are transformed into bits and bytes. This diegetically doubles the construction of the entire film, which has been recorded digitally, setting up a sort of mise en abyme. Subsequently a dialog is established between the digital camera of Jake's video log and all of the cameras that shot the film and with which we identify. The spectator has access to what transpires outside of the video log as well as to an internal limited first-person account, granting omniscience.

Jake's log gives us not only the doubling effect we have been exploring, but a fertile demonstration of the trajectory of the shot/reverse shot element essential to the cinematic concept of *suture*. The notion of suture was exported from psychoanalytic theory by Jacques-Alain Miller, a student of Lacan's. As in the apparatus theory, the concept of suture grew out of the sense of lack prevalent in Lacan's work. Miller points to the moment in which we leave our immediate experience of the world for entry into the symbolic. The intrinsic loss/lack/absence that obtains is a direct result of gaining meaning at the "expense of being."[65] Theoretician Jean-Pierre Oudart appropriated the concept of suture in his quest to identify a cinematic syntax, something that would mirror the function of language in literary texts. Contributions by Daniel Dayan, Stephen Heath and Laura Mulvey, to name a few, have enlarged and complicated the concept, but generally there is agreement that the articulation of a film and the construction of a viewing subject are facilitated by the basic element of the interlocking shot.[66]

Kaja Silverman takes issue with apparatus theorists' assertion that a primary identification takes place between the subject and camera. Looking at the subject through the lens of suture theory, Silverman sees a disjunction. There is the initial *jouissance*, the viewer's delight in all she sees, the sense of ecstatic power that comes over one who is omniscient. But sooner or later, the viewer becomes aware of the cinematic frame, suddenly self-conscious of the fact that what he is able to see has been predetermined, controlled by some "other." What was ecstasy one moment becomes loss in the next with the realization that he only has access to an enframed bit of the camera's choosing. This consciousness of the existence of all the rest, of all that he cannot see, deepens the spectator's desire to see *more*.[67] Jake's extended love affair with the Pandoran world exemplifies an extended version of the transition from initial *jouissance* to the resultant dispossession of his field. His exuberance in embodying the avatar and the heightened perceptual awareness that he achieves are manifestations of the joy he takes in his sensory world and its apparently endless possibilities. It is only after he mates with Neytiri and wakes up in the dark constraint of his linkup pod that he falls into despair. He realizes the restrictions of his broken humanness and the extent of the unbreachable gulf between their worlds. His limitations are not framed by the camera, but instead are framed by the avatar apparatus itself.

The shot/reverse shot is the ideal cinematic device to grant the viewer the "more" that she desires as well as to hide from her the fact of the controlling camera eye. This formation alerts the viewer to an "other field"—a character, a cinematic space, or an object — and links this object to the character's gaze. For example we see Neytiri high above in a tree drawing her bow. In the reverse shot we see Jake lost in the jungle. We link these shots temporally, spatially and diegetically, although logically it is entirely possible they could be occurring miles apart or temporally separated. But our impulse is to connect the two by building a story, imagining the *more* we could be seeing and linking it to what it is that we are given to see.

From the beginnings of cinema there has been motion. Figures move in the frame, the frame changes, the camera moves, or there is an edit that switches to a different shot. The problem of coherence has always existed: how is it that the spectator can maintain a unified sense of the narrative? The spectator will always tend to link images in sequence, to try to find a connection, even when there is none. We have, as an example, the experiment conducted by Russian film director Vsevolod Pudovkin.[68] Pudovkin shot the face of the Russian actor Ivan Mosjoukin in what could be described as a neutral expression. He juxtaposed this face with images of a bowl of steaming soup, a dead woman laid out in her coffin, and a child playing with a teddy bear and then showed these paired images to an audience. In each case, the spectators believed that Mosjoukin was looking at the paired object, and this transformed for them the impassiveness of his face. When Mosjoukin's face followed the bowl of soup, he was noted as looking at it pensively. When his image followed the dead woman, his expression was described as sorrowful. And when his face followed that of the child, he was seen as having a glowing smile. The sequential images cued the spectator to create narrative meaning and to cover over the impassive expression with what they imagined one might feel in such a situation. The mere juxtaposition of shots invites the suture of the viewer.

Returning to Jake's video log, it transforms the shot/reverse shot in a way that interjects the viewing subject into the film. The video log, the eye of the computer camera, and the way in which these scenes were shot *sutures* the spectator to the computer and Jake to his virtual self, doubling him in an ultimately destructive digital recording.

Jake's inaugural video log is presented in the standard, shot/reverse shot format. We first see the video monitor through Jake's eyes. He sits in front of a digital camera that is connected to a computer terminal on which he records his "scientific" observations. We are no longer outside the film looking in, but we see from the place in which Jake is sitting, speaking into a recording device, and which feeds back to him his own reflection. In this first shot we see what Jake sees: precisely what is on the computer screen. The red record button blinks back at us. The icon of Jake that identifies whose video log we are watching is visible on the desktop, as is the time stamp. And we see Jake's face and the entire lab that sits behind him. We are right in close to this particular doubling.

Then the camera angle switches, moving to the side and giving the reverse shot. Now we are outside the computer looking over at Jake and his recording setup. He sits at the computer, the camera atop its tripod, the large-screen computer monitor reflecting back what is being recorded. As Jake turns, the back of his head faces the "virtual" camera, Cameron's camera, but on the desk we can see what the computer camera sees displayed on the large-format monitor. In this particular shot/reverse shot, we are given the space between Jake and his video double and the link that is established between the two.

When we encounter Jake recording his next v-log installment, the shot/reverse shot is missing. There is only what the video camera sees, only what is visible on the monitor. We see Jake reach his hand up to turn on the monitor, which fades up from black, as if just waking from sleep mode. We see our point of view shift slightly as Jake adjusts the video camera. We are privy to the entire GUI: the time stamp, the record button, his ID picture. This video log continues as voice-over to an accompanying montage of shots of his apprenticeship to Neytiri. But we are never given the reverse shot. We are married now to the computer camera eye, and the frame that bounds what it is possible to see extends only to that end. When, in the middle of this montage, Grace interrupts Jake to tell him he has to learn to see the forest through Neytiri's eyes, we are rooted in the eye of the computer, limited by the extent of its frame. This perspective continues through his next log entry. As he confides to the video camera that he hardly remembers his whole life, that he doesn't know who he is anymore, the caroming of Jakes abound. There is Jake the marine and Jake the Na'vi, Jake the observer and recorder of his video log, and the virtual Jake of the recorded logs, assuming a life and an impact all its own, outside of the will or actions taken by the human Jake.

When Quaritch and Selfridge prepare for their impending attack on Pandora, Jake and Grace, returned for the moment to their human bodies, plead with them for a chance to salvage the situation. In this scene everyone is gathered in the command center. Quaritch, turning to the computer monitor, uses the surveillance clip of Jake destroying the bulldozer cameras to indict him. Jake sits there in his wheelchair confronting his vibrant, active double smashing the surveillance cameras with a rock, now also visible to the spectator through the back of the transparent computer monitor. In the background are multiple, intensely colored, virtual versions of Pandora, imaged on serried screens and spread out across the command center. As Grace pleads with Selfridge to reconsider, she elaborates about the exponential nature of the electrochemical network of synapses that exist within the root system of the trees on Pandora, her words doubling and redoubling, offering a verbal ripple to the reduplication of the visual representations of Pandoran data we see on the computer screens behind her.

The nail in the coffin of Grace's plea comes from an unexpected place. Quaritch accesses the file containing Jake's video logs and scrolls through them until he finds the one he needs, the one in which Jake unwittingly makes the case for the futility of a diplomatic solution. Quaritch invites Grace to look. We are now watching the projection to Jake's introjection. The monitor now says "Play" instead of flashing the red record button, and there is a real-time readout display of the "script" of his log.

Here we revisit the shot/reverse shot format, which sutures the virtual Jake to the human characters who surround the computer monitor and at the same time inserts the spectator into the scene. The viewer is initially located outside the shot: we again look through the back of the transparent monitor — a handy visual device that keeps us outside the scene but able to look in — and we can see the entire space of the command center and the ensemble gathered to watch and listen to Jake's virtual double.

A point-of-view shift brings us around to the front of the monitor, where we are in tight to Jake's log. But we are no longer restrained by the frame of the monitor, no longer wedded to the computer's camera eye. The first shot/reverse shot gives us Jake, painfully watching himself seal the fate of those he has come to love. The second shot/reverse shot gives us Grace, then Quaritch, Selfridge, and finally Norm. In each of their expressions we see their reactions to the truth of Jake's double's words and to the impending disaster. They hang on virtual Jake's words as he assures them all that there is nothing that the humans have, not Lite Beer nor blue jeans, that can induce the Na'vi to move. Jake has, contrary to what he was attempting, convinced the company men that destroying the Na'vi is the only solution. We can read on their faces the hopelessness of the situation. In this scene Jake confronts himself, squeezed in the mire of his doubling subterfuge. He has lost control of his parts: his brutally honest reflections offered in the name of science to his video log have been usurped. By virtue of this chain of shots/reverse shots, the spectator is threaded into the scene between the Jake in his wheelchair and the virtual Jake in his video log. Jake's despair, his culpability and his betrayal fill the discontinuity of the filmic moment.

There is one last video log, in which Jake literally and symbolically signs off. He says his farewells to the linkup laboratory and wheels himself off to the final ceremony and final scene of the film in which he enacts a literal suture: his ego, his consciousness, his memories, his identity — "all that he is" — travel through the "eye" of Eywa and into the body of his avatar. Jake says good-bye to the double of his virtual video self and to his disabled human body. He is unified in the container of his avatar.

In the Chinks and Cracks

This integration of his fragmented self, however, doesn't yield the "I" of Lacan's symbolic, cut off from immediate sense and from the mother. Instead, it finds Jake joined to the network of connections that is the Na'vi and their world on Pandora. Jake is one with the mother, Eywa, one with the people, and undivided in his own self. He has reversed and transformed the Lacanian entrance into the symbolic by turning to this world in which the mother is revered, in which connection is everything, in which immediate perception constitutes the Na'vi way of being. This feminist twist that here holds nature in esteem, that values the community, relationship, and the networks of connections between life forms, is presented to the spectator clearly and unambiguously.

When Jake prays for Eywa's assistance in defeating the human invaders, he tells the deity that where he comes from there is no green, that the humans have destroyed their mother. This not-so-subtle subtext of the human disregard for their own planet and its resources is threaded throughout *Avatar*, made evident in the disdain shown by Selfridge in his interactions with Grace. When she protests that the trees are sacred, Selfridge scoffs and asserts that everything on Pandora is sacred, that you can't throw a stick without hitting some sacred thing. This notion that everything is, in fact, sacred seems preposterous to him. The space that Grace inhabits in this scene has been described by Teresa de Lauretis as existing in discursive blind spots and margins; Grace is inserting herself into the "chinks and cracks of the power-knowledge-apparati"[69] of the hegemonic world that Selfridge and Quaritch occupy. And like Jake describing himself when he is cast out from the Na'vi, she is in the place that the eye can't see — especially the narrow, monocular eyes of Parker Selfridge and the colonel.

When Grace tries a different tack, playing her scientist card, Selfridge's reaction is no less virulent. When she explains to him the magnitude of the biological connections that exist in the root systems of the trees on Pandora and the ways in which the Na'vi can tap into this neural net, he deflects the value in what she is proposing with another attempt at humor. He asks her what she and her team have been smoking while on the moon's surface. Eponymously named "Self"-ridge, Parker embodies the realm of the symbolic, in which the self denies what is immediate and real and connected. In true Lacanian form, he longs for and believes that his salvation lies in obtaining what is unobtainable, the illusion of the fabulous other, in this case, the "unobtainium."

In Quaritch, too, we find an equal disparagement of that which smacks of the heart. He is quick to reduce Jake's "marriage" to Neytiri and his allegiance to the Na'vi as simply "getting some local tail." The colonel and Selfridge are dismissive of Jake's transformation and all that he has come to value; they ridicule Grace's awe of what she has discovered in the trees of Pandora in spite of its rational, scientific basis. Mammon is all that is worshiped by Selfridge, and might is Quaritch's god.

A disregard for the natural is shared extra-textually as well. In Slajov Žižek's review of *Avatar*, the Lacanian scorn seeps through. In one brief descriptive phrase, "the aborigines who live in an incestuous link with nature,"[70] Žižek slams both nature and connection. He contrasts the "fantasy" world of Pandora with what he claims to be the "ordinary" world—"true" world?—of imperialist colonialism. Of course there is no mistaking that the film *Avatar* is a fantasy, and in fact Žižek insists that in order for a concept such as reality to exist, there has to be that specific other, fantasy, or else reality has no meaning. But within the diegetic construction of the film, Pandora is just as "real" as imperialism. In his critique, Žižek suggests that Pandora be likened to the "Toon" world of *Roger Rabbit* or the digital illusion of *The Matrix*. While he initially compares *Avatar* to these films, alleging a similar "hyper-reality" achieved through the digital construction and 3-D shooting, he ultimately confuses himself and conflates the "digitally enhanced everyday reality"[71] of Pandora—diegetically as real as any other natural setting—with the digital production that created it. In the end, Žižek asserts that Jake leaves reality for an illusion, similar to what would happen if Neo chose to remain within the illusion of the matrix. Again, Žižek apparently misses the mark here. The matrix is, within the narrative construction of the film, an illusion. The viewer sees the massive rows of fettered humans providing power for the machines. The illusion of cities and "normalcy" is just that: not real. Pandora, on the other hand, within the context of the science-fiction film *Avatar*, is *not* an illusion. Jake is opting not for a fantasy, although it may seem like a fantasy to the viewer, but for a *realer* real. By asserting that in the end Jake migrates, in the "underlying symbolic economy,"[72] from reality to fantasy, Žižek denies the necessary suspension of disbelief and ultimately the spectatorial suture that must take place.

The sutured viewer can't help but also long for this appealing fantasy of a world where touch is made visible by phosphorescent response, in which life is cherished, and the connections among living things valued. *Avatar* evokes that longing and connection in the audience for an idealized other, but in this case the "other" is a fantasy world in which the mother is sacred, honored, essential: one who embodies connection, not individuation.

The Digital Double

This powerful doubling of the real and the virtual, the human and the avatar, finds its way into the making of the film as well. Shifting the focus of the infusion of doubling to the production side of the equation, each actor who plays the part of a Na'vi or of the driver of an avatar is doubled by their computer-generated character. While they are leaping about the volume in their performance-capture suits, their double — their avatar — is being formulated and refined in the virtual world of Pandora. Each of these actors and actresses has been doubled in bits and bytes.

The camera eye, with which the spectator can't help but identify, has also been reduplicated. But instead of seeing a double of the camera, we have, like our folded fan, a multiplicity of camera eyes. Dozens of cameras encircled the volume where the actors were shot. Each actor/actress had his/her own head rig, recording the minutest of their features' expressions. In the case of the way in which *Avatar* was constructed, it might be more accurate to suggest that the spectator identifies with the composite eye of *all* the cameras, created by the computer animators and ultimately photographed by Cameron's virtual camera. In watching Cameron virtually shoot *Avatar*, we turn the camera on the director setting up a ricocheting action.

This extraordinary rupture and consequent restitching in the creation of the composite image doubles the inherent fracturing and healing of the moving camera that lies at the heart of cinema. Thus, *Avatar* can be viewed as a meta-film, commenting on the nature of cinema and the construction of the filmic subject, and in some fashion breaking the cinematic mold. Similarly, the hyper-reality Jake perceives through his avatar while immersed in the world of Pandora reflects the redoubling of the spectator's perceptions in the immediacy of the 3-D experience.

No matter how many cameras are used to create the composite image that is the film *Avatar*, they all still reside within the cinematic frame, whether that is considered the frame of the film itself or the frame of the screen on which it is displayed. Anne Friedberg, in her examination of the "virtual window," insists that it is neither narrative nor projection but the frame itself that recenters the viewer. The frame holds true, no matter what the story. The perception of movement within the frame assumes a fixed edge, or as she declares, "What stays in place: the frame of the image."[73] The frame of the screen serves as the boundary between what is in the screen world and what remains in the "material world of the spectator."[74] But computer generation, Cameron's head rigs, the SimulCam system and the performance-capture suits in concert have altered the apparatus and hence the determination of the spectator as well.

This profusion of eyes fluxes the monocular view inherited from Renaissance perspective, and within the 3-D experience of *Avatar*, it opens Friedberg's boundary of the frame. The multiple cameras that create the composites that become the film break open the intrinsic frame of cinema. *Avatar* doesn't really break this frame, but it appears to. The experience of watching the film in 3-D is precisely one of the cinematic frame being pierced, the film coming out to meet the spectator. Things push out past the boundaries of the fourth wall. In her essay entitled "Floating in the Digital Experience," Manohla Dargis quotes from a *New York Times* article written in 1896 that describes the experience of Edison's Vitascope, "a machine that 'projects upon a large area of canvas groups that appear to stand forth from the canvas, and move with great facility and agility as though actuated by separate impulses.'"[75] Dargis recalls this description when recounting her own experience of seeing *Avatar* in 3-D. She finds that the 3-D images were often spectacular, and Cameron's characters, like the figures in that 1896 Edison film,

> '[A]ppear to stand forth from the canvas, and move with great facility and agility, as though actuated by separate impulses.'[76] When I watched *The Dark Knight* in Imax, I felt that I was at the very edge of the screen. *Avatar*, in 3-D, by contrast, blurs that edge, closing the space between you and the screen even more.[77]

The inviolable space between the projector and screen is now penetrated and populated by aspects of the image on the screen. These have emerged to fill the volume of the theater, to move closer to us. Thus the stream that ran from projector to screen and from screen to subject is now suspended like water droplets caught in a strobe in the empty space between, meshing projection and introjection.

In Heath's "The Imaginary Signifier," much is made of the voyeuristic nature of the cinema. The voyeur watches from a necessary distance. He can't be too close or he becomes overwhelmed. He is outside looking in and necessarily maintains "a gulf, an empty space, between the object and the eye, the object and his own body."[78] Heath and others see the gap between the cinematic spectator and the screen as mirroring that of the gaze of the voyeur and the necessary distance from the object of his look. But in the cinema, Heath asserts, there is an extra loop of doubling beyond that of the voyeur. The distance between the spectator and the screen is not equivalent to the distance between voyeur and object. The film, unlike a play, opera or ballet, is always already a "delegate." There is no real there there. The projection of the film already reduplicates what the camera eye saw.

But in *Avatar*, that redoubled distance is altered. The camera in *Avatar* no longer replicates the voyeur. The viewer of *Avatar* in 3-D is immersed in the super-reality of the film; she enters the action, feels the inherent movement, senses the permeability of the screen as the film comes out to meet her. And while the 3-D film is equally a stand-in for the objects that were created digitally and photographed virtually, the immersive experience titillates the viewer. She knows that the water droplets on the palm frond are not there, but at the same time, she sees them, close up and personal; she hears the rain droplets spatter. The frisson of the illusion transports and tickles the viewer in a manner similar to what we might imagine was experienced by the spectators of early cinema.

The Dream and the Double

The theoretical lens of the cinematic apparatus sharpens the perception of the antithetical pairs of absence/presence, introjection/projection, mobile/fixed. The apparatus of *Avatar* fluxes these polar opposites and reveals them as co-inhabiting a single space. There is an additional metaphor saturating the cinematic apparatus theory and *Avatar* that is closely connected to our experience of the visual and which subtends these antithetical pairs.

In Baudry's work on the apparatus theory, he posits a configuration — darkened room, separation from the outside world, inhibition of motoricity — that brings about what he calls "a state of artificial regression." We have looked at this state in relation to Lacan's mirror stage and the ways in which in the processes of forming an ego, the child also forms a sense of intrinsic lack. But Baudry offers another possible reason for entering a vulnerable and regressed state; the darkened theater and our immobile body replicates the conditions in which we sleep and, ultimately, in which we dream.[79] This comparison between the movies and dreams is not unique to Baudry or the apparatus theorists. It is a commonsense parallel that is often drawn and one that travels in both directions. The spectator sinks into the seat in the darkened theater much the way he sinks into sleep. The dream is often described as being like a movie, appearing on the dream screen.

While asleep we have the experience of incoming perceptions — we imagine that we are seeing, feeling, sensing — when in actuality there is nothing coming in. The dreamer mistakes the mental representations of the dream for a perception of reality. The representations of the dream *seem* to be perceptions. However, in the cinema we *do* perceive projected light and amplified sound. In spite of this distinction, Baudry posits the effects of the cinema as comparable to the impression of reality created in the dream. In both cases there is nothing *really* there, but we experience a presence in this absence that, Baudry asserts, is "over-cathected."[80]

The dream, according to Freud, equals projection in the analytic sense of covering over an exterior representation with something we refuse to acknowledge or bring to consciousness, and in the cinematographic sense, since once "projected, images come back to the subject as a reality perceived from the outside."[81] The dreamer "sees" and is immersed in the dream that she is projecting; she takes it in, introjects it as if it were coming to her from some external place.

The dreamer, when awake, understands that what he dreams is a projection of his own making, just as the spectator knows that the film originates in the projector behind his head. But like the viewing subject who receives the images that are projected as if they themselves were a "second screen," the dreamer, too, perceives the dream images as if they were deposited in his psyche.[82]

This notion of the cinema screen as a double for the dream screen is central to Baudry's argument.[83] And while this argument wanders into areas of excess — for example the film screen as symbolizing the mother's breast — the notion that while dreaming we regress to a state *in which self and environment are undifferentiated*, a state in which perception and representation merge, has particular pertinence for the representation of the dream in *Avatar*.[84] Jake's journey exemplifies this state in which the discrete boundary between self and environment begins to blur. On Pandora, Jake's self is less differentiated due to the interlinking of the living world surrounding him. Jake satisfies, in his migration to the Na'vi, his "regressed"— if one accepts Baudry's perspective — desire to return to a sense of undifferentiated wholeness.

The dream — as desire, as illusion, as hope, as a metaphoric motif— pervades *Avatar*. The film is bracketed by Jake's dreams, real and imagined. The opening scene of the film is Jake's voice-over narration of the recurring dreams he had while in the VA hospital, recovering from the injury to his legs. This dream, in which he is flying over jungles eerily like those of Pandora, presages his adventures to come. Jake tells us that in these dreams he felt "free," but sooner or later he had to wake up. This opening narration establishes the trope of dreaming/waking that carries us through the film. The cryo-sleep induced to transport Jake and the mercenaries is a dreamless sleep, but a sleep nonetheless. The cryo-tube and the linkup pod are places in which sleep is simulated, and the darkened immobilized state of the cinema spectator is mirrored. But in the linkup pod, Jake lives the dream of life on Pandora. While it is a "real-life" dream, that is, Jake isn't really sleeping or dreaming, we get the sense that when his time in the avatar is interrupted, or he is pulled out of the link, he emerges as if he had been in a deep sleep, groggy, unfocused, not present yet to his surroundings. At one particular point after his first meeting with Neytiri, Grace has trouble "waking" him and claims he was dug in like a tick. At the other end of the linkup, when Jake arrives in his avatar, he also simulates a kind of coming to, an awakening. So the linkup simulates a sleeplike state in which Jake experiences the freedom that was once only possible in his nocturnal dreams.

The opening dream sequence bookends Jakes prophetic "dream" of being a warrior who would bring peace to the Na'vi, a dream that was thwarted toward the end of the film, a dream from which he himself admits he has to awaken. There are many other points in the film where the dream motif is visible. As Jake begins to lose his sense of himself, he states that everything seems all turned around. His life on Pandora appears more real to him, his experience in the pod and on the base more like a dream. And in his last-stand battle with Quaritch, the colonel accuses Jake of living a dream by insisting that it was finally time for him to wake up.

The dream can also been seen as metaphoric, as a way of denoting Jake's misaligned loyalties to Quaritch and the way of life he has known as a marine. As he wakes up, he sees the value in life as the Omaticaya live it, and he becomes aware of the lack in his old way of living. In the scene following the one where Quaritch becomes convinced that diplomacy is not an option, Jake explains it all to Grace, telling her, "This is the way it is done." If someone has something you want, you make him or her your enemy and then you feel justified in taking it. At this point, Jake is waking up from a long sleep in which he was responsible for implementing that ideology. In the end, he suc-ceeds in bringing his dream of peace on Pandora to life.

In responding to the question of what makes it possible for the dreamer to believe his dream is real, Freud posited that sleep "is a reviviscence of one's stay in the body of the mother." The conditions of the position in which we rest, the warmth of the bed, the lack of the daily "excitement" remind us, according to Freud, of our time in the womb, our time within the mother. Jake's transposition into the body of his avatar, like the dream state, brings him home to the body of the mother as personified by Eywa and life on Pan-dora.

Extra-textually, James Cameron shared the story of the origin of the Na'vi with James Lipton in an interview on the Bravo TV show *Inside the Actors Studio*.[85] In 1975, Cameron's artist mother had a dream one night of a tall, blue woman warrior. When she described her dream to Cameron, he was moved to create a painting about this warrior woman, which he describes as attenuated and somewhat like a Giacometti sculpture. And he surrounded her with the purple skies of an alien world.

When Cameron first wrote the screenplay for *Avatar*, he felt he needed the aliens in the story to resemble humans, to have faces that revealed the depth of what they were feeling so that the audience would make an emotional connection. He wanted to tell, among other things, a love story, and he wanted the spectator to be able to relate to the humanoid creatures who would fall in love. This impulse to preserve what inheres in the human experience kept Cameron from moving forward on this project until he could accomplish this goal. When the time was right and when the technology was finally ripe, he retrieved that image he painted of the tall blue woman warrior to use as a model for the alien race that would people his love story. In *Avatar*, Cameron summoned the memory of his mother's dream and, in the end, created a fantastical, dreamlike world that honors the mother.

Chapter Six

Receptions and Representations

The Reception

It was from a weekly visit to the cinema that you learned
(or tried to learn) how to walk, to smoke, to kiss, to fight, to grieve.[1]
— Susan Sontag

In her 1996 essay, "The Decay of Cinema," Sontag bemoans the loss of the cinematic experience, of sitting in the dark among anonymous strangers, "submerging yourself in lives that were not yours."[2] Sontag insists that from the advent of television on, rituals that once surrounded that weekly visit to the movies have vanished. But if we once learned from our regular excursions to the enveloping darkness of the theater, the utter ubiquity of images in our current daily lives theoretically should be teaching us plenty. If inscribed in the flashing frames were lessons about love and power, about sex and being sexy, about good and evil, what might we be learning when every day we are assaulted by endless images on our computer screens, our smart phones, in the backseat of a taxi, on an airplane, in our dens, kitchens and bedrooms, at the bus stop, hanging high above the field at Fenway Park?

Movies, television, computer, and advertising images mediate our experience. No matter how evolved or conscious we may be, these images with which we are bombarded funnel our perceptions, shape our identities, and serve as the skewed other through which we come to see ourselves. In her *Killing Me Softly* series, Jean Kilbourne suggests that all these images, but particularly those in advertising, serve to instill in us a sense of normalcy by repeatedly showing us images of what is neither normal nor natural.[3] Kilbourne focuses her insights on images of woman and the ways in which it is impossible for a real live woman to compete with an airbrushed version of "woman," no matter how young, thin, or beautiful she may be. But it is not just representations of women that are visually encoded. In the images that surround us we find representations of race, masculinities, sexual orientation and gender identity, and of degrees of able-ness. Just as Sontag remembers how she learned to smoke or to grieve, we learn from this plethora of images who we are, how we do or do not fit, how we do or do not have agency in the world in which we live.

As Stuart Hall has noted, "Representation *is* an essential part of the process by which meaning is produced and exchanged between members of a culture."[4]

Meaning Floats

Throughout this volume, structuralist and post-structuralist lenses have served to make visible the binaries that are necessary to meaning-making processes. Chapter one looks at the relationship of the seer and seen, revealing the Aletheic approach to apprehension suggested by the Na'vi in *Avatar*. Chapter two uncovers the fluxing of nature and technology and the ways in which they each emerge out of one another. In investigating the nature of representations in general and specifically in *Avatar*, it may be useful to employ the oppositional pairs of encoding/decoding and sending/receiving. These pairs veer off from the traditional binary in the sense that there seems to be no hierarchical imperative. Sending is not necessarily privileged beyond receiving. Decoding is a necessary concomitant of encoding.

The meaning of what has been sent or encoded resides in the receiver or the decoder — in the case of the cinema, in the spectator. And the process of making this meaning, of decoding the signal, relies on retrieval from an archive of shared meanings, in other words, from a culture of which one is a member. It is one of the great frustrations of all artists, perhaps even of all humans, that there is no assurance that what we mean to communicate will be received in precisely the way we intended. As Stuart Hall suggests, *meaning floats.*[5] It drifts and morphs among decoders, but also from moment to moment, from era to era in relationship to historical contexts. There is no accounting for, no way of controlling the experience, belief system, knowledge, or the circumstances of the person who will be making the meaning. The artist can offer up his or her vision, but then the thing takes on a life of its own.

Mikhail Bakhtin, Russian linguist and critic, argued that meaning is established through dialogue. "Everything we say and mean is modified by the interaction and interplay with another person."[6] No one group can control or fix or completely determine *the* meaning. Hall draws on the example of the fact that the British, (or any nation, for that matter) no matter how they would prefer to be perceived, can't control how anybody else in the world represents or thinks of "the British."[7] The meaning of British-ness is always being negotiated between those who are representing British-ness and those who are attempting to make meaning out of those representations. And the meaning makers bring to that task their own vast experiential storehouse of stereotypes and cultural codes.

Sharing codes is essential to sharing meaning making, and one can never be completely assured that an overlap of understandings will be the case. An episode from the first season of the TV series *Bones* illustrates the difficulties that arise when encountering an absence of shared codes.

Temperance "Bones" Brennan is the hyper-rational protagonist of the TV series. She is a forensic anthropologist, best-selling author of murder mysteries, self-proclaimed genius, and talented martial artist who has teamed up with an emotional spiritual FBI agent to solve murders based on the forensic evidence that resides in the skeletal remains of the deceased. Temperance is socially awkward and is portrayed as being woefully ignorant of almost all of the tropes of popular culture. The show's allure relies on unique twists and turns that turn sex-role stereotyping on its head.

But in this particular episode, Brennan's very normal Asian-American co-worker and friend, Angela, has convinced Brennan to take the night off and go out dancing at a venue where a famous hip-hop artist is the DJ.

As Angela and Brennan make their way out onto the dance floor, Brennan tries to explain to Angela why she is so taken with hip-hop music. "It is so tribal!"[8] Angela quickly and quietly tries to discourage Brennan from analyzing her experience, tries to dissuade her from using the heavily encoded word "tribal" in that milieu. But Brennan is on a roll. She excitedly explains to Angela, having to yell to be heard over the loud rap music, that African Americans aren't the only ones with a tribal heritage. A black woman dancing nearby overhears Brennan and responds angrily, asking if Brennan was insinuating that they were "natives of some tribe."[9] Brennan goes on to explain that anthropologically speaking, we are *all* members of tribes. Another angry bystander warns Brennan to shut up. But she persists, trying to make her point. She tells them that she sees hip-hop as mirroring the direct visceral connection found in tribal communication,[10] confident that if she can just clarify, all will be understood.

A third angry bystander approaches. Brennan is now surrounded, but not deterred.

"After the Cartesian split in the 17th century we separated our minds from our bodies, the numinous from the animalistic."[11]

In response to this mini-treatise, one of the African American women in the crowd challenges Brennan, asking if Brennan meant to be calling her an animal. As tempers start to flare, yet another black woman in the club tries to intervene. She explains, "She's using Descartes' philosophy to say that she's down with the music."[12] Before Angela can safely extract her friend from the fracas, the crowd erupts in a slugfest that results, predictably, in the unearthing of a body mummified in the disco's wall — the real focus of the episode.

This snippet of dance floor chatter reveals the tip of the encoded iceberg that is the discourse on race in America today, as well as exemplifying miscommunicated representations due to a lack of shared meanings. In Brennan's specifically scholarly and personally relatively sheltered world, "tribal" is understood as an anthropological term, not as a racial slur. But to the bulk of the patrons on the dance floor of the hip-hop club, the unselfconscious, naïvely assertive delivery of the white lady's "tribal," "visceral" and "animalistic" was seen as blatantly racist. The viewing audience is constructed in this instance to cringe along with Angela — hip, worldly, bisexual — who just wants Brennan to stop talking. And even though, along with Angela, we know that there is not an intentionally racist bone in Brennan's body, we, too, want her to shut up before she gets herself in trouble.

In the dialog between Brennan and the dancers who overhear her conversation, there is an absence of shared code. Brennan doesn't understand that the words she is using are encoded to reinforce racial stereotypes, and the dancers in the club for the most part don't get Brennan's references to the Cartesian split — which in and of itself could be construed as bolstering a particular racial stereotype — nor the fact that she is bemoaning this disconnect between mind and body and rejoicing in what she perceives as its reconciliation on the dance floor. Our interlocutor, the black woman who has access to the encodings of both "cultures," tries to translate as a way of diffusing the mounting tension. She understands that Brennan is trying to give voice to the pleasure she is experiencing, and she understands the racial stereotypes Brennan is sketching with her choice of language. Unwittingly, Brennan is evoking a deep-seated power dynamic that is layered upon the "civilized/primitive" dichotomy, typified by an Enlightenment that extolled the rational, the logical and the scientific above all else, at the expense of embodied experience.

"Savage" versus "civilized" has been a powerful opposition at the heart of a racialized discourse that has oft been conflated with that of black/white. On the surface, the simple binary black/white could refer to the reflection or absorption of light. But due to the archives of representations to which we have been endlessly exposed, multiple "supposed" meanings also dwell in each pole. Certainly within a pre–civil rights era America, white was aligned with refinement, a civilization based on reason and law, and a restrained expression of the emotional and the sexual, while black was associated with the primitive, with the instinctual, open expression of feeling over intellect, with a privileging of custom and ritual. White was equated with the idea of culture subduing nature, black with the notion of culture being equal to nature.[13] Global citizens of a post–civil rights 21st century, we have ostensibly transcended these stereotypical associations, but their imprints linger on.

In *Avatar*, when Jake suggests that if something you want belongs to others you make the other your enemy in order to justify taking it, he was actually understating the case. You don't *just* make them your esteemed enemy. You demonize or demean or in some way undervalue them. If they are "fly-bitten savages," then you need not treat them with the respect and fairness an equal would deserve. You can ignore the injunction to "do unto others" because this other is not equal to you.

While Temperance Brennan is trying to give voice to the great loss that the Western civilized world endured due to its alienation from its physicality and its over-restraint of emotional expression — particularly ironic given that these are precisely the issues with which the character of Brennan struggles — this physicality and intense emotionality have been stereotypically assigned to people of color and in many cases are the very qualities feared by their white counterparts.

In his book *Heavenly Bodies*, Richard Dyer quotes black actor and musical performer Paul Robeson as saying,

> The white man has made a fetish of intellect and worships the God of thought; the Negro feels rather than thinks, experiences emotions directly rather than interprets them by roundabout and devious abstractions, and apprehends the outside world by means of intuitive perceptions.[14]

Robeson's quote comes pretty close to mirroring what Dr. Brennan was trying to communicate. Stuart Hall maintains that this stance gave Robeson's performance a kind of "vibrant emotional intensity," but at the same time reinforced the racial stereotypes of the binaries black/white, emotion/intellect, nature/culture.[15]

The scene from *Bones* serves multiple purposes. In the context of the TV series, it adds dimension to the characterization of Dr. Temperance Brennan. It also demonstrates meaning-making practices and the necessity of shared codes. Encoded in the scene are signs associated with Angela — free spirited, artist, bisexual — and those connected to Brennan mentioned above, which are only accessible to faithful viewers of the series. In addition, figures connected with hip-hop music and attributed to the population likely to frequent a hip-hop club are being signified to any viewer familiar with those tropes. But the scene also speaks to the fluxual quality of meaning and Bakhtin's notion that meaning is found/made through a process of negotiation, through interaction and interplay.[16] In the nightclub scene, we have not only the interplay between the characters on the dance floor but the interplay between the encoding of racial discourse within the TV series and the ways in which this discourse lives and has lived in the world outside of its media representations.

Just as Sontag suggested that she learned to smoke and to kiss from watching movies, the flip side is also true: the movies attempt to represent a vision of kissing and smoking. This active dialog between media representations, which have the power to effect change through their representations, and social change that has the power to affect representations in the media, is ongoing and reciprocal, dialogic.

This interplay is visible in the various ways in which identities are encoded in cinema, TV and other media. Reaching all the way back to the pivotal 1927 film *The Jazz Singer*, which will figure prominently in the discussion of representations of the "other" in *Avatar* that follows, we note the immigrant experience was drawn in stark detail. In his 1981 article in the *Village Voice*, J. Hoberman claims that *The Jazz Singer* was "the bluntest and most resonant movie Hollywood ever produced on the subject of American Jews."[17]

The film's privileged place in cinematic history as the first feature-length "talkie" notwithstanding, it surfaces not only the Jewish immigrant experience, the clash between Old World values and new, between father and son, but most importantly the overlay of representations of the white Jew and the black-faced minstrel. This portrayal of blackface and its relevance to *Avatar* will be explored later on in this chapter. Speaking more directly, however, to the impact of the interaction between social discourse and its dialog with filmic representations of identity, it is important to note the larger conversation that followed on the heels of *The Jazz Singer*. A climate that may have been conducive to the continued representations of the Jewish experience in film abruptly dissipated. In its place was the flourishing of the anti–Semitic, anti–Catholic Ku Klux Klan of the 1920s, the closing down of immigration from Southern and Eastern Europe, and the executions of Nicola Sacco and Bartolomeo Venzetti.[18] As Michael Rogin recounts in his book *Blackface, White Noise: Jewish Immigrants in the Hollywood Melting Pot*, the 1930s led to broad assimilation, intermarriage among the bulk of the Jewish Hollywood producers and in their effort to wish away an insidious anti–Semitism, they instead disappeared the Jew from the silver screen altogether for quite some time.[19] At the same time, "talking" films moved the cinematic industry toward the more authentic. According to Rogin, the white actor in burnt cork was at cross-purposes to a convincing counterfeit of reality because of its transparency: it called "attention to the figure behind the mask."[20] Far better, Rogin asserts, to "bequeath spoken blackface to actual black people."[21] In this way, screen portrayals reflected and effected representations of race and ethnicity.

A more recent case in point is Lisa Cholodenko's 2010 film *The Kids Are All Right,* which portrays the life of an alternative family comprised of two lesbian mothers and their two children, conceived via insemination by an anonymous donor.

The award-winning film was the first of its kind. It did not in any way pathologize the lesbian mothers, their choices, or their right to have and raise their children. And while gay characters — think Ellen and Will and Jack — have been on their way to becoming somewhat "normalized," the issues surrounding same-sex couples, marriages and child rearing have been a lot slower to move to the mainstream. Lesbian couples have been raising their children in any number of familial configurations for decades. The 1989 children's book *Heather Has Two Mommies*, by Lesléa Newman, was written in part for the children that comprised the lesbian baby boomlet of the early 1980s. Yet it took over 20 years from the time of that book's publication until there was a prime-time, mainstream cinematic release about lesbian mothers and their families in American theaters. The raging debate over same-sex marriage that grips the United States today has gone a long way toward making these relationships, if sometimes still despised and feared, at least visible, opening the space in which this film could be made and marketed. At the same time, the film shifts viewers toward normalizing by representing *as* normal those very alternative family structures. There is an active dialogic pendulum swinging back and forth between social change and cinematic representation.

And whether we are talking about the conversation among the characters on the dance floor in *Bones* or the larger discussion between media representations and social change, we can assert that meaning arises through the "'difference' between participants in any dialog."[22] Within the representations of identities lies the power to mark or assign meanings,[23] even it they are ultimately indeterminate.

Audience Reception of Avatar

Conversation, interplay, or discursive spaces then produce, through different practices of representation, a knowledge of the "other."[24] This discernment, however, is always colored by and situated in the beholder. Nowhere is this clearer than in the vast and rambling interpretations of the representations of identities in *Avatar*. The utter breadth of responses to the film is staggering, and the extent to which bloggers and critics alike speak with conviction that their own interpretation is correct gives one pause. But as was made clear in the earlier discussion of Heidegger and his views on technology, "correct" is not all that it is cracked up to be.[25] Embracing the task of critical discourse as outlined by Teresa de Lauretis, it is necessary to oppose final statements — those that are totalizing or closed, or borrowing Heidegger's terminology, *circumscribed*.[26]

In equal measure, viewers have found *Avatar* to employ racial stereotypes and to defy fixed ideas about race and identity,[27] to offer strong female characterizations and at the same time to reinscribe the male power dynamic, to place at the center of a fantasy a hero who is disabled and to still imply he is lacking as a human being. *Avatar* has carved out a discursive space with wide and fuzzy margins. There is a flickering that peppers perceptions across the entire spectrum of representations of race, gender and ability. The critical reception of *Avatar* holds both awe and disappointment in almost equal measure, and often simultaneously held in a single viewer. There appears an almost palpable tension between the strangeness of 3-D digital performance capture and the familiarity of the old-fashioned story, between the euphoria induced by the lush, immersive visual experience and the disappointment engendered in some who expected something equally radical in the narrative's unfolding.

It has been suggested throughout this volume that *Avatar* is a film about difference — certainly it is a love story between two different species, but it is also about the difference between nature and technology, the seer and what is seen, the difference of the alien "other." More importantly it articulates the ways in which perceptions of difference are bracketed by ensconced binaries. *Avatar* gently suggests that this approach may not be serving us all that well. By fluxing traditionally entrenched polarities the film opens up the possibility of seeing difference differently.

In reviews and blog posts, the sheer volume of comments points to nothing less than a hunger to be in conversation and to, as a community of viewers, make collaborative meaning. Manohla Dargis sees Cameron as a filmmaker whose ambitions include embracing cinema as a social experience.[28] In its multi-layered presentation of the perception of and relationship to the other, the film has provided more than enough to discuss and has extended that social experience beyond the edges of the film itself. Across the blogosphere, readers and writers and viewers seek the kind of connection represented in the living network of Pandora and, within the discourse surrounding *Avatar*, have found it there. If Sontag rued the loss of the "social" of which her weekly visits to the movies consisted, this experience is being reconstituted — in blog posts, tweets and comments — across the Internet.

In attempting to determine if there are particular meanings that *Avatar* privileges, this chapter explores not only the signification of the Na'vi, but incorporates meanings created by bloggers, reviewers, theorists, and those who have commented on and participated in the larger conversation of *Avatar* which first raged following the release of the film in December 2009. As Courtland Milloy of the *Washington Post* noted, to the extent that there exists a national discussion on race, Hollywood serves as the moderator, and "the Internet is the forum."[29] Milloy advocated seeing the film, "not only for the sensational special effects but also to participate in an important discussion about race." It is this discussion about race that many have perceived as simply racist. Afro-Canadian sci-fi writer Nalo Hopkinson observed, "In the U.S., to talk about race is to be seen as racist. You become the problem because you bring up the problem. So you find people who are hesitant to talk about it."[30] Clearly Cameron lacks the hesitancy of which Hopkinson speaks and has provoked that conversation about race.

This chapter pulls apart some of the more salient threads crisscrossing through cyberspace, an appropriate method for investigating a film that envisions a future networked existence. Identity politics has always been deeply encoded in cinema, and unpacking representations of race, gender, and ability in *Avatar* leads to the overarching question of how otherness is constructed. Finally, this chapter retrieves from the archive of filmic representations *The Jazz Singer*, which like *Avatar* incorporated groundbreaking technological innovation in the service of poignantly focusing on the construction of the "other."

A Love Story

In the process of working with the artists who sketched and sculpted and programmed the Na'vi into existence, Cameron urged them to clarify the metaphoric meaning underlying the creatures' creation. So for example, the banshee might ultimately be understood as bird of prey, and it signals all that we understand about the raptor's existence.[31] The plainest, and therefore most malleable, metaphor for the Na'vi is that of the "other."

In creating the Na'vi, Cameron was certain of only one thing: the color blue. In the final chapter of this book, Cameron's directorial oeuvre is surveyed. His repeated use of the same powerful cobalt blue is threaded throughout the films he has directed. He claims that his choice for this skin color was based on its total alien-ness. But the soothing effect it has, the associations with cool water and clear skies, with truth and loyalty can't be overlooked. By the same token, the blue skin brings to mind the Hindu god Vishnu, who symbolizes the infinite, or the ancient tribe of pirating Picts living in Scotland, who tattooed themselves with woad, turning their skin blue.

Early sketches of the Na'vi included more reptilian or amphibian forms, aquatic creatures with gills, antennae and lozenge-shaped heads that sat atop elongated necks.[32] In the end, though, it was more important for Cameron to be assured that his audience would be able to relate to these creatures, to find them attractive enough so that the love story aspects of *Avatar* would prevail, than it was to just create cool alien creatures. In spite of this fact, many a critique of the film goes out of its way to underscore the utter cool-ness — or hotness — of the Na'vi. Wesley Morris of the *Boston Globe* sees in the Na'vi "a little boy's wish to shed his skin and not only live with blue people but become one of them. Their bodies look so cool."[33] When blogger Robert E. Kelley of the *Asian Security Blog* sees the Na'vi, he sees "hot native" babes,[34] and even David Brooks characterizes the Na'vi as having "hot bodies."[35]

While some found the Na'vi hot or cool, others were disappointed with how unalien they appeared. Blogger "Jesse," who was pleasantly surprised generally by the film, posted in a comment on Rembrandt Smith's *Filmsmith* blog, "I hate it when aliens are so human."[36] Cameron has certainly paid his dues with alien aliens. The alien creatures in *Aliens* and *The Abyss* didn't resem-ble humans in the least. But it is true that given the opportunity to create an entire universe from scratch it might have been exciting to see something akin to the alien Drac in the film *Enemy Mine.*

In this film, Dennis Quaid plays a pilot who is shot down and finds him-self stranded on a harsh planet with his alien enemy whom he dubs "Gerry." The Drac, played wonderfully by Louis Gossett, Jr., was reptilian — an option that Cameron rejected — spoke a language that included all kinds of nonhu-man trills and guttural sounds, but more interestingly was unisexed. In the Drac world, all Dracs reproduce asexually.

From the original *Star Trek*'s Tribbles — small furry asexual critters — to Spielberg's *E.T.*, the possibilities of envisioning alien life on a faraway moon are limitless. Cameron might have taken a cue from science-fiction writer Nalo Hopkinson and her inventive *douen*, who inhabit a penal colony in an imagined future world in her novel *Midnight Robber.*[37] Hopkinson spawned an alien race in which the male of the species was small and reptilian with suctioned fingertips and a long snout on either side of which protruded round lizardlike eyes. Their spouses, referred to as *hinte*, have legs like the male douens, with knees that bend toward the back, but otherwise resemble large packbirds. In puberty, the female douens' snouts turn to beaks and their arms become wings. The douen men fly under cover of night upon the backs of their wives.

The Na'vi, on the other hand, not only reproduce heterosexually, but on the face of things, they are *exclusively* heterosexual, a choice that does seem a particularly conservative one to make. While Cameron has typically peopled his films with strong, interesting, powerful female characters, and some might even claim he has a feminist bent, he chose not to open the homosexual can of worms. It seems just as likely that the Na'vi might travel in large female clans or herds, mating only when they want to bear children, since they are strong warriors and hunters and could clearly fend for themselves. Or why not portray the Na'vi as polymorphously perverse, without any limitations on with whom they chose to connect, physically, emotionally, psychically, as well as through their fiber-optic braids? If they share a close psychic bond with the trees and animals, why not with each other? It seems as likely, more likely perhaps, than the slim chance that they might have developed as heterosexuals living in the kind of nuclear families that have evolved in our capitalist world.

Thinking about a race of beings who are not limited in their social structures or sexuality doesn't require much of a stretch. Even Oprah is doing it. The July 2011 issue of her magazine *O* featured an article by Amy Bloom that focused on what comprises an alternative family. The essay opens with a scan of the natural world and the extent to which variety is favored by nature.[38] In his talk at the Technology, Education, Design (TED) conference, Cameron himself emphasized that "nature's imagination is boundless compared to our own meager imagination."[39]

Bloom regales with tales of the desert grassland whiptail, a lizard that is an all-female species. The reptiles reproduce by parthenogenesis, but apparently this process is enhanced by female-to-female courtship rituals.[40] There is the anglerfish in which the female is so much bigger than the male that he is almost invisible — a little blob of a thing attached by his teeth to the larger, spiny exterior of the female. And there are the saddleback tamarins, monkeys who form families with an extra male whose job it is to please the mother sexually and tend to the young.[41] (And of course we all know about the well-documented bonobos, the African chimpanzee whose social structure is matriarchal.) Bloom goes on to add to these exemplars of the animal kingdom many human examples of family structures that make obsolete the *Ozzie and Harriet/Father Knows Best* models of the past.

Additionally, many native cultures are also matrilocal and matrilineal. Cameron, with his concern for authenticity in everything from getting the detail right in the smallest leaf to assuring that the ways in which the vehicles are assembled makes good engineering sense, with his fascination with both flora and fauna, might have been inspired by the more diverse vision of alien culture at which nature points. This degree of invention would have lifted up the narrative to the same level as that of his technical innovation.

And none of these more "alien" relationship structures would have gotten in the way of the movie becoming the love story Cameron wanted to tell. *Enemy Mine* certainly was a love story, all the more powerful because the viewer has to transcend, in concert with the human character Davidge, the strangeness of "Gerry." Davidge comes to love him quite profoundly. When Gerry dies in childbirth, Davidge swears to raise the Drac's child and pass on Gerry's lineage, an important spiritual rite in the Drac culture. When the child is captured and enslaved by human miners, Davidge risks his life to save and return the child to its home. It is a great love story.

Who Are the Na'vi, Really?

The Na'vi indeed are blue with decorative striations across their skin and iridescent markings that glow at night. They are tall and thin; everything about them is elongated: their torsos, their necks, their limbs, fingers and toes. This attenuation brings to mind a Giacometti sculpture, a super leanness that is strong and spare, with an absence of excess. The Na'vi are ultra-fit. There is no fat or flab, or extra body weight. It could be argued that this "natural" strength and agility signals stereotypical tropes of perceptions of African Americans' "natural" ability in sports and on the dance floor.

Cameron's choice to meld traits from animals — the catlike ears and tail, the "lemur-like" eyes — with the humanoid bipedal form may be read as evoking a negative racial stereotype. While their facial structure is uniquely "alien," each feature points to some critical quality of the Na'vi. The extra voluminous and brilliant eyes reiterate the underlying message of the transformative power of the visual. If the eyes are the windows to the soul, the Na'vi have picture windows letting us reach right in. The twitch of a Na'vi ear or the switch of a tail can point to fear or wariness, excitement or anger. The Na'vi's noses are broad — like a large feline's — between their widely spaced eyes, tapering as they approach the lips. They hiss and bear their canines when angered or threatened. There is, in all this animality, the risk of signaling another prominent racial stereotype as exemplified in the *Bones* episode above. Brennan alluded to a fixed and rigid boundary between what is a primal, visceral expression and what is the contained demeanor that the more "civilized" among us deem appropriate. The Na'vi, in their raw expression of rage, grief, passion, and exuberance cross that border — of which Dr. Brennan might approve — but which has the capacity to make some squirm in their seats.

In the discursive space surrounding the film, however, most claims of racism or racial stereotypes emerge not from the physicality of the Na'vi but instead from the white messiah figure as outlined by David Brooks and discussed at length in Chapter Four. While they have been called "blue cat people" — *Washington Post* film critic Courtland Milloy characterized the movie as more than a "3-D fantasy flick about nice cat people vs. mechanized mad men"[42] — there is little in the physical manifestation of the Na'vi that supports claims of negative racial representations. When Milloy addresses how one gets from a film about blue cat people to a film about oppressed people of color, he points to their accessories.[43]

The trappings of the Na'vi strongly suggest an indigenous/native/primitive culture. Many have noted the use of arrows and bows, a direct link to the Native American peoples — although the poison-tipped arrows smack of the poison blow darts of indigenous people of South American jungles — and their scantily clad bodies point to a plethora of primitive cultures in the Americas, in Africa, and in the Pacific Islands. Their dreadlocks signal an African or Afro-Caribbean descent, while the decorative feathers and loincloths again mimic Native American tribes. Their reverence for life, their connection to the spirit world, their rituals and rites of passage surface an amalgamation of indigenous cultures.

The Blank Canvas

What is most wonderful about the translation of Cameron's early vision of giant blue aliens into their fully realized computer-generated existence is their indeterminacy. They are neither completely human nor ultimately alien, completely humanoid nor totally animal. They are an encoded canvas on which most spectators are more than happy to paint their projections.

One blogger is stunned by the fact that he is the only one to notice that "na" stands for Nam and "vi" equally obviously points to Viet, clearly indicating that the story is an allegory, like *Apocalypse Now*, of the Vietnam War.[44] Some, like critic Milloy, can't help overlaying the heritage of the actor playing the Na'vi with a determination of race: he recognizes African American, Native American and West Indian voices and aligns those ethnicities with the corresponding characters.[45]

If the spread of the commentary online may be likened to a neural net, then we can identify some nodal hubs out of which have spoked hundreds of comments. These include David Brooks' white messiah piece, a review by philosopher Slajov Žižek, and the critique by Annalee Newitz, editor in chief of the *IO9 Blog* that covers science, science fiction and the future.

In true viral style, Newitz's post, entitled "When Will White People Stop Making Movies Like 'Avatar'?," was picked up on scores of websites and commented on by hundreds of readers. Newitz, like Brooks, took issue with the premise that a white man was the necessary savior of the indigenous. As detailed in Chapter Four, this is a relatively shallow interpretation of the narrative of *Avatar*. Newitz's claim that *Avatar* is "a fantasy about race told from the point of view of white people"[46] is essentially self-evident. Cameron is a white guy, and Jake, the protagonist and in some sense the viewer's avatar — a way into the film — is also white. That *Avatar* is a fantasy is also indisputable. Newitz's observation that "*Avatar* imaginatively revisits the crime scene of white America's foundational act of genocide, in which entire native tribes and civilizations were wiped out,"[47] is one that most viewers will have little trouble accepting. But Cameron's narrative paints a picture of predatory imperialist posturing on the part of the RDA that resonates with any number of colonizing ventures, not just the genocide of Native American peoples.

Newitz's unique contribution to the discourse surrounding the film is her emphasis on the notion that white guilt is the source from which the invention of *Avatar* sprang. Newitz suggests that it is out of an overwhelming sense of guilt that the hero "switches sides."[48] While it may be true that "white guilt" plays a part in the conception of a story like *Avatar* or *Dances with Wolves* or *Last Samurai*, Newitz overlooks the diegetic logic that places these white heroes among indigenous peoples. Nathan Algren was conscripted to teach Japanese soldiers to shoot guns, was critically injured and rescued by the Samurai. John Dunbar slowly develops a friendship with Native American Kicking Bird and becomes immersed in his culture. And finally Jake does not choose to visit the Na'vi due to his pangs of guilt. Not totally discounting the possibility that the "white guilt" of these protagonists may predispose them to be open to seeing things from an other's point of view, a more accurate portrait of what occurs in these narratives is alluded to when Newitz recognizes that when these white heroes live among the indigenous people their perspective is altered. How we see and the meaning we make about what we see shifts based on from *where* we are looking. Our perspectives are imbricated in our identities; when our sense of who we are changes, our circumscribed view is loosed and we can see with a softer circumspect gaze.

In closing, Newitz yearns for a movie about people of color by people of color, without the filter or mediation of the white guy.[49] Two thoughtful responses to her disappointment floated to the top of the blogo-soup. The first resides in *Boston Globe* film critic Wesley Morris' rejection of the narrowness of an interpretation like Newitz's. In a *Globe* review of *Avatar*, as well as during an NPR radio dialog with Courtland Milloy, Morris makes the case for the elasticity of the signification of the Na'vi and claims that *Avatar* "defies fixed ideas about race and identity."[50] Taking a broader, metaphorical view, Morris suggests that the Na'vi could be "American Indians, Polish Jews, or bald eagles."[51] Morris allows that each viewer will have his/her own interpretation and that this meaning making is a complicated process. In an interview with Michel Martin on NPR's *Tell Me More*, Milloy and Morris agree that the Na'vi can be understood as the "other."[52] But in Morris' view, the "other" is an elastic metaphor and shouldn't be looked at simply through "the prism of race." The Na'vi could stand for "race, ethnicity, civilization, political situations, non-human species, environmental care."[53]

In a blog post entitled "*Avatar*: A Story of Transformation and Struggle," Eric Ribellarsi offered the thought that perhaps it was better to make stories, even if they arose out of a place of privileged guilt, than to not feel any complicity at all. He agrees with Newitz that there aren't enough movies that are written from the perspective of the oppressed but asks why that would mean that there is no value at all to a film like *Avatar*. "Is there really no value to the stories of John Brown? Of Jews in Israel who side with and defend the Palestinians? Of Germans who refused to go along in Nazi Germany?"[54] Ribellarsi makes several important points here. First, as exemplified by the *Bones* scene described, we live in an imperfect society. Today, in most places on our planet, there are vast and dismaying inequalities of power, agency, freedom, and consequently of access to the kind of resources Cameron had at his disposal to make this movie. If we accept that media reflects and effects representations of our reality, then it is logical to see these unfortunate inequalities in our entertainment. But as Ribellarsi suggests, isn't it better that someone make films out of white guilt, than to be totally oblivious to the oppression privileged white people have engendered?

Like Wesley Morris, Ribellarsi also pushes past the limited view that *Avatar* is only about the decimation of America's native tribes. It could be about a warrior for race equality like John Brown or it could be about the French resistance to the Holocaust. It is interesting that Ribellarsi includes in his list the Israeli/Palestinian conflict. Following *Avatar*'s release, a small group of Middle Eastern activists embraced the Na'vi as a symbol of liberation. Adopting blue garb, these Palestinians and Israelis together demonstrated against the Israeli West Bank barrier. One of the marchers, Mohammed Khatib, is quoted as saying, "When people around the world who have watched the film see our demonstration and the conditions that provoked it, they will realize that the situations are identical."[55] The Na'vi, then, have become visual code for some kind of recognizable oppression. Several weeks after this anti-barrier demonstration, a group of activists from the Centre for Orangutan Protection striped their faces blue and voiced opposition to the Indonesian government's illegal deforestation endangering the lives of orangutans.[56]

On the opposite end of the spectrum from those who were inspired to take up the blue mantle and act for the benefit of some greater good were those who left the theater after *Avatar* just plain blue. These spectators became depressed because their real lives paled beside the luminous intensity of Pandora. According to the *Huffington Post*, there were over a thousand posts on a fan forum site from those experiencing post–*Avatar* depression.[57]

Avatar is a film that affected people. It made them angry, it disappointed them, it inspired and depressed them. It sparked passionate conversation and debate. There is, of course, no "correct" interpretation of or reaction to *Avatar*. If we grant the film the elasticity Morris attributes to it, and perhaps that Cameron has intended, we find that audience reception is unsurprisingly based on audience predisposition. There is no absolute neutrality; this idea of an objective perch from which to judge, famously formulated by Thomas Nagel is none other than a myth. There is, as philosopher Mitchell Silver has wisely noted, "no view from nowhere."[58]

Apprehending the Other

It is no surprise then that what Rabbi Fred Guttman found in *Avatar* was a "spiritual message that spoke to his Jewish soul."[59] Guttman and others were quick to point out that in Hebrew *Navi* means "prophet." In the "deep type of seeing" in which the Na'vi engage, Guttman recognized what Buber has called the "I-Thou" relationship. In the prominence and sacredness of trees, Guttman finds a connection to a pro-environmental message, to Torah as the "tree of life" and to the Kabbalah. He points to the root connections that Grace explained as "signal transduction," as reflecting the Kabbalistic teaching that we are all connected to the Source.[60] Instead of seeing white guilt as a motivating source for wanting to lead an oppressed people to freedom, Rabbi Guttman saw in the fact of Jake, Grace, Norm, and Trudy's switching sides, Cameron's "nevuah" or prophesy and a timely warning to his audience. "Will we be able to come together to save and heal the planet and humankind?" Rabbi Guttman asks. "Will we be able to learn how to truly see the "other," not as an opponent, but as part of the Oneness of God's creation?"[61]

Avatar unveils many modes of seeing. There are those who see narrowly, who look with blinders on, or not at all. There are those who see with care and patience, and expectancy, in the way of the Na'vi. There are those who are given the opportunity in certain moments to alter the way that they see. In her essay "Giving an Account of Oneself," Judith Butler suggests that we can only recognize an "other" when we become disoriented from ourselves.[62] In other words, when we hold on to our circumscribed notions of our identity and of those around us, it is not possible to really see the "other." We see only our frozen concepts of them. And this rigid notion, this thinking that we know the "other" does violence to their being, clearly illustrated in the ways in which Selfridge, because he *knew* the Na'vi as "fly-bitten" savages, couldn't connect his actions with the harm he was inflicting.

Butler suggests that it is not until we are decentered, in some way unable to grasp on to our own solid identity, that we are able to recognize the "other."[63] We see this decentering occurring in several of the characters in *Avatar* and the resultant transformation in their ability to give and take recognition.[64] Norm, who brings to his avatar driving years of studying the language and customs of the Na'vi and hours of testing his avatar, initially sees Jake as interloper, intruder, and usurper. He understands himself to be skilled and learned. It is not until Jake's unprecedented penetration of the inner circles of the Na'vi that Norm feels displaced. His sense of himself as knowledgeable and deserving is undone, and he reacts with petty irritation to Jake's ignorance of the Na'vi language, customs, and beliefs. Ultimately, however, his take on

Jake's abilities are refigured, and he compassionately comes to alter his appraisal of Jake. As he loses his own sense of entitlement, he begins to be able to see Jake as a friend, as a mentee whom he can help to accomplish his mission, and ultimately as his ally in the fight to save Pandora.

Grace similarly rejects Jake in a knee-jerk fashion because she believes she knows who he is: jarhead flunky, trigger-happy ex-marine, etc. As Grace begins to see Jake as an asset to her project, she gets wind of the fact that Jake is also doing reconnaissance for Quaritch. Her sense of herself as being in charge is challenged by the subterfuge surrounding her. At that point Grace acts to take responsibility for removing Jake from close proximity to the colonel. In this way, her re-visioning of Jake allows her to remove the linkup pods to the camp in the mountains, in defiance of protocol. But it is during their time together in the shack that their relationship is transformed. Grace comes to appreciate Jake and even toward the end to "mother" him, making sure that he eats and sleeps and takes better care of his human container. In turn, Jake tolerates Grace's ministrations. This is a major shift away from his militantly self-sufficient self, established early on in the film. In seeing Grace more clearly, he yields to her efforts to assist him.

Grace's ultimate dislocation is more profound that Norm's, in that she is mortally wounded and finds herself at the Tree of Souls confronting her own death. If ever there were a situation in which we are disoriented and decentered, a situation which pushes us to conceive of ourselves and others in the largest, most generous way possible, which raises the question of who or what we are, really, it is our own impending death. Grace finds herself with Eywa, convinced of the reality of the Na'vi deity, as she awaits the transfer of *all that she is* into the body of her avatar. All that she thought she knew, as a scientist, slips from her grasp.

Trudy is singled out early on as the one pilot who is not tethered to a reliance on the instrument panel. She is the "science sortie" pilot, flying all the avatar drivers and their instruments out to the wild, often through the flux vortex that she has learned to navigate. She has an appreciation for the beauty that is Pandora, but she is first and foremost a soldier. When she and the fleet of helicopter pilots are ordered to fire upon Home Tree, Trudy has a moment of dislocation from her identity. She has seen the Na'vi as living sentient beings, and her idea of herself doesn't include being a murderer. At the same time, she is a soldier who has been trained to follow orders. With her finger on the trigger, she can't abide the consequences of her actions if she were to follow the given orders and shoot. This decentering brings her the strength and courage of her convictions and a clarity in which she understands that this is not what she had signed up for. She chooses not to fire and turns her helicopter around, leaving the devastation behind. In her unanchored moment of not knowing who she is as a soldier, she is able to take responsibility for saving what lives she can. In these moments of uncertainty, of a limited self-knowledge, these characters are subject to a critical opening in their identities and are able to take an ethical stand. Or as Butler has pointed out "a certain risking of the self becomes, as Levinas claims, the sign of virtue."[65]

In Jake's attachment to his experience in his avatar and his neglect of his own physical body, his decentering is perhaps the most visible and the most potent. When he claims that he doesn't remember his whole life prior to Pandora, that his existence in the avatar seems more real than his other reality, we know his grasp on his identity is slipping. As he loses his sense of self, he becomes "other" to himself and is sufficiently disoriented that he ironically begins to be able to see more clearly. He is pulled outside of himself and transformed by this process. Or as Butler would have it, "recognition becomes the process by which I become other than what I was and, therefore, also, the process by which I cease to be able to return to what I was."[66] Jake could not return to being a jarhead, could hardly return to being human. His dislocation — physical, mental and spiritual — metamorphosed him into something other than what he was.

Jake's split self enables him to re-cognize those around him — Quaritch, Selfridge, Grace and the Na'vi — and allows him to take the important ethical stand — not because he is guilty, not because he wants to be "the man," but because he has failed to achieve self-identity, and according to Butler this facilitates the emerging of a new sense of ethics.[67] Out of his limited self-knowledge arises a humility, a generosity, and a need to be forgiven for this lack. This, Butler suggests, fosters a willingness in turn to forgive others who also lack complete self-transparency. "As we ask to know the Other, or ask that the Other say, finally, who he or she is, it will be important not to expect an answer that will ever satisfy."[68] Here Butler makes a case that supports Wesley Morris' take on the elasticity of for what/who the Na'vi stand. They stand for letting the "other" be, in all his or her glorious indeterminacy.[69]

Avatar *and Identities*

It is not simply that the encoded identity politics of *Avatar* represents the elastic "other." Embedded in the characters in the film we can unearth figures that adumbrate the performance of gender as well as tellingly hint at what it means to be differently abled. Across the board, Cameron's characters — men and women alike — are tough. No one in the ensemble comes across soft or effeminate. The extreme representation of a sort of pervasive, subterranean machismo is found, of course, in Stephen Lang's performance as Colonel Quaritch. The colonel warns Jake early on that the gravity on Pandora will make him soft, although there is no evidence of that effect on anyone. The soldiers are in tip-top shape, and the Na'vi could never be considered soft in any regard. And everything about Quaritch is hard—his body, his resolve, the AMP suit in which he fights, his heart.

While the performance by Lang is powerful, the character of Quaritch borders on stereotypical, a form of hyper-masculinity that some could find offensive.[70] (It is important to note that the encoding of types is a device that the cinematic relies upon. Unlike the novel where the nuances of a character can develop over pages and chapters, a film or TV series relies on the reductive in order to get its message across quickly and efficiently. It is when this typing crosses the line into stereotyping that we run into trouble.)

Gary Westfahl of *Locus On-Line*, the "Magazine of the Science Fiction and Fantasy Field," found in the colonel an outdated stereotype that might have been acceptable 30 years ago but not, he felt, today.[71] Quaritch's blanket disregard for the lives of the Na'vi, whom he referred to as roaches, goes beyond what Westfahl finds believable. And yet the character of Quaritch is a necessary yang to Jake's yin. Jake experiences a metamorphosis while Quaritch stays rigid and inflexible.

There is a certain singularity about Quaritch, a super soldier, which is almost asexual in nature. There is nothing about him that objectifies or demeans women. They are not even on his radar. He is equally uninterested in anyone who doesn't figure into furthering his mission. He'd just as soon shoot Grace as negotiate with her, and he is virulent in his attack against Trudy in the final battle. If anything, his misogyny makes him oblivious to the women around him, and one wonders if there might be some latent homoeroticism at play. There is certainly an undercurrent of homoeroticism among the mercenaries who greet the new recruits by smacking their lips with relish at the arrival of "fresh meat." And in the scene in which Quaritch is pumping iron and Jake wheels himself into the caged space where Quaritch is working out, we see Quaritch's appraising gaze dart downward. We assume, in the context of their conversation, that he is checking out Jake's withered legs, but he might just as easily be sneaking a peek at Jake's crotch.

Quaritch is incensed when Jake sleeps with Neytiri, as if his choice to be sexual, to actually engage with a "woman," especially an alien woman, is an indication of some mortal weakness. The implication that because Jake gets some "local tail" he has lost his way underscores the colonel's conviction that Jake has, in fact, gone soft. Quaritch infantilizes Jake by calling him "son," doubling the power-over effect of his higher rank with a paternalizing stance. Underneath this veneer of affection, Quaritch holds disdain for Jake's flaccidity. In the scene where Quaritch interrupts a linkup in progress because he has found Jake responsible for disabling the dozer's video feeds, he punches him in the face, accusing him of crossing the line.

This metaphoric line is polysemic. It stands for disobeying the father figure, for disregarding orders, for joining with the Na'vi and destroying the dozer feed, and ultimately going over to the other side. When Quaritch orders one of his officers to wheel the meat — Jake — out of the linkup shack, his utter disgust for Jake's broken embodiment is laid bare.

Quaritch's hardness and intractability serve as narrative foil to Jake's perceived weaknesses — he is a paraplegic; he is recruited to be one of the "limp dick" scientists; he is seduced by the "fake legs" of the avatar, clearly inferior to the real legs offered by Quaritch; and he ultimately loses his way in the woods. This adversarial relationship is clarified in the way the scenes which feature them both are shot and edited, as examined in Chapter One. Quaritch's over-the-top hyper-machismo is necessary so that Jake's performance of masculinity stands out in relief.

From the moment Jake wheels himself off the transport vehicle and onto the tarmac at Hell's Gate, he is the object of derision. The veteran mercenaries call him "meals on wheels," doubling his vulnerability. He is both fresh meat, like all the new recruits, but also prey. One of the soldiers comments that Jake's presence in the wheelchair is just wrong. While never dealt with directly, there is always the looming question of the extent of Jake's paralysis. How pervasive is his injury? Is he able to perform sexually? If not, this would add weight to his already fierce desire for transformation and would go a long way to explain his shift in realities, his disorientation.

In his human, disabled body, Jake is lacking not only a working pair of legs and perhaps a functional penis, but he is read as embodying what Lee Edelman has identified as "codified anxieties about masculinity."[72] Jake's disability makes him something less than a man and perhaps something less than heterosexual.

When Jake returns from his first foray in his avatar, he returns as somewhat of a hero. As the group sits around eating a communal meal, Grace tells the story of how he was last seen with a wild Thanator on his tail. Jake's survival and return with the news that not only had he survived, but the beautiful Neytiri was going to train him, was greeted with hearty approval from his peers, all except for Norm. The tension between the two of them erupts when Jake teases that he has a date with the chief's daughter. While this is said lightly, it speaks to Jake's ability now to feel and act, if not manly then schoolboyishly, now that he has been made temporarily whole by having access to the avatar's completely functioning body.

In his *New Statesman* review of *Avatar*, which he is rumored to have written without seeing the film, claiming that the "idea" of the film was sufficient,[73] Slavoj Žižek gets a lot about the film wrong. But one true note his review sounded was what he called "the Hollywood formula for producing a couple."[74] There is a pressing heteronormativity required by the structure of the classical Hollywood film. And as discussed above, Cameron here opted to ride that wave in rather than fight the tide.

For Žižek, though, there is a twist on the white messiah myth. The white guy doesn't "go native" to be the hero or to assuage his guilt or to lead the indigenous population out of the proverbial desert to freedom. He goes to find "a proper sexual partner."[75] In his rant against what he perceives as a "rather conservative, old-fashioned film,"[76] Žižek loses his way and attributes, quite insensitively, a diminished status to Jake precisely because he is disabled. While Žižek is appalled by the "array of brutal racist motifs"[77] in *Avatar*, he thinks nothing of devaluing a man because his legs don't work. Žižek notes, "A paraplegic outcast from earth is *good enough* to get the hand of a beautiful local princess,"(emphasis added)[78] dissing both Neytiri and Jake in one fell swoop. Since Neytiri is *only* a "native" princess, she will settle for less, for the disabled man. And, clearly, Jake is damaged goods. But by coupling with Neytiri, Jake becomes fully masculine, fully heterosexual, undoing any trace of his lack, as long as he remains in his avatar.

Again, here is evidence of Cameron's propensity to blur boundaries. On the one hand, he elevates the paraplegic ex-marine by making him the hero, the guy who gets the girl and fulfills his dream of becoming a warrior for peace. At the same time, critical disability theorists would be quick to point out that it is precisely because Jake is paralyzed that he is portrayed as "needing improvement."[79] Jake is broken and needs to be fixed. This equation of disability and a lack of wholeness is essentially so troubling because on the surface it appears almost commonsensical, until we consider the multitudes who live with all manner of disabilities and consider themselves to be whole, functioning members of society. It is only the fully able-bodied spectator that sees in this difference an intrinsic lack.

As noted earlier in this volume, Jake's confinement to a wheelchair reduces his white male privilege and makes him a more sympathetic protagonist. As the marine in the wheelchair, as the grunt who isn't a scientist, as the "dream walker" among the Na'vi, Jake gets what it means to be the "other." As an outsider he has the creds that enable him to enter the world of the Na'vi and empathize with their otherness to a certain degree. At the same time, the implication that his life is worth less as a differently abled man makes Quaritch's offer to restore his "real" legs appear all the more believable and enticing. If the spectator didn't also believe Jake was lacking, this ploy wouldn't have resonated.

On another level, Jake's paralysis adds to the power and poignancy when he is able to relocate his consciousness into the body of his avatar. Able-bodied spectators and those who are differently abled alike can imagine the exhilaration of that first run that Jake takes out into the fields of Pandora. Blogger "Harry" who writes the blog *Ain't It Cool* and is a self-identified four-wheeler is quick to remind that in the 21st century, it is not uncommon to be or to know a soldier returning from Iraq or Afghanistan who has been maimed in war.[80] Harry notes Jake's disaffection for the way that he is being treated — as a "cripple," as someone who needs to be helped — simply because he is in a wheelchair. From the moment he wheels himself off the transport ship he is the butt of jokes, he is dismissed by Grace, and everyone tries to "help" him. It is precisely the nature of his assignment as avatar driver that allows him to transcend his physical limitations, which are legible on his body, but which stand in *Avatar* for the larger limitations of our human fragility. So we all can relate to that moment when Jake wiggles the toes of his avatar. But for those similarly restricted, we can only imagine. Harry's blog enlightens us, "People in wheelchairs dream of running. Trust me on that. I know I'm a fat geek in a wheelchair, but we all dream of running.... Hell, I doubt I'd ever want to wake up if I could have a Na'vi body that was as nimble, fit and amazing as this."[81] There is then this multi-layered appreciation of fleeing the constrictions of our humanity on top of the harsh reality of the opportunity for a paralyzed man to regain — even temporarily — his full mobility.

Jake is queered by his outsider status and by questions of the status of his virility. In his avatar he becomes whole and fully heterosexual. All the more reason, when it appears that he will lose everything — when Neytiri rejects him and he is cast out by the Omaticaya — that the story requires an epiphanic moment to restore what was lost.

Robert McRuer, author of "As Good as It Gets: Queer Theory and Critical Disability,"[82] points to the intense desire for the epiphany created by the structure of the classical Hollywood narrative. This moment is often described as one in which a person loses themselves, one in which the past, present and future collide and temporarily offers the protagonist exceptional clarity.[83] The protagonist then is able to move forward with "a sense of subjective wholeness that he or she lacked previously."[84]

Jake has such a moment when Grace is mortally wounded. He is "in the place the eye doesn't see,"[85] in other words banished from the Na'vi, rejected by Neytiri who feels betrayed by him, and AWOL from his previous connection to the marines via his intelligence gathering for Quaritch. He is split between his human self and his avatar self, and he is desperate to get the help needed to save Grace. But as Grace is wise to point out, the Omaticaya have no motivation to assist them. And Jake realizes that she is right. With no plan in mind, Jake wanders among the ashes of Home Tree aware of his utter alienness. This scene is devoid of color, gray and ashen, dead in contrast to previous scenes of Pandora that exuded abundant and vibrant life. When his ikran finds him, Jake has his epiphany and in voice-over observes that there are times when your whole life boils down to a single moment. This is the turning point for Jake. His decision to attempt to ride the great Leonopteryx and his successful bonding with the giant banshee garners him reentry to the Na'vi, forgiveness from Neytiri, and admiration from Tsu'tey. His epiphany, according to McRuer, could only have happened in a "flexible" body, that is, one that is read as heterosexual and able bodied. The only way Jake could have this moment, the epiphany on which the classical Hollywood narrative insists, was if he could leave the confines of the wheelchair. The epiphany is not available to the disabled, for it is that "sense of subjective wholeness" that the hero carries to the end of the narrative[86] that remains just out of their reach.

Chick Flick

The completion of his apprenticeship confers upon Jake the status of man and warrior. This achievement grants him the privilege of choosing a mate. Even though at the moment Neytiri places the choice before him Jake softens the dominance encoded in this privilege by emphasizing that this choice must be reciprocal, it can't be entirely ignored. As Malinda Lo has made plain in the title of her blog post, "Native Women Are Not Trophies,"[87] this retro moment sticks in your craw. And while the moment is veneered with the feminist gesture of Jake insisting that Neytiri choose him as well, in the context of the rest of the film it stands out as a reactionary glitch. It is doubly troubling when looked at juxtaposed to the similar language used in the choosing of an ikran.

Neytiri tells Jake that when he is ready, that is, when he has demonstrated his prowess as a warrior, he may choose an ikran. Neytiri cautions him that he must feel the choice inside — she gestures to her heart — and that the ikran must also choose him. When Jake asks how he will know if the ikran has chosen him, Neytiri explains that it will try to kill him. It is worth noting that Neytiri, too, almost tried to kill Jake. The parallels between bonding with a banshee, which Neytiri explains is a monogamous, lifelong bond, and the bond between Jake and Neytiri are just a tiny bit too close for comfort.

The choosing of a mate that becomes the prerogative of the Na'vi man smacks of anthropologist Claude Lévi-Strauss' project, in which he hoped to uncover universalizing structures in all cultures. His overall observation was that while women are no doubt human beings like men, their social function is generally much closer to that of chattels (or perhaps ikran?), "whose regulated possession and exchange among men ensures and maintains social order."[88]

They are part of an exchange economy, giving status to the men who "own" them, and according to Teresa de Lauretis, women therefore can only be seen as objects. They can't be producers of culture, nor can they be subjects. The subsequent status acquired by men may be understood, as in Gayle Rubin's assessment, as the phallus. Rubin suggests that the phallus is more than simply a way of discriminating between the sexes. It is what assures the males' right to a woman.[89] We can see this exemplified in both the harmless banter between Jake and Norm, when Jake teases that he has a date with the chief's daughter, as well as in Tsu'tey's outrage when he realizes that Neytiri has mated with Jake. By "choosing" Neytiri, Jake has usurped Tsu'tey's power. And nothing in how strong, brave, smart or passionate Neytiri is can transfer the phallus to her.

In most other respects, however, Cameron has made a film peopled with unusually strong, vibrant, fleshed-out women characters and in a fashion has resituated Laura Mulvey's "bearer of the look" in these women. In the section of her seminal essay, "Visual Pleasure and Narrative Cinema," entitled "Woman as Image, Man as Bearer of the Look," Mulvey instructs, "In a world ordered by sexual imbalance, pleasure in looking has been split between active/male and passive/female."[90] According to Mulvey, it is the man who acts in response to whatever the woman — who is displayed there for his pleasure — provokes. She is essential to the narrative film, but only to the extent that the hero is moved — out of love or out of fear for her safety — to act. As Budd Boetticher, director of classical westerns, noted, "In herself the woman has not the slightest importance."[91]

Mulvey suggests that the woman is an "alien presence" in cinema — ironic especially when juxtaposed with *Avatar*—"freezing the flow of action" because her visual presence on screen forces an "erotic contemplation" which fights against the forward narrative thrust.[92] In other words, female characters are likely to be made into a spectacle, but rarely *act* in a way that forwards the story.

While Mulvey's observations were fodder for feminist film theorists in the 1970s, questions remain. Can women *be* the bearers of the look? How is a female viewer constructed? And pertinent to our conversation, how is the feminine constructed in the diegetic world of *Avatar*? Is it possible to square the disturbing regression of the scene where Jake is told he may choose a mate, with the undisputable fact that Cameron has a history of writing "feminist"— admirable, embodied, smart, interesting, and even sometimes lesbian — women?

The women of *Avatar* are no exception in Cameron's oeuvre. Grace is a successful world-renowned botanist who has been working on Pandora for a decade. She is tough, dedicated, compassionate, brusque, and fiercely committed to her research and to the well-being of her team. The brittle exterior is simply the clichéd shell beneath which is a tenderhearted caring woman who also happens to be a brilliant scientist. Her capacity for growth and change has been detailed in Chapter Two, but let it suffice here to note that it is that aspect of her character that keeps her from being a one-dimensional reiteration of Cameron's earlier Ellen Ripley from *Aliens*. It is Grace who first and foremost, with her scientific faith in the data that she has obtained, surmises that the wealth of Pandora is not to be found in the unobtanium. Grace undoes the notion of the spectacle of the woman stopping the action. Grace acts. She argues with Selfridge, she stands up to Quaritch, she takes the initiative in moving the linkup shack to the floating mountains; each action furthers the plot.

Trudy is physically fit, an ace helicopter pilot, and a soldier. Her actions, too, are instrumental in key plot points on which the narrative turns. Trudy brings Jake to Quaritch. She flies the science sorties and transports Grace, Jake and Norm into the jungle and back. When Grace moves the whole team out from under Quaritch's nose, it is Trudy who flies the shack out to the flux vortex. Trudy runs interference for the science team and warns them when Quaritch is going to initiate the destruction of Home Tree. And it is a deeply compassionate Trudy who undertakes her own personal mutiny when she refuses to shoot at the Na'vi. Trudy's tactical cunning gets Grace, Jake and Norm out of the brig. She is also the only one of Quaritch's minions — not including Jake — who turns against him. She is portrayed as dedicated to what is good and right and true, and poignantly, Trudy ultimately gives her life in the fight for Pandora.

Moat is the shaman of the Omaticaya, spiritual advisor and co-ruler with her husband, Eytukan. While he is hemming and hawing about what to do with the alien dream walker, Moat goes right to the source. She is intuitive and decisive. Like Trudy and Grace, she takes action, and these actions again serve not to arrest the plot but to move it forward. She devises the scheme of Jake's apprenticeship, and she defies Eytuakn's rule by setting Jake and Grace free when they have been captured and bound.

Lastly, Neytiri is portrayed as a fierce hunter, a practiced warrior, a dutiful daughter; she is a consummate teacher. Anyone who has studied martial arts will recognize in her constant poking and prodding of Jake's core, her corrections to his stance, the instruction of a master. She is impatient with him, laughs at his foibles, but stays on course. She is honest, transparent, passionate, and fair, and she has a sense of humor. Like all the Na'vi, she moves with strength, agility and grace through her world.

Each of the four main female characters is beautiful in her own way, yet none of them are objectified or fetishized. They are portrayed as whole beings, shot in a manner that underscores their being-ness rather than the commonly fetishized point of view that tends to fragment, or crop women's bodies to accentuate their parts in an attempt to eroticize them. In fact, if anything, Cameron tends to focus on the heads and facial features of all of his characters — the intensity of the work of rendering these faces with the head rigs not lost!— zooming in on their emotive capacities.

But where the paradigm shift occurs is in each of these four major characters functioning as a "bearer of the look." This switch up of Cameron's serves several purposes. When women do the looking, it upends the dominant power balance. By establishing in the characters of Grace, Trudy, Moat and Neytiri the locus of the gaze, these women are also imbued with power. And while there are certainly ways that Jake, Tsu'tey, Quaritch, and so forth are also powerful characters with the agency to move the narrative forward, by displacing the gaze so that it inheres in the women, Cameron constructs a female viewer as well.

Grace, Trudy, Moat and Neytiri are shown seeing, and the spectator is complicit in identifying with their gaze. Grace looks at plants. She investigates the root systems and discovers the signal transduction that is Pandora: a connective network. Grace looks into her microscope, at her field computer, at her samples, at the video logs. She searches for Jake through binoculars when he is lost in the jungle of Pandora. She sees the Na'vi, their beliefs, their rituals, their connection to their world. She sees the mistakes that Selfridge and Quaritch are making, and she sees enough to know that she needs to move Jake away from Quaritch to protect her research and finally Jake. Ultimately, Grace sees Eywa and in her death is given a transcendent vision.

Trudy is the only pilot that has learned to see in the flux vortex, the only one who has transcended reliance on the instruments that are supposed to enhance what is visible. Trudy sees what is happening all around her; as Quaritch mounts his offensive she sees the need to intervene by warning Grace and the others. When faced with the dilemma of killing Na'vi or disobeying a direct order, Trudy is able to see her way clear to make the right choice, in that instant, regardless of the cost to her career as a soldier. Trudy clearly sees her moral duty as superseding her obligation to her commanding officer, and by doing so, she makes both the dilemma and the ethical choice stand out in high relief for the spectator.

Moat is by definition a seer. As shaman of the Omaticaya clan, she, even more than your average Na'vi, sees *into* the people. She sees the meanings in the signs of Eywa, and as Shaman, she has the last word in interpreting them. When Eytukan is questioning Jake, Moat announces that she will be the one to *look* at the alien. As she encircles Jake, examining him from every angle, she sees in him a being worth investing in, worth trusting, worth curing. When she cuts him down to free him, she does so because she sees in him hope for her people. Moat sees what most are unable to see, and the power of her vision lies in her faith: in Eywa, in her people, in life.

And while Grace, Trudy and Moat each see in important ways that offer a woman's purchase on *Avatar*, it is ultimately Neytiri that is the bearer of the look. And in that, Jake is constructed as the object of her gaze. When Jake and Neytiri first meet, it is Neytiri who is the voyeur. She peers down at Jake through a screen of ferns, before drawing her bow to take aim. She watches him as he wrestles with the viperwolves, for just long enough to recognize his courageous strong heart and just short enough to have time to rescue him from their midst. As Jake is traipsing behind Neytiri, they are interrupted by a snow shower of seeds from the sacred tree. When these iridescent spirits alight, covering Jake's head and torso, Neytiri steps back. Like the artist working on her canvas, Neytiri needs to create distance so that she can see, in its totality, what is happening to Jake. She takes Jake in; she introjects him in that moment, covered with the floating seeds.

As his teacher, Neytiri always has her eyes on Jake. She watches him progress and get stronger. She watches him and makes corrections; she instructs him. She watches him to evaluate his progress and determine his readiness to move forward in his apprenticeship. She watches him fail. She sees him fall in the mud and bump and bounce his way to the ground when he leaps out of the tall trees.

The first time we see Neytiri showing Jake how to use the Na'vi bow and arrow, she again steps back to take in the whole of him. She shows him with a swat, with a push, where he is not strong enough, where he needs to be connected, how to breathe. The second time we see him drawing back his bow, Neytiri puts her face next to his so that she may see along the line of his arrow. When he looks at her looking at his point of view, she becomes aware of how close they are, aware of the intimacy, and again she steps back. Jake watches her watching him.

From this point on, she sees Jake differently. When he makes his first clean kill, she looks on with quiet appraisal. She deems him ready to choose his ikran, and she watches him make the bond. As Jake dives and struggles with his flailing banshee, Neytiri gazes down from atop the cliff, glowing with pride.

While *Avatar* is clearly Jake's story, prior to his epiphany in the ashes of Home Tree, it is a story within which he has little agency, a story that happens *to* him. His brother's death gets him to Pandora. Trudy gets him to Quaritch. Grace keeps him safe. Moat accepts him as a pupil. Eywa anoints and chooses him to help protect Pandora. Neytiri saves his life, time and again, and teaches him the way of the Na'vi, which in the end sets him free — from his withered body and from his previously meaningless life.

In the very last scene of the film, as the spectator is awaiting Jake's migration into the avatar, Cameron zooms in tight on the avatar's closed eyes. We see Neytiri's palm cupping his face and can only assume she is bent over his face, awaiting the outcome. We wait with Neytiri. Jake's eyes flash open, large and luminous and yellow and looking directly into the camera. Which means they look directly at us. But it also means, if Neytiri is in fact bent over Jake, that Jake is looking directly into Neytiri's face. This places Neytiri in the same location as the camera/director/spectator. If only for a split second, Jake looks directly at us. The film quickly fades to black.

If we consider that the bearer of that spectatorial gaze is and has always been male, then we are faced with a moment of untenable homoeroticism, Jake holding the gaze of another man. And if we consider that Neytiri is looking into Jake's eyes, then we are usurping the power of the male gaze and relocating it in the eye of woman. In either case, those last seconds challenge the normative power dynamic and the traditional masculine prerogative all at once.

Avatar is Jake's story, but in spite of this, or perhaps because of it, Jake is constructed as spectacle within it. From the close-ups of his withered legs, to his shocking blue embodiment in his avatar, it is Jake who is arresting. He is framed, captured, enlarged, and on display. While these are processes intrinsic to cinema — the larger-than-life projection of narrative — in this case it is Jake who is objectified, and electrifyingly so. It is to Cameron's credit that his use of the performance capture process[93] to create the Na'vi resulted in a fully embodied portrayal, despite its being computer generated. The spectator is struck by the intense physicality of Jake in his avatar, and this intensity overshadows the plot that revolves around it. From his early moments in his avatar, when he swats at everything in his path, to the culminating ride on the great Leonopteryx, we are riveted to and by Jake's body. How it moves, senses, sees, and reacts, how his toes curl with the ecstasy of bonding with the direhorse. Whether we see him through Neytiri's loving eyes, through Grace's watchful eyes, through Quaritch's outrage as he watches Jake captured on the video surveillance tapes, or speaking to us in the recordings of his own video logs, Jake is the spectacle, and we can't help but be in his thrall.

Pandora

There is in *Avatar* the representation of a final feminine presence that must be addressed: Pandora. According to Dr. Jennifer Nesbitt, associate pro-

fessor of English at Penn State, York, naming the moon on which *Avatar*
unfolds "Pandora"—after the mythological woman who was responsible for
introducing evil into the world—was no coincidence. All of the pro-female
characters notwithstanding, Nesbitt sees in Cameron's "conservationist, anti-
imperialist economy of looking" a subsuming of female power.[94]

Nesbitt rightly points out that in the myriad critiques, reviews, blog
posts and comments, nary a mention of the significance of naming the moon
Pandora has been touched upon. She attributes this deliberate omission to an
"unconscious, misrecognition of the full range of gender politics in the film"[95]
and maps the moon Pandora to its mythological namesake. Nesbitt suggests
that like the character in Greek myth,

- Pandora is "new," compared to Earth, which Jake assures us has been
  damaged beyond repair.
- Pandora is dangerous, which Quaritch has emphasized.
- Pandora is female. If a moon could have a sex, then Pandora would be
  a *she*. The colors, apart from the opulent greens of the Na'vi's' jungle
  homeland, tend to be, as was noted by critic Daniel Mendelsohn, "lus-
  ciously 'feminine' on the flora—violet, mauve, delicate peaches and yel-
  lows."[96] Nesbitt argues that since Eywa, the deity of the Na'vi, is female
  and is essentially "in" and "of" Pandora, then Pandora *must* be female.
- Pandora is desirable. Just look at how Jake can't keep his hands off of
  her![97]

Nesbitt goes on to argue that the "rape" of the planet at the hands of the
RDA is further justified when one thinks of Pandora as feminine. Then the
moon becomes "chattel" and at the mercy of those who believe they have the
right to control and possess her.[98]

Without fully fleshing out Nesbitt's arguments, she concludes that
although the RDA is expelled from Pandora, Jake, whom Nesbitt interprets
as Pandora's caretaker, is still a man. She asserts that to take pleasure in *Avatar*
is to "acquiesce to female disempowerment."[99]

Nesbitt's argument is particularly compelling due to the stark absence
of discussion around the meaning of Pandora in the context of the film. However, if Jake is to be "caretaker" of Pandora, in the diegetic logic of the film,
he was chosen, perhaps even engulfed, by Eywa. While Nesbitt claims that
Pandora needs Jake more than he needs her, it seems apparent that the opposite
is true. Jake was saved—from his loss, from his alienation, from his meaningless, lonely life—by Pandora. Jake was transformed and emboldened, finding purpose in the task of saving the moon and the Na'vi way of life. If Nesbitt
is right in her conclusion that by migrating his essence into his Na'vi avatar,

Jake becomes feminized and part of Pandora — and in her words is "subject to a penetrating gaze which others and possesses him"[100]— then in fact his caretaking of the moon ceases to be problematic!

Blueface/Blackface

Avatar has been linked with a host of narratives that have at their diegetic core the hero's quest overlaid with anti-imperialist and pro-environmental tropes. *Dances with Wolves, The Last Samurai, Pocahontas,* and *FernGully,* among others, have figured prominently in these comparisons. It is the hero-ine's quest, however — Dorothy's journey through Oz — that *New York Review of Books* critic Daniel Mendelsohn insists is the story that Cameron keeps try-ing to tell.[101] An encounter with "otherness"— Dorothy's companions, the munchkins, witches and of course the wizard himself— is what Mendelsohn believes Cameron is striving for in *Avatar.*

Underscoring the references to *The Wizard of Oz* threaded through *Avatar*— Quaritch's new arrivals aren't in Kansas anymore, Selfridge calls the Na'vi "blue monkeys"— Mendelsohn also highlights a cinematic echo of *The Wizard of Oz* in *Avatar.* By shooting the "human" realm of Pandora — the inside of the helicopters and transport ships, the labs and linkup suites — in dull grays and washed-out blues, Cameron evokes the opening black-and-white scenes of Kansas in *The Wizard of Oz.* When Jake links into his avatar for the first time, the intensely brilliant full-color spectrum of the Pandoran flora and fauna amaze and delight by contrast, just like when Dorothy exited her tornado-swept house and steps out into Oz.

Both *The Wizard of Oz* and *Avatar* rely upon the singular monomyth of the quest, but in this case the quest is to find "home." Dorothy searches for the literal home to which she has lost her way, and Jake seeks a bodily home, in which he may find a truer expression of his self. Mendelsohn sees Cameron's oeuvre of films as "avatars" of *Oz,* his "beloved model," and locates within these "the yearning, by us humans, for transcendence — of the places, the cul-tures, the very bodies that define us."[102]

It is in a most unlikely film — Alan Crosland's 1927 *The Jazz Singer*— that the yearning for transcendence that unfolds in *Avatar* finds a sublime and related expression. Like *The Jazz Singer, Avatar* is a liminal film that employs the innovative in the service of the representation of otherness, strad-dling old-fashioned storytelling and new-fangled technology. And like *The Jazz Singer, Avatar* also hovers over a threshold of indeterminacy that some have found disconcerting.

The Jazz Singer recounts the moving story of Jakie Rabinowitz, a young

Jewish boy whose heart is captured by jazz, "the misunderstood utterance of a prayer."[103] While his father has taught him that music is holy, the raggy-time music that young Jakie sings, according to his father, "debases the voice that God has given him."[104] His father banishes Jake from home, declaring his son dead to him.

Leaving the East Side of New York, Jakie moves to the West Coast, changes his name to Jack Robin, and becomes a successful entertainer. When offered a chance to open in a Broadway show a decade later, Jack returns home to New York. He is reunited with his mother, but his father still refuses to accept his son. When his father becomes deathly ill, Jack is forced to choose between his deep ties to his Jewish heritage, what he describes as "the cry of my race,"[105] and his passionate yearning to sing jazz.

In his illuminating study, *Blackface, White Noise*, Michael Rogin highlights the alterities between which *The Jazz Singer* oscillates. It is the first "talkie," the first full-length feature film in which the audio is synchronized with the image. Rogin considers *The Jazz Singer* to be cinema's transitional object. The film is structured as a classic silent film, inserted into which are several scenes with synchronized sound: both dialog and musical numbers. Diegetically, it lingers in the space between black and white, between Jew and Gentile, between the street and the stage, between man and woman, between the sacred strains of "Kol Nidre" and the plaintive wail of "My Mammy."[106]

With the heft of history on his side, writing some 70 years after the film's release, Rogin stakes his claim that *The Jazz Singer* has retained its magic. Mendelsohn and others have suggested that *Avatar*, too, will "change permanently the nature of cinematic experience henceforth."[107] Only time will tell how *Avatar* will stand its test.

Avatar holds a similarly liminal space to that of *The Jazz Singer*. In *Avatar* we move not from silence to sound, but from the shooting of live-action scenes to the generation of digital simulacra. In reading *Avatar* we are invited to inhabit the interstices between nature and technology, between human and alien, between seer and seen, between fixity and elasticity, and between mind and body.

The apparatus of the avatar linkup signals the essence of cinema.[108] Rogin makes a similar comparison between *The Jazz Singer* and the movies. "Jack's putting on and taking off of blackface is synecdochic for the movie's reversibility, its promise that nothing is fixed or lost forever."[109] The fluxing of absence/presence dwells in cinema: the necessary and paradoxical re-presentation of that which is not there. Rogin points to this quality in Jack Robin's transitioning in and out of blackface: he is black, but not. He is Jewish, but not. Similarly, when Jake Sully moves in and out of the apparatus of the avatar, he is there and not there, confined to the linkup apparatus and running free through the trees and mountains on Pandora.

In the narrative of *The Jazz Singer*, Jack's application of blackface first serves the function of Americanizing him.[110] As a Jew, as an immigrant, Jakie is othered and the perks of melting-pot culture are out of his reach. When he appears on Broadway behind his burnt-cork guise, Jack is no longer Jakie Rabinowitz, the cantor's son. The application of blackface gives Jack access to a uniquely American identity, affording him access to Broadway, opening the way to his major success as an entertainer. Ironically, Jack can only rise by donning the mask of a group that remains "immobile, unassimilated, and fixed at the bottom."[111] By appropriating all that has been assigned to the "negro" minstrel—"intense emotionality and the musical expression that results from it"[112]—he paradoxically finds his way back to his Jewish soul and makes amends with his father.

Similarly, Jake's application of "blueface"—his linkup in the avatar—can be read as a futuristic technologically improved blackface. It is not just the smearing of burnt cork to mask one's whiteness, but an immersion in the body of the other that restores Jake to himself. It is not too terribly much of a stretch to hear in Jake's impassioned call to the Na'vi a distinctly American voice. Perhaps this is why it was so pertinent that Sam Worthington *play* an American, not an Australian, Jake Sully. Rallying the Omaticaya, Jake gives voice to the original revolutionary spirit upon which the United States was founded, in opposition to the iron grip of corporate greed and imperialism that threatens the Na'vi. In blueface, Jake, too, is re–Americanized.

The story of Jakie Rabinowitz/Jack Robin is, much like *Avatar*, a story of doubles. From the souvenir program in which both a white-faced and blackfaced Al Jolson are featured, to the split reflection in the mirror in which Jack sees himself in blackface superimposed onto his father in his cantor's garb singing "Kol Nidre," *The Jazz Singer* is about the fulfillment of a transgressive desire.[113] As Rogin asserts, "The interracial double is not the exotic other, but the split self."[114] Jakie longs to be Jack, longs to be American, and longs for expression through the "plaintive wailing song of jazz."[115] Jakie is forced to choose between his Jewishness and his Americanness, between life on the Lower East Side and the glamour of Broadway, between his dream of becoming a jazz singer and his father's dream that he become the sixth in a long line of Rabinowitz cantors.

Blackface lubricates the slip and slide between the selves of Jack Robin, instead of fixing his identity in one place or the other. When, toward the end of *The Jazz Singer*, Jack darkens his hands and face, he suddenly aches for his Jewish "race," is nostalgic for his abandoned past. Blackface gave him a boon on Broadway and by extension had landed him the (gentile) girl. Moments before its application, Jack was determined that nothing, not even Mary, should impede his path to success. But blackface, with its (imagined) connotations of emotionality, amplifies for Jack "the call of the ages."[116] It is not until he darkens his skin that he realizes his pressing need to reconcile with his father, to sing Kol Nidre for his community. Blackface gives Jack back to his father but also gives him to Broadway.

Estranged from his mother for the decade following his banishment, Jack returns home when he is offered the Broadway gig. In his parents' living room, on the piano where his father taught him the lilting Jewish liturgy, Jack serenades his mother with Irving Berlin's jazzy tune, "Blue Skies." When his father interrupts the music and yells "Stop!" the power of his voiced command is doubled. It sends Jack into exile again, and it literally silences him for the rest of the film. With the exception of the musical numbers, Jack's father's "Stop!" is the last synchronized dialog in the film.

When Jack's mother ventures to the theater to implore him to sing "Kol Nidre" in his ailing father's stead, she comes upon him rehearsing in blackface. Perplexed, she observes this person who sounds just like Jakie, but who looks like his shadow. Blackface, as Jack's mother makes clear, is metonymic for the flickering shadows of cinema itself. Jack's blackface performance brings a tear to his mother's eye, doubling the "tear" his girlfriend Mary hears in his voice. His mother, now firmly on his side, declares that if God had wanted Jakie to sing in the shul, He would have kept him there. She encourages Jack, then, to do what is in his heart.[117]

Jake Sully, too, slips between split selves, is doubled throughout *Avatar*: Jake the paraplegic and Jake the embodied Na'vi, Jake the soldier and Jake the avatar, Jake in actuality and Jake captured on video. By figuratively applying blueface, Jake uncovers a self of which he had formerly only dreamed, and he, too, gets the (alien) girl. Jake's blueface heals the rift between himself and his figurative mother, Earth. When Jake explains to Eywa that the humans had killed their mother, he admits his own complicity, his own personal loss. Jake's ultimate migration into the avatar solidifies his link with and returns Pandora/Eywa/the mother to him as well.

But reparation of mother love is not the only love making under way. The overt miscegenation hinted at between a blackfaced Jack and his white girlfriend Mary covers the real transgressive love between the Jew and the gentile. While Jack's blackface expresses Jewish solidarity with others who are also marginalized, it more importantly obscures his Jewishness, eliding the difference that would have kept him from pursuing the gentile love interest. Similarly Jake's blueface blankets the miscegenation that is starkly visible in the scene where Neytiri cradles Jake in the linkup shack and we see them for the first time as they truly are.

In Jack Robin's blackface we are given a white fantasy of blackness replete with a reduction to the stereotypically iconic clownish white mouth,[118] exaggerated gestures, and large rolling eyes. In Jake's blueface we are given the white fantasy of the indigenous warrior, replete with a reduction to the stereotypically iconic nudity, feathered adornments, war whoops and the ferocious hissing and barring of the teeth of which the Na'vi are so fond. In *The Jazz Singer* and *Avatar*, black/blueface doubles for an ethnic/racial variety that frees Jack and Jake from the restraints of their own otherness.

Under his burnt cork, Jack is free to be an entertainer, an assimilated American, the man with a tear in his voice. Disguised, the Jew can be gentile. In his avatar, Jake is freed to become the warrior for peace, free to run and climb and jump, to protect Pandora and to fall in love. In blueface, the paraplegic regains his ability to move. Blue/blackface offers each protagonist a new identity that saves him from suffering a divided self.[119]

The performance of black/blueface is available to Jack and Jake due, to a certain extent, to their reduced white male privilege. While Jack is diminished by his Jewishness and Jake by his disability, their whiteness still affords them access to what Rogin suggests might be understood as a form of racial cross-dressing.[120]

Sexual cross-dressing grants one sex access to the qualities s/he fantasizes belong to the opposite sex, all the while being safe within the bounds of their true identity.[121] If we substitute racial cross-dressing, we have a similar equation; the white man embodying his fantasized version of the racial other, without endangering his privileged white status. He plays at being the other, trying it on for size but, ultimately, can slither back to the reassurance of is original self.

However, in both *The Jazz Singer* and *Avatar*, the cross-dressing conflates the racial and the sexual. In both cases the double opens the way to a forbidden woman (the gentile, the alien) and to a personal transformation (the jazz singer, the warrior) and returns them to the mother. Recent turns in queer, feminist and gender theory see the cross-dressing phenomenon as more of a reflection of the fluidity in the performance of gender than a usurpation of power.[122] Both Jack and Jake have run the risk of feminization in their cross-dressed selves. As Rogin points out, Jack is submissive, feminized by the "black mask of deference," in contrast to his "white-face" assertive aggressiveness in the scenes preceding his transformation.[123]

Jake Sully's feminization, alluded to above, is a by-product of his performance of blueface. In his avatar he is linked with a feminine Pandora, with a feminine Eywa, and has become the objectified other of Neytiri's gaze. Engulfed by the feminine, his avatar also restored Jake's functional manhood, destabilizing any inherently clear gender boundaries.

Whether the split self is achieved through a low-tech application of burnt cork or a high-tech transfer of consciousness through an avatar linkup apparatus, the underlying story — the longing to become other than what one is, to transcend the limitations of gender, race, class, ethnicity, or ability, to follow one's dream — is the same. *Avatar* and *The Jazz Singer* each tell a tale that reflects the spirit of the innovative technology that brings the story to light. *The Jazz Singer* changed the course of cinematic history with its synchronized sound. It was the first feature-length film in which gesture and sound were paired to simulate a more authentic and complete representation of reality. When Al Jolson finishes his rendition of the soulful "Dirty Hands, Dirty Face," he speaks directly to his cabaret audience, but his words are meant for the spectator of the film. His famous line, "You ain't heard nothin' yet!" functions within the context of the story but signals the big changes to come, as cinema becomes something to listen to as well as something to see.

By the same token, Jake's "I see you" points not only to the expanding awareness available to him through the vehicle of his avatar, but hints at a future in which cinema, like the avatar apparatus, will launch the spectator into a virtual space that ravishes their senses and staggers their imagination.

Chapter Seven

James Cameron, Auteur and Inventor

What's often missing is awe.... [Cameron] hasn't changed cinema, but with blue people and pink blooms he has confirmed its wonder.
— Manohla Dargis[1]

While it remains to be seen if *Avatar*, like *The Jazz Singer*, will be recognized as a transitional object as cinema shifts toward a more immersive experience, the fact of its impact is indisputable. Cameron has the distinction of having written and directed the two top-grossing films of all times, *Titanic* and *Avatar*. Produced twelve years apart, both were nominated by the Motion Picture Academy for Best Picture — which *Titanic* won, along with ten other Oscars — and both received Best Picture and Best Director Golden Globe awards as well as other prestigious nominations and awards. The two films each cost over two million dollars to make, and each grossed in the neighborhood of two billion dollars. Altogether Cameron has won three Academy Awards, was granted two honorary doctorates and is a member of the NASA Advisory Council.[2] Two of his films, *Terminator 2: Judgment Day* and *Titanic*, have graced the American Film Institute's top-ten lists for the categories of Science Fiction films and Epic films respectively. *Titanic* is one of the very few films made in recent decades to sit on the AFI's list of the top 100 films of all time.[3]

A 2009 *New Yorker* profile of Cameron, published on the eve of *Avatar*'s release, dubs him "A Man of Extremes." In her article, Dana Goodyear shared the perception of a small group of actors and technicians who repeatedly work with Cameron. They see in him that famous doubling of which he is so fond and refer to his darker, more impatient and critical side, as "Mij — Jim backwards."[4] The *Boston Globe's* Wesley Morris categorizes him as embodying an epic conflation of "hawkish and dovish sensibilities. The muscled trigger-happiness of *Terminator* meets the humane scientific wonder of *The Abyss*."[5]

Indeed a man of extremes, he is able to subtend these apparently contradictory qualities, and, either in spite of them or because of them, Cameron lives large. He hasn't let much stand in the way of his narrative, technical or artistic dreams. He explores, invents, creates, perfects. He has been interviewed by publications as diverse as *Popular Mechanics* and *Vanity Fair*. He is a dreamer *and* a doer. He is old-fashioned *and* cutting edge.

In February of 2010, following the success of *Avatar*, Cameron was invited to speak at the Technology, Entertainment, Design (TED) Conference. His talk zeroed in on the autobiographical synthesis of his childhood passions, art and science fiction. The very streamlined trajectory from his youthful frog-snagging forays into the woods to director of blockbuster films included a fascination with the underwater world of Jacques Cousteau and his perceptions that the deep oceans were alien territory. He revisited the wreck of the *Titanic* after finishing its namesake film, a dive which was documented in his film *Ghosts of the Abyss*.[6] His fascination with life in places that the light of the sun cannot reach was the subject of another of his documentary films, *Aliens of the Deep*.

Cameron brought his TED talk to a close with a piece of advice by which it is apparent that he lives: "Failure has to be an option, but not fear."[7] Jake, leaping into thin air after Neytiri, hoping that the canopy of enormous leaves below will slide him safely to the ground, can be thought of as metonymic for Cameron himself. Or perhaps there is a bit of Cameron in the character of Jack Dawson, the young artist who falls in love on the *Titanic* and dies in the icy waters into which it plunged. Dawson admonishes Rose's family and friends — the upper-class passengers with whom he is invited to dine — to make each day, every moment count. In agreement, they all raise their glasses and toast "To making it count." Cameron has evidently embraced that philosophy as well. To a greater or lesser extent, the combination of great courage and fierce attachment infuses all of his projects and serves as the warp through which the weft of Cameron's imaginative narratives have been woven.

Cameron's listing in the Internet Movie Database cites him as having written 22 films/TV episodes, directed 20 and produced 23 projects, as well as having multiple credits for visual effects, editing, acting and cinematography.[8] In Chapter Three of this volume, a great deal of attention was paid to his innovations in cinematography, performance capture, computer character generation, and the employment of the 3-D SimulCam system that in combination elevated *Avatar*. But this geeky side is only half the story.

Cameron is a romantic at heart. Steven Spielberg sees Cameron as both a "techno-brat" *and* "a very emotional story-teller."[9] Goodyear concluded in her interview that Cameron's rock 'em sock 'em pyrotechnics have "romance at their molten cores."[10] Cameron claims that he set out in making *Avatar* to counteract the schmaltz of *Titanic* and to do a "classic guys' adventure story."[11] In spite of himself Cameron admits his attempt at making a "testosterone movie" ended up being a chick flick.[12] The beauty and power of *Avatar*, however, and of many of Cameron's other projects is that they straddle that boundary between high-tech gadgets that go boom and the human heart. When critic Daniel Mendelsohn complains that Cameron's thinking is muddled because he portrays a civilization — the Na'vi — that is both "hypercivilized and precivilized," that is "atechnological and highly technological," he inadvertently homes in on the interstitial space that Cameron is compelled to explore.[13] Throughout this book there has been a focus on the fluxing of what have traditionally been understood as structural oppositions. In inhabiting and inspecting these in-between spaces, Cameron's work is infused with an energetic torsion, the push-pull that defines most binary pairs. And while Mendelsohn interprets these apparent conflictual stances as evidence of something "deeply unself-aware and disturbingly unresolved within Cameron himself,"[14] they can also be appreciated as a fluctuation of our hegemonic either/or paradigm.

Whether Cameron merits the moniker *auteur* or not, there is no question that his contributions to cinema cannot be overlooked. His almost fanatical attention to detail makes him an extraordinary metteur en scène, and while on the surface his films can be seen taking place on distant planets, at sea, in the future and in the past, in cities and in the desert, it is possible to skim, from this apparently disparate body of work, his unique aesthetic style.

The auteur theory is notably diffuse and open to revision. In his essay "Auteur Theory," Peter Wollen points to two main branches into which this theoretical approach has split. There are those who look to a "core of meanings" or a repeated thread of motifs and those who focus more on style and mise en scène to define the work of the auteur.[15] Wollen consequently sees the former as yielding meaning only a posteriori — the meaning is constructed after the fact by the critic in the context of examining the entire body of the director's work. The films of a metteur en scène, on the other hand, are formed a priori. In the case of *Avatar* particularly, one can see the fluxing of even these theoretical models. Cameron had to design/invent/create — from the leaves on every plant, to the flying twirling iridescent creatures of the Pandoran night, to the complex computer-imaging systems of Hell's Gate — every computer-generated thing in advance, an extraordinary feat of mise en scène. It is only after it had all been rendered in bits and bytes that he was able to go back with this virtual camera and shoot the film, exemplified particularly clearly in the flights of the ikran discussed earlier.[16]

Wollen resurrects Jean Renoir's thinking that over the course of his or her career, the director *really only makes one film* "which it is the task of the critic to construct."[17] It is only over the trajectory of multiple projects and from a perch somewhat removed that the "esoteric structure" of this meta-film manifests or "seep[s] to the surface."[18]

According to Wollen, the director is not always aware of his or her conscious intent, and therefore this deep structure can only emerge through a process of repetition over the course of multiple films and only be perceived across the intrinsic gap between the critic and the film. Wollen insists, however, like de Lauretis, that there is no one true interpretation of a film. Meaning can only be gleaned if the spectator commits to work at reading the film in the larger context of the director's oeuvre.[19] It is only within the viewing context of an entire group of films that the spectator is able to perceive the individual film's imbrication in the complete body of work. In encountering a series of works, the viewer undergoes what might be understood as a hermeneutic spiral. Each time the viewer watches a film she is changed. When she sees a subsequent film by the same director (or for that matter any director!), she brings to that film all that she has already read in the first film. The second film, then, also retroactively alters what she saw in the first film.

Perhaps an example will make the effects of this hermeneutic spiral clear. If *Avatar* is the very first film of Cameron's that one has seen, the extra-textual references to *Aliens*' Ellen Ripley will be missed. Grace's character will stand on its own, as will the performance of Sigourney Weaver. But if this same spectator, taken with Cameron's direction, were now to choose to watch *Aliens*, he would see Ellen Ripley in light of what he observed about the character of Grace Augustine. Changed by his viewing of *Avatar*, his perception of Ripley would be colored by his knowledge of Grace. If he rescreened *Avatar*, he would now see the film, and Grace, from his changed horizon. Each film and each subsequent viewing can be read as a palimpsest through which all the previous projects can be detected.

In spite of its indeterminate nature and emphasis not on the masterpiece but on the entire body of work, auteur theory has survived and, according to Geoffrey Nowell-Smith, has become indispensible. Beneath superficial disparities between films, Nowell-Smith asserts that "a hard core of basic and often recondite motifs" can be uncovered.[20] The particular pattern formed by these themes structures the director's work and comprises that "one" film that he or she aspires to make.

Cameron relayed to interviewer Dana Goodyear that *Avatar* is a film that integrates his life's achievements.[21] In order to see this more clearly, this chapter draws on Andrew Sarris' visual model for unpacking auteur theory, a model that relies on a figure of three concentric circles. In the outermost ring,

Sarris locates the technical competence of the director. The middle ring illuminates what is distinguishing in what Sarris calls "recurrent characteristics of style."[22] And embedded in the central circle, Sarris locates what he understands to be an interior meaning, extrapolated from the tension between the director's personality and his or her material, something ambiguous and not easily rendered in non-cinematic terms.[23] François Truffaut referred to this inner core as the "temperature of the director on the set," and Sarris called it the élan of the director's soul.[24]

This chapter analyzes the works of James Cameron in the light of Sarris' paradigm. With a cursory look at Cameron's very first film, *Xenogenesis*, written in 1978, and some of his television and documentary work, the focus of this chapter will fall on the major films that Cameron has written and directed: *The Terminator, Aliens, The Abyss, Terminator 2: Judgment Day, True Lies, Strange Days* — which Cameron wrote but did not direct — *Titanic*, and *Avatar*.

The Outer Circle

Writing in 1962, Sarris' idea of what might have been included under the heading "technical competence" would, at the very least, be a lot less complex than it is today especially with a film like *Avatar*. It is safe to assert that in the area encompassed by Sarris' outer circle, Cameron excels. Known as a consummate storyteller, his mastery of the technique of moviemaking is apparent. Whether we address the hard-core essentials of the filmmaker — shooting, editing, lighting, and so forth — or the very high-tech world of computer-generated special effects, one would be hard pressed to make the argument that Cameron is anything less than an innovative master of all things technical.

Sarris makes the point that because films are made — and here he is talking about films made in 1962 — by crews, not individuals, it is possible for a good cinematographer, editor, or actor to cover up for an incompetent director. He stresses, in this case, the importance of viewing the director's work across numerous films to observe patterns that speak to his or her competence that may surface in spite of the collaborative nature of the medium.[25] The comparison between the massive number of credits on today's films, especially those with special effects or computer-generated/animated aspects to them, and the credits of films of the early 20th century is stunning. The crew of *The Jazz Singer* consisted of 26 members, 12 of whom were musicians. The crew of *Avatar* had closer to a 1,000 members, not including the cast or Cameron, who wrote, directed and co-edited the film.

How does one, then, discern the role of the director? Managing a crew of hundreds is a talent all its own. Cameron, though, has distinguished himself as a technician throughout his career, with multiple nominations and awards for his direction, writing, and filmmaking. His cast and crew anecdotally comment that because Cameron knows it all — from makeup to lighting to editing to creature design — there is no fudging, no getting away with being or doing anything less that one's best and then some. Beginning with *Xenogenesis*, co-written with Randall Frakes, Cameron has consistently pushed against the boundaries of technical filmic conventions.

In this short science-fiction film lie the seeds that grew into much of Cameron's subsequent work. A low-budget, low-tech film, *Xenogenesis* opens with titles typed out in a computer font accompanied by the sound of a ringing phone. (A cursor was added to this font when it recurred in the title sequence to Cameron's 1984 *The Terminator*.) The first section of the almost twelve-minute-long film consists of detailed, comic-book-like illustrations of the characters. Accompanied by a voice-over, opening pans of the lush illustrations provide the backstory. The film proper appears to be a stop-motion clash between a young man, Raj, who is introduced as being "made" by a machine, but for all intents and purposes appears human, and a machine that was left behind to clean and guard an abandoned outpost, which has been uninhabited for 50,000 years. Raj comically notes how "clean" the place is, and sure enough a robotic duster emerges and goes about the business of cleaning up random detritus. When Raj himself is detected, the machine attempts to vacuum him up as well.

Raj's partner Laurie, within earshot at the other end of a walkie-talkie, comes to his aid inside what is undoubtedly the prototype for Ripley's power-loader and Quaritch's AMP suit. Her mechanical vehicle resembles a spider with six legs and a central compartment in which she sits and from which she pilots the thing by moving her arms in a bicycling fashion.

The short film's ending is a cliffhanger. Literally. Raj is hanging by his hands over an abyss of endless computer schematics, while Laurie, after initially losing battery power, appears to be making considerable progress kicking the cleaning robot toward the edge of the cavernous space. The film ends abruptly with the robot almost on top of Raj, just short of toppling over the edge into the abyss.

In this stripped-down tale that takes place in a virtual space — within a computer's innards — it is easy to spot the tropes that would compel Cameron to deeper and continued exploration: the antagonism between the human and the machinic, the heroine who comes to the rescue — capable, technologically savvy, brave — as well as the implied warning of a future at the hands of technology gone awry.

The motifs of *Xenogenesis* function as the paper cone around which the

cotton candy of Cameron's imagination was spun. The film lays the ground-
work for Cameron's affinity with all things mechanical. When Linda Hamilton
began working with Cameron on the first Terminator film, she was purported
to have commented, "That man is definitely on the side of the machines."[26]
The stop-motion robots of *Xenogenesis* make the mechanical sense necessary —
have moving parts that work in concert — to achieve a kind of technological
verisimilitude. The robot's obsessive vacuum arm, its disabling light, and its
blasting laser beams are all legible in their functionality. The mechanical "exo-
skeleton" in which Laurie maneuvers has jointed legs, which crawl the thing
crablike across the floor, but also serve as weapons, when push comes to shove,
and it becomes necessary for her to disable the cleaning robot. These robotic
aspects of the film were meticulously assembled by Cameron.[27]

As discussed thoroughly in chapters Two and Three, the interweaving
of the technological as both diegetic figure and a critical aspect of how Cameron makes the films he makes, is consistent throughout his career. In each
of his films, with the possible outlier being *True Lies*, Cameron raises the bar
for what is technologically possible in cinema as well as continuing to poke
and prod at the question of how it is that we relate to our machines, how they
enhance and/or detract from the way we live our lives.

It is pretty much a straight shot from *Xenogenesis* to Cameron's 1984 *The
Terminator*, in terms of the technological trajectory. While in between these
projects, Cameron created special effects for "B-movie king" Roger Corman
and directed the horror picture *Piranha II: The Spawning*, it was *The Terminator* that put Cameron on the map as a director.[28] Anecdotally the manifestation of a dream that Cameron had about a metallic man emerging from a
wall of flames, *The Terminator* broke new ground where animatronics were
concerned. The story revolves around a cyborg sent back from a future in
which the machines have destroyed the world and are at war with a small surviving group of humans who are determined to resist them. This band of
resistance fighters was led by John Connor. The target of the Terminator's
mission in the present was Sarah Connor, John's mother. His mission: to go
back in time before she had given birth to the future revolutionary and murder
her.

Working with the late Stan Winston, Cameron created animatronic dummies of the Terminator character, famously rendered by Arnold Schwarzenegger, that were used to reveal the underlying mechanical man that he was.
These duplicate dummies allowed his surface humanity to be literally peeled
away, graphically exposing his robotic metal skeleton and his mechanical eyes.
While Arnold reminisced that when he watched the film in retrospect he
couldn't tell when he was playing the role and when it was the dummy —
quite the comment on his own mechanical acting — in the scenes where the

Terminator is excising his own eye, it is obvious that we are not looking at a living, breathing actor.[29]

To recreate Cameron's dream scene, a 200-pound, electronically controlled robot was constructed by Stan Winston. Taking over a year to build, the robot consisted of more than 1,000 handcrafted chrome parts.[30] The "injured" metallic skeleton of the Terminator emerges from a fiery explosion in which his human covering has melted away and he limps menacingly toward the characters of Sarah Connor and Kyle Reese, taking special effects to a new level. Stan Winston won the Academy of Science Fiction, Fantasy & Horror Films' Saturn awards for Best Makeup for *The Terminator* and Cameron, for Best Writing.

When Cameron took on the job of directing *Aliens*, he decided to simplify the original design of the eerie extraterrestrials so that the actors who played the parts of the aliens would have more mobility and flexibility. In this sequel to the original *Alien*, which was directed by Ridley Scott, Sigourney Weaver's Ellen Ripley is found after floating for decades in space. She is recruited to search out a human colony that may have been decimated by the very same frightening aliens whom Ripley had attempted to destroy. Reluctantly, she agrees to accept the assignment. Foreshadowing Cameron's attention to the precision of performance capture in *Avatar*, he focused, in *Aliens*, on the ways in which light could reveal and obscure the creatures all at once. Playing with camera angles, he shot the costumed actors crawling on the floor with his camera upside down to simulate their creeping along the ceiling.[31] In 1986, *Aliens* won Academy Awards for Best Effects, Sound Effects Editing and Best Effects, Visual Effects as well as the Hugo Award for Best Dramatic Presentation.

The breakthrough technology of *The Abyss* in 1989 and *Terminator 2: Judgment Day* in 1992 was touched on in Chapter Three in the context of the history of computer-generated characters. Working on the material plane with animatronic creatures, costumes, and makeup is a world apart from manipulating data digitally in order to arrive at the underwater alien of *The Abyss* or the liquid metal of the late-model Terminators. While *The Abyss* was not a blockbuster by any stretch of the imagination, it did garner an Oscar for Best Effects, Visual Effects. The Academy of Science Fiction, Fantasy & Horror Films awarded Cameron another Saturn Award for Best Director for *The Abyss*. Like *2001: A Space Odyssey*, *The Abyss* was a slow-moving, but according to film critic David Chute, "meticulously crafted" film with "utterly gorgeous special effects."[32] Chute's assessment of the painstakingly sharp and detailed images and performance only underscores Cameron's technical directorial competence. *Rolling Stone* critic Peter Travers claims that is was *The Abyss* that confirmed Cameron's status as a "world-class filmmaker."[33]

The loss of a nuclear submarine in *The Abyss* occasions a group of Navy

SEALs to be sent to the aid of the underwater oil-rig grunts to help retrieve the sunken nukes. Lindsey, the architect/engineer of the oil platform, and her estranged husband, Bud, the captain of the oil-rig, band together to avert a nuclear disaster. In addition to the threat from the mentally deteriorating Lt. Coffey, the crew find that they have "non-terrestrial" company.

The Abyss was shot almost entirely underwater in the containment building of an abandoned nuclear power plant and was unusually stressful to make technologically, physically and emotionally.[34] Before the shoot began, the cast and crew were flown to the Caribbean to become scuba certified. They worked with actual diver propulsion vehicles and traveled in real submersibles. The camera crew, the lighting crew, and sound crew all worked underwater, sometimes for hours at time.

For *The Abyss*, Cameron recorded the first underwater dialog for a film. In addition, his brother, Mike Cameron, designed a special camera with an airtight housing that could withstand the underwater shoot. In the scenes where Bud or Lindsey had to swim without tanks — in the first case because Bud was swimming through the flooding ship and in the latter because Lindsey had "apparently" drowned — the actor and actress undertook these rigorous and somewhat dangerous stunts themselves.[35] Cameron sometimes spent upwards of twelve hours a day underwater on this besieged shoot, trying to recreate an authentic deepwater milieu. Taking underwater filmmaking to a new level would serve Cameron in his future shooting of *Titanic* and two of his underwater documentaries, *Ghosts of the Abyss* and *Aliens of the Deep*.

When it came to the creation of the NTI — non-terrestrial intelligence — as the underwater alien was called, Cameron turned to CGI, creating what he referred to as the first "soft surface character animation."[36] Under the supervision of Dennis Muren, ILM created a "transparent water worm" that interacted with Mary Elizabeth Mastrantonio and Ed Harris. This shimmering, slithering creature not only displayed emotion but also accurately mimicked their facial expressions. This pushed CG into alien territory, setting a high bar that was soon surpassed by Cameron's T-1000 model of the molten metallic Terminator man.

Again working with Dennis Muren at ILM, the shape-shifting silvery cyborg offered a glimpse into what digital effects were apt to offer in years to come. In *Terminator 2: Judgment Day*, two Terminators are sent back into the past this time, one whose mission it was to kill the now 10-year-old John Connor and one, resembling Schwarzenegger's original Terminator, to protect him. The newer Terminator model, the T-1000, was a chameleon-like cyborg capable of not only shifting its shape but also able to mimic the qualities of whatever it touched.

In *Terminator 2*, computer-generated effects were intrinsic to the film's huge success and necessary to the cohesion of the narrative, not simply the frosting on the cake. Cameron's work in *Terminator 2* was recognized with Oscars for Best Effects in Sound Effects Editing, Visual Effects, Best Makeup, and Best Sound. Cameron also won another Saturn Award for directing and several more for special effects, as well as another Hugo Award for Best Dramatic Presentation.

In the six intervening years between *Terminator 2* and his next blockbuster, *Titanic*, Cameron worked on two films. He wrote and directed *True Lies*, a comedic spy/action film starring Jamie Lee Curtis and Arnold Schwarzenegger, and he wrote and produced *Strange Days*, which was directed by his ex-wife Kathryn Bigelow. According to the Internet Movie Database's website, Cameron also was involved in extensive editing on *Strange Days* but was not able to receive a credit for this because at that time he was not a member of the editors' union.[37]

The 1992 film *True Lies* takes as its premise a secret agent who hides his work as a spy from his wife who believes he is a computer salesman. When Harry Trasker (Schwarzenegger) suspects his wife (Curtis) of cheating on him, he turns his spy prowess on her only to learn that she is being conned by Simon (Bill Paxton), a used car salesman pretending to be an undercover agent. When Harry pretends to engage Helen's help as an undercover agent, they inadvertently get tangled up with real terrorists. Playing with themes of deception, subterfuge, and mistaken identities, Cameron's delight for the double is evident in this farce.

While *True Lies* begins and ends with enough pyrotechnics to satisfy any action film fan, it is the one film of Cameron's that stands apart from the rest of his work. It isn't science fiction, there are no oceans deep — although the film opens with a diving scene!— no adventures in outer space and, except in the most minimal way that any comedic spy worth his salt must have his gadgets, it doesn't feature much in the way of technology. And while the figures of romantic love and deceptive doubling are central to the story, for the most part the film is a silly spy romp that serves as a vehicle for Schwarzenegger's stilted acting and in which Jamie Lee Curtis is simply brilliant.

Strange Days, on the other hand, although not directed by Cameron, is marked by more of his signature motifs: a dystopian future in L.A.; an innovative technology by which one person can virtually "jack-in" to the experience — physical, emotional, psychic — of another in a process called "wire-tripping"; the redemption of a loser protagonist; and sufficient romantic longing, idealism, corruption, and fulfillment to satisfy any viewer. The diegetic space of *Strange Days* allows for the repetition of many of Cameron's standard tropes, and these shall be explored later on in the context of the inner circle of Sarris' paradigm.

While *True Lies* was far more of a box office hit, it was shooting the first-person "point of view" shots for the wire-tripping sequences in *Strange Days* that required yet another innovation by Cameron. The point of view of the person making or playing back the wire-trip tape was difficult to represent. The research arm of Cameron's production company, Lightstorm Entertainment, took a year to invent a super-light 35 mm camera that could fit in the palm of a hand and which had the stability and mobility to replicate the human eye, lending verisimilitude to the wire-tripped sequences.[38]

In "The Heart of the Ocean: The Making of Titanic," Cameron said that as far as he was concerned there was no point in making a film if you weren't going to break new ground. And break new ground he did with the film *Titanic*, as much of the original ship was reconstructed. The enormous "floating city of light" was built on hinges that enabled the shearing of the ship in two under the pressure of the encroaching waters. *Titanic*'s engines, four-story-high crankshafts, and its fiery furnaces were all built to scale. Cameron worked with historians of the *Titanic* to assure that every detail — the linens, crockery, the beading on the women's dresses, carpets, and woodwork — was authentic. Another new camera with a housing that could withstand the crushing pressure of the depths of the actual dive to the wreck of the *Titanic* had to be invented. Remotely operated underwater vehicles (ROVs) with hundred-foot tethers were used to explore the decrepit remains for the initial dive scenes in the movie.

Titanic won Oscars for Best Art Direction-Set Decoration, Best Cinematography, Best Costume Design, Best Director, Best Sound Effects Editing, Best Visual Effects, Best Film Editing, Best Original Score, Best Original Song, Best Picture, and Best Sound. It won an additional four Golden Globes and a Grammy for the song "My Heart Will Go On." And until *Avatar* came along, *Titanic* had broken all box office records.

Mise-en-Scène

It should be clear slipping down into the second ring of Sarris' concentric circles — that of mise-en-scène or the director's style — that these rings are not completely discrete. Cameron's technical prowess is asserted precisely in his almost fanatical obsession with getting it right. And getting it more than right he does. Each of Cameron's films is marked by his attention to detail, his perfectionism, and his accuracy. Working, for example, with historians on *Titanic* or a linguist on *Avatar*, Cameron takes no shortcuts, cuts no corners. To honor his commitment to authenticity, no matter what the cost, requires immense effort and attention oft hidden by what Sarris refers to as the "film façade." The viewer is meant not to notice the blood, sweat and tears that returns the film in its final form, and yet, Sarris maintains, there is always something of the director's unconscious that seeps through. The film then, Sarris argues, "is not a communication, but an artifact which is unconsciously structured in a certain way."[39]

A few examples will elucidate the extent to which Cameron's devotion to replicating reality — or perhaps what he has imagined as reality — seems to have no bounds. In *The Abyss*, an important plot element contains the real but still experimental procedure in which a human can "breathe" an "oxygenated fluorocarbon emulsion."[40] Bud, Ed Harris' character, will need to breathe this emulsion in order to dive deep enough to disarm the dangerous nukes in the trench. One of the Navy SEALs introduces and demonstrates the procedure on a white rat named Beany, the oil rig's mascot. Cameron consulted with scientists at Duke University to be assured that (A) this would actually work, and (B) that no harm would come to the rats. The folks at Duke explained that they had had success, hadn't harmed any rats in the process, and instructed Cameron and crew in the necessary technique, including squeezing the liquid out of the rats' lungs when the procedure was completed. The rat we see on the screen actually undergoes this procedure, does breathe the liquid fluorocarbons, and is, except for those anxious moments when it can't breathe, relatively unscathed.[41]

Cameron's preparation of his casts leaves nothing to chance. As mentioned in Chapter Three, Cameron took the entire cast of *Avatar* to the rain forest of Kauai so that they could experience — mentally, physically, and emotionally — what life in the jungle might be like. Cameron worked to train the cast in the use of weapons — shooting a bow and arrow, Na'vi style — and all things military. But *Avatar* was not the only film in which he took such great pains to prepare his actors and actresses.

The cast and crew of *The Abyss* all became competent scuba divers. Sigourney Weaver, a self-professed gun control advocate, had to learn how to shoot all manner of flamethrowers and assault rifles on the set of *Aliens*. She described working on that film as her most physically challenging work, since much of the time she was carrying the young girl "Newt" around as well as toting a massive flamethrower. The film was shot in a deserted power plant in the middle of winter, and Sigourney had to wear a T-shirt just as if she were in an overheated space station. In the scene where she frees Newt from being enshrouded in the cocoon of the aliens, she tears away at what appears to be alien ooze. Though the ooze looks like gooey stretchy stuff, the alien threads were simulated using a kind of fiberglass on which, when tearing frantically to rescue Newt, Weaver inadvertently cut her hands.[42]

Edward Furlong, the young actor who played John Connor in *Terminator*

2, worked with a trainer who made him do sit-ups and lift free weights. Linda Hamilton's comfort and competence with automatic assault weapons was acquired at the hands of an ex–Israeli commando.[43] When observed in early scenes of *Terminator 2* doing pull ups in her cell in the mental institution, there is no mistaking the extent to which Hamilton had to work to get her body to be that lean of a machine.

Kate Winslet recounts her challenges in the scene where she is rescuing an imprisoned Leonardo DiCaprio. Jack is handcuffed to a pipe in a room quickly filling up with icy water. Rose runs to find an implement to break open his handcuffs and returns carrying a wooden-handled fire axe. In this scene she is forced to swim with one hand shimmying along a ceiling pipe, the axe in her other hand. The water was freezing. They were not able to heat it because that would have resulted in steam rising off its surface, denying the plausibility of being in icy waters. Winslet laments the fact that while everyone else was able to wear wetsuits underneath their costumes, she was wearing a flimsy dress that precluded that option. Not all of the prep is painful, however. Leonardo DiCaprio seemed to quite enjoy his instruction in Irish step dancing for the scene of the steerage party on the *Titanic*.[44]

No matter what kind of preparation is undertaken, there are limits to what makeup and human bodies can do. At this point Cameron turned to working with both Stan Winston and Dennis Muren; what could be created with models and puppets and animatronics was, but when it was necessary they switched to optical or digital representations. For *Terminator 2*, Winston and his minions constructed duplicate bodies of the children in the playground who turn to ash and disintegrate when exposed to the nuclear blast in Sarah Connor's recurring nightmare/vision. They built elaborate, detailed miniature cityscapes that were blown to bits in the imagined holocaust. It was not enough for Cameron to just have a metallic dude emerge from the flaming inferno; it had to be a T-1000 who walked and moved exactly like actor Robert Patrick. Predating an effective motion-capture system — this was done in 1992 — they turned to working with multiple — up to 60 — laser scans of Patrick's face, his expressions, the way he strutted, the tilt of his head.[45]

Cast, Crew and Characters

In countless interviews, actors and crew speak to the arduous, challenging aspects of working on a Cameron film. Long hours, shooting at night, challenging environmental conditions, demanding feats of strength and agility are all de rigueur. Yet as is typical of any auteur, Cameron often works with the same crew and members of the cast across various projects. Stan Winston and members of his studio, people from WETA and ILM, and Dennis Muren all contributed to special effects across films. James Horner did the music for both *Titanic* and *Avatar*, and these movies were both produced by Jon Landau, among others. Cinematographers Adam Greenberg and Russell Carpenter repeatedly worked with Cameron, as did producer and ex-wife Gale Anne Hurd. In spite of the grueling conditions for the cast, Arnold Schwarzenegger, Linda Hamilton, Michael Biehn, Bill Paxton, Sigourney Weaver, Jenette Goldstein, and Lance Henrikson all came back for repeat performances.

In addition to working with the same people, Cameron also has a pre-dilection for casting a similar type of character. *Avatar, Aliens, Strange Days, Titanic*, and the TV series Cameron created, *Dark Angel*, all are peopled with unusually strong female characters. While this was explored in some depth in Chapter Six in relation to the women characters in *Avatar*, it merits mention-ing here because it speaks to something that infuses all of Cameron's narrative work. Cameron is playing with and extending the boundaries of what is allow-able in the portrayal of women. It is not just that they are drawn with physical strength, although that is certainly part of it. In each of his films, beginning with *Xenogenesis*, at the very least we are seeing women as exhibiting agency, power, courage and intelligence. Laura comes to the rescue of Raj. In *Aliens*, Ellen Ripley conquers her debilitating fear of the aliens and leads what is left of the crew to safety, rescuing both Corporal Hicks and Newt in the process. Lindsey, who it just so happens engineered and designed the oil rig on which the story unfolds, sacrifices herself in the hopes that Bud can resuscitate her and destroy the nukes in *The Abyss*. Fighting machine Sarah Connor sacrifices herself on multiple occasions to save her son and in the process manages to destroy two of the Terminators. In *True Lies*, in spite of her love for Harry, Helen displays rare courage when she believes she is helping Simon to save the world and when she tries to protect Harry, believing that she had gotten him into a mess by playing at secret agent, not realizing that he actually *was* a spy.

In *Titanic*, the character of Rose risks her life for an opportunity to expe-rience joy, love, and freedom, standing up to her dominating fiancé, her con-trolling mother, and the conventions of her time. The character of Mace, in *Strange Days*, rescues her schlemiel of a friend Lenny countless times and in the end takes on the entire LAPD to bring the truth to light. And of course the transgenic character Max in the TV series *Dark Angel*, which Cameron created, is nothing less than a woman warrior.

These examples alone would be sufficient to underscore Cameron's fas-cination with and commitment to creating complex and compelling female characters. But it is in the writing and casting of some of his more minor characters that Cameron really pushes the boundaries of what has traditionally been an acceptable portrayal of women. Private Vasquez, played by Jenette

Goldstein, who leads the squad into the processing station to flesh out the aliens, is a case in point. Vasquez is an extraordinarily buff and butch woman who is accepted by her peers and valued as a comrade. A fellow soldier jokes with her, asking if she had ever been mistaken for a man. Without missing a beat, Vasquez responds, "Have you?" She is first in every reconnaissance mission, leading the way through the dark, dank, and dangerous passageways, and ultimately she gives her life to protect her fellow soldiers. The character of Trudy stands in the shadow of Private Vasquez.

Titanic's unsinkable Molly Brown, played by Kathy Bates, offers a different slant on pushing boundaries. Molly doesn't endanger traditional representations of gender but pierces entrenched class boundaries. Her honesty, her willingness to assist Jack by dressing him appropriately for his dinner with the first-class passengers and helping him decipher the riddles of cutlery use, label her *outsider*. She is the only person in her lifeboat that can't stomach sitting there without doing something to try and save the hundreds who were jumping to their deaths. Understandably, she was not willing or able to risk her own life to save theirs, but she at least made an effort.

In *Dark Angel*, Max's best gal pal, Original Cindy, is a lesbian. While she is not a mutant like Max and her allies, she stands by Max, serving as her body shield in the very last episode when they are under siege. She is out about her sexuality, often joking with Max about it, as when she finds other women characters attractive. In a show that draws on the antipathy between the humans and mutants, it is refreshingly novel to have the lesbian sidekick portrayed as one of the normal ones.

Cameron's second wife and the producer of his first three films, Gale Anne Hurd, told Dana Goodyear for her *New Yorker* article that Cameron had always seen women as much more interesting than men as protagonists. "He felt that they were underutilized in sci-fi, action, and fantasy," she said. "And that just about everything you could explore in a male action hero could be explored better with a woman."[46]

Cameron's affinity for specific actors and specific character types is matched in the costume and prop arena by his attraction to all things that smack of the military. While an anti-war message rings out loud and clear from *Avatar*, Cameron's fascination with the aura of the soldier is unmistakable. Enamored of all things that explode, shatter and/or go up in flames, Cameron is also taken with the camaraderie of the warrior. Incorporating military signals and jargon—Cameron's character's sign to one another and speak of distances in "klicks"—fatigues and briefings, mess meals and of course the endless explosive battle scenes of both *Terminator* films, *Aliens*, *True Lies*, and *Avatar*, it is the delight he takes in all manner of headgear that crosses over the boundary from fiction to reality.

In the future from which the Terminator comes, the resistance fighters are hatted with helmets that include built-in binoculars or night goggles, lights and microphone headsets. The headgear in *Aliens* is remarkably similar, with video and infrared cameras and an added light that sits perched on their shoulder to guide the way. The wire-tripping device of *Strange Days* is made of thin strips of wire, almost spiderlike, that grab the top the head of the person recording or playing back the tape. This construction foreshadows the array of wires that surround the head in the avatar linkup apparatus as well.

In the icy underwater opening of *True Lies*, Harry Trasker's diving apparatus is accessorized to the max with lights and camera lenses galore adorning his diving helmet. Harry's partner Gibson, who is often in a surveillance van nearby, is seen wearing the requisite audio headset. And finally in *Titanic*, the "driver" of Duncan, the robot that precedes the submersibles into the wreck, is wearing some far-out virtual reality goggles.

This fetishizing of headwear comes to fruition with *Avatar*. The Na'vi warriors who fly their ikran wear decorative gear as well as their brilliantly colored war paint. Sitting on their brow and encircling their heads are beads and bone and teeth and feathers woven into hemplike macramé tiaras. While Quaritch's pilots are seen in the requisite helmets and headsets, his troops on the ground are wearing the streamlined Bluetooth earpieces along with their exo-packs. But what is most telling is that Cameron's penchants for head wear led him to invent the head-rig cameras that enabled the astounding realism of the facial performance capture of the characters of *Avatar*.[47]

Cameron Blue

Manohla Dargis noted, "The movie's truer meaning is in the audacity of its filmmaking." Cameron is nothing if not intrepid. But in addition to his films being marked by absolute authenticity and remarkable rigor on the parts of cast and crew, there are also visual tropes, stylistic notes which Cameron has repeatedly played and on which he has relied, the most blatantly obvious of these being the almost ubiquitous use of what it makes sense to christen Cameron blue.

In almost every one of his films, we find some indication of this rich, deep, mesmerizing blue. In *Avatar,* it becomes a primary signifier, but in many of his preceding films, it serves as "spot color," more akin to a signature at the bottom of an oil painting. What it means to Cameron we can only guess. Perhaps it evokes his early immersion in the underwater world of Jacques Cousteau or the imagined vastness of deep space. Or perhaps it is the painter in Cameron, flexing his color muscles. But in spite of its origins or import to

Cameron, its effect can't be minimized. The particular blue that recurs throughout Cameron's projects is warm, inviting, enveloping. Like his restrained use of 3-D in *Avatar*, this blue meets the viewer more than halfway and welcomes her in. The blue is reassuring, even as it hints at the steel edge of determination of the Terminators, the depth of the abyss, the iciness of the waters surrounding the *Titanic*, the expansiveness of infinite space.

The first blue appears in *The Terminator* title sequence, as the metallic blue words scroll forward and backward across the screen behind a cursor and computer font in which the credits are displayed. The monochromatic opening scenes in both Terminator films are shot in a steely metallic blue; the Terminators arrive in the past amid a cobalt lightning storm.

The title sequence for *Aliens* is also done in Cameron blue, and the film opens onto a saturated bluish cloud in outer space. Ripley, 57 years in hypersleep, is covered in an icy crystalline blue when her return pod is rescued. The background of the title screen for *The Abyss* is a darker shade of Cameron blue, while the title font fades to baby blue. The bulk of this watery world shimmers with an underwater blue tinge. *Titanic*, too, sails on a sea of blue. The initial bluish cast of the underwater scenes, the dark thalo blue of the churning Atlantic beneath Rose as she threatens to jump, the hue of the side of the ship at night that silhouettes people jumping to their deaths. Even the mammoth iceberg itself is shrouded in an icy blue. But perhaps most poetic of all is the royal blue of Rose's diamond that is reflected in her eyes.

Again in *True Lies*, the title sequence is done in 3-D block letters in shades of blue. In the opening sequence Harry Trasker escapes his pursuers through a blue-tinged snow-covered wood, with help from his buddy in the bluish light of a surveillance van near by. Many of the night scenes — think slick inky black streets — are shot tinted blue, as are the warehouse scenes where Trasker is held prisoner in a lovely blue button-down shirt.

Lines of Sight/The Center Circle

Another stylistic device that Cameron frequently draws upon is the point of view that has been usurped by technology. In earlier chapters the narrative force of Jake's video blog and surveillance files was examined for the ways in which it particularly displaced the viewer from the eye of the director's camera in *Avatar*. Cameron often relied on this shift to the eye of the computer or to the point of view of those reviewing a videoed segment to serve a stylistic function. Displacing the spectator's eye and pointing to its displacement serves as a meta-comment on the structure of the cinematic apparatus as well as on our contemporary scopic regime. An unexpected shift in the place from where we are looking or the devices and substances through which we see can't help but bring our attention to that seeing. By highlighting these, Cameron brings our awareness not only to what we are seeing but also to our practices of looking.

As we focus on the deeper meaning of these shifts in our seeing, we are also blurring the boundary between Sarris' second ring of stylistic attributes and the central circle where the internal meanings of Cameron's work as an auteur are signaled by the visual figures. We now can attend to Nowell-Smith's "hard core of basic and often recondite motifs."[48]

In both Terminator films, Cameron places us in the eye of the cyborg. The Terminator's visual experience is made explicit by saturating the screen with a red tint. As he chases after Reese and Sarah in the first Terminator film, a grayed-out target covers their figures as they run in front of him, but this is just a fraction of what can be seen within the Terminator's visual field. There are multiple data readouts including a compass, an angular measure, and a list of the sizes and distances of the objects in the visible field. The data fluctuates as needed, not only offering quantitative information about what is visible, but the readout offers the Terminator choices of appropriate verbal responses. In other words, Cameron has conceived of a cyborg whose input device relies on processing visual cues to deal with his changing environment. When the protective, "good" Terminator of *Terminator 2* is lowered into the molten soup, we are shown his red screen growing smaller until it becomes just a blip and then disappears, signaling that he is no more.

A displacement or multiplication of perspectives fleshes out the spectator's point of view. One-way mirrors — practically a requirement for any replication of police interrogation — and video monitors were part of the police station scenes in *The Terminator* and grant the spectator four simultaneous points of view. We are able to see through the one-way mirror into the interrogation room where Reese is being questioned, as are the police officers who watch the questioning. We can see the reflections of these observing officers in the glass on the reverse side of the one-way mirror. On the black-and-white monitor we can see the video of Reese's interview as it occurs in real time, and we can step back and see the entire scene from the director's-eye view. (This effect is also used in *True Lies*, when Harry Trasker is interrogating his wife, Helen. To that set, Cameron has added an infrared monitor that records Helen in pulsating psychedelic colors.) This refraction or multiplied view of what it is possible to see gives the spectator a *rashomon* of the moment. By offering a kaleidoscopic instead of one-pointed perspective, Cameron is signaling the complex meaning not only of the moment, but of the essence of cinema and ultimately of life.

The seeds of the idea for Jake's undoing by video blog double can be found in *The Terminator* scene in which cops, police shrink, and Sarah Connor gather to watch a previously recorded Reese ranting on the black-and-white video monitor. When Reese realizes that his pleading is falling on the deaf ear of the shrink who is interviewing him, he turns and yells directly into the camera, underscoring levels of displacement. Reese is talking directly to whoever is viewing the video: the room full of cops, Sarah, and of course the audience. When he becomes overly agitated and starts to describe how the Terminator will tear out Sarah's heart, someone hits the pause button, and Reese is reduced to the staticky lines of which all video images are comprised.

Video feeds become plot agents in *Aliens* as well. Each soldier has a video camera attached to his or her headgear that streams back to an individual video monitor with the date and time stamp, as well as the soldier's name in the readout across the bottom of the frame. Ripley and Lieutenant Gorman watch from the relative safety of the armored vehicle as the soldiers encounter the remains of the human population cocooned in alien ooze. They also watch as one by one the video monitors flatline when each subsequent soldier meets their end at the hands (or mouths) of the aliens.

Later, Carter Burke, in an effort to assure that he will be able to take alien specimens back to Earth with him, releases the "facehuggers" and removes Ripley's gun from the lab while she is asleep. When she and Newt are attacked by the impregnating aliens, they wave and scream at the video camera in order to get Corporal Hicks' attention. Burke reaches up and calmly turns off the closed-circuit monitor. By controlling who sees whom, Burke potentially controls the life-or-death outcome.

While *True Lies* tends to be the odd film out in Cameron's oeuvre, its secret-agent-man plot affords lots of opportunities to play with the idea of displacing the point of view. In the opening scenes of the film, secret agent Harry Trasker is on assignment in wintry Switzerland accompanied by his colleagues nearby in a surveillance van. His partner, Gibson, follows Trasker's exploits through the acid yellow night-vision light of a high-powered scope, starkly contrasting Cameron's cool blue of the snowy night.

When they return to their civilian life after an unsuccessful assignment, Gibson stops by at Trasker's home to pick him up for work. He shows Harry a spiffy new surveillance camera disguised as a pack of Lucky Strikes. The cigarette pack–camera transmits its image to a pair of sunglasses. The portable hidden technology helps Harry to keep track of two terrorists who are following him and to outwit them when they try to ambush him in the men's room at the mall. The spectator watches their approach and the ensuing battle through the point of view of the black-and-white image of the Lucky Strike camera.

Cameron likes the effect of the displacement afforded by incorporating the point of view of the video camera, surveillance camera, or the built-in camera eye of the computer. During the opening scenes in *Titanic*, there is an almost tongue-in-cheek sequence in which the character Brock Lovett, who captains the dive down to the wreck of the *Titanic*, is documenting his adventure in the submersible. Waxing poetic, he narrates their descent and arrival at the site of the wreck. His mate watches in disbelief as Brock tilts and pans to tape himself looking out of the porthole. Here again Cameron provides the spectator with multiple perspectives. We see what the video camera is recording — including the frame of the video shot and flashing record button — and we are able to see the recording taking place. We see Lovett in his submersible, and we see what he sees out the porthole window. This outside/inside play is something that Cameron has used frequently with great effect, a constant reminder of the fact that everything we see is bound by the "inside view" of the director, bound by the frame of his camera lens; we never get to ultimately step outside to see the whole shot.

When Lovett excavates what he believes to be the safe that will contain the "heart of the ocean" — the valuable missing diamond — he has someone videotaping him as he reaches into the waterlogged safe. When he comes up essentially empty-handed, the first thing he does is turn to the cameraperson and tell them to turn off the camera, underscoring the control which only the director has. We see what the director decides he or she wants us to see, nothing more and nothing less.

As if to make sure we are aware of those limitations, Cameron gives us the mise en abyme of the camera recording the camera. Cameron shoots Brock shooting himself. He shoots the videographer shooting Brock opening the safe. And in an early glimpse of the *Titanic* preparing to set sail, Cameron pans the crowded docks and frames the back of a man who cranks his ancient motion-picture camera, possibly for a newsreel about the departure of the great ship. We are situated behind Cameron, who is behind the cameraman watching him shoot the *Titanic* as Cameron shoots him shooting.

In the early dive scenes of *Titanic*, Cameron shoots the ROV — the remotely operated underwater vehicle. Essentially eyes on a tether, the ROV explores the cracks and crevices of the wreck where humans dare not go, revealing to Lovett what remains of the luxury liner at the bottom of the sea. One of the ROVs dubbed Duncan sported its own pretty nifty headgear, adorned with lights and camera lenses anthropomorphically arranged on its front end. Duncan is additionally equipped with "hands." In a manner similar to the way Laura drives her exo-skeleton in *Xenogenesis*, Lewis, a member of Brock's crew, grabs the mechanical arms that direct Duncan's hands. A hundred yards ahead in a decrepit stateroom of the Titanic, Lewis instructs Duncan to lift up a wardrobe and uncover the safe hidden beneath. Here we have

Cameron shooting Lewis moving his hands to make Duncan's hands move. It is not too much of a stretch to see the logical next step in this progression: the extension of the eye, the extension of the hand, Ripley in the power loader, Quaritch in the AMP suit, and finally the projection of Jake into the body of his avatar. These chains of linkage portend Jake linking into his avatar into the ikran. In his TED talk, Cameron spoke about his own experience piloting the ROV during his dive to the *Titanic*. He said that it felt as if his mind was projected out into the robotic explorer, inside the wreck of the *Titanic*. He felt like he was out there in his little robotic "avatar" immersed in what he described as a "post human future."[49] Displacing the point of view and sending it outward ahead of what is humanly possible to see is a figure that has captivated Cameron's interest and shows up in his documentaries as well as in his narrative films.

When salvage workers come upon Ripley's module in the opening scenes of *Aliens*, they send in a robot whose job it is to determine whether the men can safely enter the capsule. In *The Abyss*, a robot is dispatched to check out the reactor on the submarine to ascertain that it is safe for the divers to enter. When Bud is trying to discover what Coffey is planning to do with the warhead he rescued from the wreck of the *Montana* he dispatches an ROV to spy on Coffey and determine what he is up to. Finally, a remote robot sent out by a deranged Coffey is equipped with a nuclear warhead and heads to the deepest part of the trench where the NTIs have settled. It is that warhead that Bud ultimately has to find and disarm.

Cameron offers the intermediary step between sending out one's eyes and sending out one's entire being in *Avatar* with the wire-tripping apparatus of *Strange Days*. The character Lenny Nero, played by Ralph Fiennes, is an ex-cop who makes a living selling wire-tripping tapes. In a fevered sales pitch he tells a potential client that jacking-in is not simply like TV, but better. *It is like life. You feel it, taste it, smell it. You are doing it.* The technology that ostensibly had been developed by the government to replace wire-tapping had been usurped by a raging black market amid the chaos of Y2K in Los Angeles. The SQUID — Superconducting Quantum Interference Device — is yet another of Cameron's headgear fetishes. Its wire prongs sit on top of the head, and whether you are recording what you are doing or playing back someone else's event, theoretically the device interfaces directly with the cerebral cortex. You get not simply a visual but an embodied, experience.

The narrative of *Strange Days* coalesces around two wire-trip tapes that end up in Lenny's possession: one reveals a brutal rape and murder and one that uncovers the political assassination of a radical black rap artist at the hands of two corrupt cops. The two narratives wend their way toward a frenzied conclusion, in which Lenny and his partner in this escapade, limo driver

"Mace," played by Angela Basset, try to bring the perpetrators of these crimes to justice.

These "tapes" become vehicles for displacing oneself either into the past — which Lenny does obsessively, trying to relive his failed relationship with his ex-girlfriend Faith — or into the experience of another. With the development of the point-of-view camera mentioned above, it was possible to place the spectator in the space of the wire-tripping recorder/viewer, accentuating what is typically accomplished with the shot/reverse shot. The viewer is used to "seeing" through the eyes of the characters in a film. But in the shot/reverse shot we are still outside of the character; we share her point of view, but we are not seeing "out of her eyes." In this instance, though, the lightweight 35 mm camera brings the spectator right into the character's lap.

What we see out of our own eyes includes our appendages coming into our field of vision as they emanate out from our bodies. We see a wisp of our own hair; we might see from a shoulder down, from our thigh out. We can't see our faces or our necks; when we look down, our bodies begin somewhere near the sternum. There are parts of our own bodies we can't see without a mirror. This unique perspective was replicated by the point-of-view camera.

Lenny longs for Faith. He watches and rewatches old wire-trip tapes of the good times they had, and we watch playback of them Rollerblading together that was recorded by Lenny. He falls and we fall with him. We look down and see his legs splayed on the sidewalk. With this visual perspective we are left to imagine the physical sensations that are purported to accompany the "jacking-in."

The entire jacking-in concept serves as the diegetic ancestor of the avatar project, but with a slightly different emotional cast to it. Emerging out of an imagined dystopian future of 1999 (*Strange Days* was made in 1995), jacking-in or wire-tripping was an escape from the riots and violence and ugliness of the world on the eve of the millennium. But it was an escape that, when over, left you exactly where you began. The avatar apparatus may still have been an escape from a dystopian future, but diegetically speaking, it actually transported Jake to an Edenic realm that, in the end, he was able to inhabit.

Like *Avatar*, *Strange Days* also fluxes the inside/outside binary. With the introduction of the wire-trip concept, Cameron raises all the concatenating issues of escapism, of what is real and what is virtual, of the tension between the urge to escape and the rewards of living in the present. Interestingly, there is a brief scene between Lenny and his friend Keith, a man in a wheelchair who works at the nightclub to which Lenny returns in the process of stalking Faith. We presume that Keith could be a veteran of some war when we see that he has lost both his legs from the knees down. Lenny brings Keith a playback of a man running along a pristine beach as a present. Keith dons the headgear, and as he runs, we look down and see strong, whole legs connecting with the wet sand beneath our feet. We notice an attractive young woman running toward him/us, passing, and glancing back at him/us smiling as she goes by.

The camera abruptly cuts back to the present, and we are now outside again, looking at the expression on Keith's face, pained and grateful all at once. Lenny had given him a millennial gift of legs for a moment. It doesn't take much imagination to trace the trajectory from this scene to the scene in which Jake first experiences his avatar's legs in the red clay of Pandora.

The character of Mace who we are meant to surmise is in love with the hapless Lenny tries to get through to him. He spends his days mooning about and chasing after Faith who has left him for the scumbag record producer, Philo. Faith won't give Lenny the time of day, though. Waxing philosophical and more than a little self-reflexive, Faith tells Lenny why she likes the movies better than "playback." "The music comes up and the credits roll and you always know when it is over."[50] But Lenny can't let go. He retreats into a world of fantasy and memory as he clings to Faith through the playing back of old tapes of their relationship, all the while ignoring Mace who is right there, flesh and blood, and in love with him. Mace tries to explain to him that "Life is here right now" in real time and that memories were meant to fade, that they were in fact designed that way.[51] A more direct comment on the allure that the media asserts—film, TV, video, the Internet—and the force it exerts to drag us away from being present to what life offers is hard to imagine.

The controversial tapes that end up in Lenny's possession have the power to change history. When Mace risks everything to get the tape of the dirty cops to the police commissioner, it speaks to her conviction but also to the power of the media in general to elicit change. The whole time the crowds are celebrating in the streets of L.A. and the riot police are right there beside them with shields and night sticks, in the background is an enormous screen — think Times Square size — broadcasting the latest news and entertainment. The playback tape functions as ersatz cinema evoking the potential to seduce and distract as well as the power to transform the ways in which we see.

After Lenny plays back the tape of the execution-style assassination of the rap singer, Jericho One, he tells Mace to watch it. She refuses because she wants no part of the wire-tripping experience. She asks Lenny to just tell her what is on the tape. He is adamant that this is something that has to be *seen*, has to be experienced to fully comprehend; it is *that* important, he tells her. Here Cameron forcefully outlines our complex relationship with our practices of looking and the objects at which we are compelled to look. This theme has long continued to occupy his imagination. One might even surmise that this was his aspiration in *Avatar*, to create a film that transcends the purely visual. If *Philadelphia Enquirer* critic Carrie Rickey's assessment is any indication, we might assume that Cameron succeeded. Rickey told Tom Ashbrook of NPR's *On Point*, "You can argue with the narrative, but as a movie going experience, I was physically involved."[52]

The Eye of the Beholder

The eye as the locus of our vision has fascinated Cameron on two counts. It signals seeing, the physiological process. But for Cameron it also underscores how we look at one another, what we are able to see and what we aren't, who determines what is seen and what is hidden, and ultimately what is beneath the surface. As a filmmaker he has to make both work. The surface of the film must be pristine; it must be authentic, beautifully shot; it has got to be "right." But that isn't enough for Cameron. Cameron is fascinated — as his use of underwater imagery hints — by what lies beneath the surface of the "film façade."

Much has been made in earlier chapters of this book of Cameron's fluxing of the visual paradigm in *Avatar*, where at every turn we are shown how to look at seeing. Cameron points to the ways in which the power-over paradigm is problematic and posits alternative ways to see. In a video about the making of *Avatar*, Cameron inadvertently gives us some insights into this passion of his. He suggests that when we allow ourselves to become the other and see the world with the eyes of an alien, we see anew.[53]

In Chapter One, Cameron's engagement with the eye as symbol and as a representation of what is given to see was explored. While the eye of Jake's avatar has come to stand for the film *Avatar*, it is simply the tail end of a long line of eyes into which Cameron has zoomed.

In *True Lies*, Harry uses a dentist's mirror to look around the corner into a corridor and make sure the coast is clear. Cameron gives us a close-up of the spy's blue eye encircled by the sterling rim of the dental tool. *Strange Days* opens with a tight shot of Ralph Fiennes' green eye and the voice-over, "You ready? Boot it." Lenny closes his eyes and the image turns to static as we shift into virtual reality. This ancestral static begets the wormhole that carries Jake into his avatar.

Cameron uses the eyes of the old and young Rose in *Titanic* to bridge the intervening decades. Soon after we first meet the older Rose, she is examining the drawing that has been recovered from the wreckage as it floats in a tray of water. Cameron zooms in on her blazing blue eyes from the point of view of the drawing in its tray. As her papery thin lids cover them, he cuts to her memory of the drawing as Jack is executing it, followed by another quick cut to Jack's artist eyes as he looks from the paper to the younger Rose and back again. Later on in the film, Cameron superimposes the eye of the young Rose as she poses for Jack with older Rose's eye, as she regales the crew with her memories of that moment.

In both Terminator films, Cameron not only shows us how the Terminator sees, but he juxtaposes the human eye and its mechanical counterpart. When the first Terminator's eye is injured, he retreats to repair it. In a particularly gruesomely graphic scene, the Terminator removes the human facsimile of an eyeball with an exacto knife and throws it into the sink. He scrapes away any loose flesh from the eye socket revealing his real machinic eye underneath. A close up of this glowing red mechanical eye exposes the opening and closing of the aperture. This eye does not have the limitations of the gelatinous orb with which humans are graced. This eye resembles nothing as much as a miniature camera, with powerful zoom capabilities, linked to the computer chip brain of the Terminator which makes visible the data readouts described above.

To the Terminator, the human eye was simply cosmetic, dispensable. Its loss does not disrupt his ability to see. But the scene raises the issue of the relationship between our human eye and its machinic extensions. All of the video footage, surveillance, ROVs, sonar, radar, computer screens, one-way mirrors, night goggles, binoculars, and microscopes together point to Cameron's engagement with our practices of looking, the ways in which our seeing is extended by mechanical eyes and the ways in which those eyes keep us from seeing clearly. Cameron is pointing to both. Yes, he is impressed with machines that extend what we are given to see. As a filmmaker he relies on and even improves on them with his innovations. But his is also a cautionary tale. There is a warning here, at times metaphorical, and at times in his films it is explicit.

The metaphorical "eye" — in other words, the ways in which we see — also figures prominently in Cameron's films that pre-date *Avatar*. Rose is surprised and impressed with Jack's drawings as she thumbs through his sketch pad on the deck of the *Titanic*. She sees his mastery of line, his "good eye," and tells him, "You really *see* people." The drawings themselves speak to what and how Jack sees, focusing on the gnarled hands of an old woman holding an infant, the sad woman bedecked in jewels who sits at the bar night after night waiting for her lost love, the elegant long fingers of the one-legged prostitute who has agreed to model for him. "I see *you*," is Jack's prescient response to Rose's observation.

Jack draws Rose languishing nude on the stateroom divan. Cameron's camera eye lingers on the artist's tools — the charcoal, the conté crayon he sharpens, the nib of a pen, all tucked neatly in place in a well-worn pouch —

as Jack caresses Rose's body with his eyes and the stick of black in his hand. Nothing shows us seeing as purely as this scene, cutting back and forth from Rose to Jack's eyes, to his hands, and finally to the drawing that comes to life.

That Jack does indeed see through to what is essential reverberates throughout *Titanic* in the motifs that rely on both the imagery of the sea as well as the tiered system of decks pointing to the class stratification and its transparent inequities. The technology of the *Titanic* offered the promise of speed and luxury, of a record-breaking crossing splashed out in headlines, but delivered a sobering and humbling return. Cameron brought this home by juxtaposing what lay beneath — the red-hot fiery world of the furnaces in the engine room — with the cold blue waters surrounding the ship. The discrepancy between the lively celebratory reveling of the steerage class and the stuffy constrained "deadness" of the first-class passengers is made vivid as Rose distractedly watches a very young girl in white cotton gloves smooth her napkin on her lap while her mother admonishes her to sit up straight at the table.

The shiny veneer of propriety blinds many on the ship to what is just. As the water floods the luxurious floating city of lights, it covers all of what had glittered, all of what had been extolled beyond the value of human life. Gold-rimmed china clanks beneath the rising waters; Monet's lilies float helplessly as the sea surges. When all that was believed to be of value is washed away, what is left to see?

In the sandy floor beneath the wreckage, Cameron's lens finds a pair of broken spectacles. The destruction — the exploding, shattering, smashing — of glass has become a Cameron trademark. But if we understand the function of glass as a barrier, the smashing of it becomes a sign of connection, of seeing more clearly, and as Jack does, more thoroughly. A pointed example of this occurs during *True Lies*, when Jamie Lee Curtis is being interrogated.

Harry and Gibson are hidden behind the two-way mirror. On their side of the glass, there is all manner of recording apparatus — a video recorder, infrared scans, and so forth. Their voices are electronically modified and distorted so that Helen has no idea that her husband Harry is her inquisitor. In the guise of an interrogation, Harry is trying to find out whether his wife still loves him. Here Cameron's doubling will be recognized, as Harry's whole life as a spy is a double life and here again we find him dissembling. Harry keeps poking and prodding and trying to ascertain whether or not Helen has had sex with Simon — used car salesman cum spy — until finally she loses her patience. She picks up the metal stool that she has been sitting on and hefts it into the one-way mirror, shattering the glass as she does so. At this point, Harry is convinced that she still loves him and all that was hidden from him — her loyalty and unflagging love — becomes visible. The doubt and duplicity shattered like the two-way mirror.

The entire Russian/U.S. conflict played out in the background of *The Abyss* is the result of faulty seeing. They both have picked up evidence of an unidentified object moving at impossible speeds through the deep, and each believes the other is behind it. Suffering from high pressure nervous syndrome, Lieutenant Coffey loses his ability to think clearly and sees enemies every-where. While strategizing with Bud to come up with a way to prevent a nuclear event, Lindsey casts their predicament in terms of how they see. She tells Bud, "We all see what we want to see. Coffey looks and sees the Russians. He sees hate and fear. You have to look with better eyes than that."[54] Looking with better eyes is what Cameron would have us all do.

The theme of how we see, in other words whether our vision is circum-scribed or circumspect, wends its way throughout Cameron's films. Obviously the theme of what is visible and what is not is etched into the narrative of *Strange Days*. The wire-tripping tapes that fall into Lenny's hands threaten to make visible the brutal rape/murders, Jericho One's assassination, and the racist corruption of the police. Lenny can't see Mace and the love she has for him. The black-market popularity of the wire-trip tapes speaks to the desire to escape, to "see" someone else's life. Cameron suggests here that we look at how we relate to our screens, to the ubiquitous media shower, to television, and asks in turn, are we escaping? Are we tuning out by tuning in? Are we forgoing our lived experience for something virtual? All of these questions are revisited and resonate strongly in *Avatar*. But there is also another side to the question of how we see.

Cameron inserts a line in *Strange Days* that speaks to his artist's eye, the cameraperson's eye, the eye whose job it is to see. In a playback tape that Lenny revisits of him and Faith about to make love, Faith looks directly into Lenny's eyes — which due to the innovation of the point-of-view camera is tantamount to looking into the eyes of the spectator — and tells him that she loves his eyes. She loves the way he sees. And while he continues to "see" her with loving eyes, she becomes blind to him and his feeling for her. Here we might notice the nascent idea for the "I see you" of the Na'vi, a recognition of the correlation between *how* we see and how we are apt to treat one another.

In several of his films Cameron highlights a type of hubris that results in a vision clouded by a stubborn refusal to see. We have looked at this in *Avatar* in the characters of Selfridge and Quaritch. But it finds its way into the rest of his work. Carter Burke, the head of Ripley's expedition, believes he knows what is best with regard to the aliens, as does the inexperienced Lieutenant Gorman. Together they refuse to see and acknowledge the danger, and consequently the results are disastrous. Lieutenant Coffey, in *The Abyss*, doesn't see that he is losing his grip on reality and almost causes a nuclear holocaust. Bruce Ismay, chairman of the White Star Line that conceived of and financed the *Titanic*, was more concerned with the headlines that would be made if the ship arrived early. He presses the captain, against his better judgment, to light the last four boilers even though the engine hasn't properly been "run in." Cameron hits two birds with this one stone of a scene, hinting at the pressures, even in the early twentieth century, that the press can exert, as well as pointing at Ismay's foolhardy illusion of invincibility. It was Ismay's shortsightedness that was also responsible for reducing the number of lifeboats from 48 to the 16 mandated. He didn't want the lifeboats to clutter the luxurious deck of the behemoth. Finally, in the Terminator series, even Sarah Connor becomes so blinded by her love of and determination to save her son that she terrorizes and almost kills the inventor of Skynet, Myles Dyson.

The Human and the Machinic

Across Cameron's body of work, he brings into focus both the human and the machinic eye. In *Avatar*, Cameron brings the two together. He tells us, "The eye came to life in *Avatar*."[55] But it is not only the eye that Cameron zeroes in on. Right from his first film he has been enthralled with the complex relationship between human and machine. This motif infuses much of his work and becomes central in the two Terminator films, in *Titanic*, *Strange Days* and of course in *Avatar*.

A stripped-down parable, *Xenogenesis* offers up little more than the battle between the human and the robot. But even in this first short adventure in filmmaking, Cameron is melding the human and machinic, specifically in the case of Laura who extends her human capabilities through the use of robotics. Cameron uses the human who relies on technology and the machine who exhibits human tendencies to blur the boundaries between the two, evoking the cybernetic and the post-human, raising questions as pertinent to our lives today as they were in 1984 when the first Terminator film was released.

Cameron alludes to his own childhood in which he was steeped in the science-fiction genre where abundant warnings prevailed "about technology, about science, about the military and the government."[56] A marriage between dire alarm and the human/machinic interaction produces the progeny of the Terminator series located in a post-apocalyptic future in which machines have all but destroyed the earth, but the surviving humans have banded together and resist the rule of Skynet. Cameron blurs the human/machinic boundary by giving us the Terminator, a cyborg that appears human on the surface, and Sarah Connor, a human who becomes almost machine-like in her ruthless attempt to save her son at all cost. In the first Terminator film, a tongue-in-cheek outgoing message brings the slippage between the two into focus. Sarah

Connor's roommate's phone answering machine announces, "Fooled you. This is just a machine, but machines need love, too."[57] John Connor connects deeply with the second Terminator who has traveled back in time to protect him. His mother observes this affection and realizes that, in some bizarre sense, this Terminator may be the best father figure possible. He will always be there, he will never desert John, and he would — and does — give his life to save John's. Sarah notes, "In an insane world, it was the sanest choice."[58]

Of all the Terminator's attempts to fit in and to learn to be more human — like *Star Trek*'s Data, humor eludes him — it is his sacrifice at the end of the film that speaks most eloquently to his acquired humanity. Similarly, in *Aliens* we have Bishop, the "synthetic" to whom Ripley initially has an averse reaction. But it is Bishop who volunteers to crawl 180 meters through a claustrophobic tunnel to readjust the satellite dish so that he can remotely pilot the second ship and bring it to the surface of the planet for their escape. Impaled by the deadly alien's tail and torn in two, he still manages to grab Newt and hold her fast, keeping her from being sucked out the airlock and into deep space.

Cameron has suggested that these tales of machines are meant to be allegorical, meant to symbolize our own tendency toward dehumanization. When a cop lacks compassion, when a therapist is without empathy, Cameron sees them as a machine in human form.[59] This, then, is the rigid mechanical behavior evidenced in the characters of Quaritch, Selfridge and Carter Burke; in the police who find Reese's tale of the future too unbelievable to be anything but madness; in Ismay's pressure to push the *Titanic* in ways that may have increased the likelihood of its colliding with an iceberg.

But Cameron is also fascinated by the smudging of the ostensibly clearly drawn line of demarcation between the human and the machine. This was examined in detail in the discussion of the relationship between nature and technology in *Avatar* in Chapter Two. But Cameron's propensity for extending human perception by way of the machinic seeps into many of his stories. And no wonder, given the extent to which today we are all extending our virtual selves out into the ether in bytes and bits, on blogs and in tweets, the extent to which most of us are always just a click — and not the military kind — away from almost anything.

In *The Abyss*, the ROVs extend what the crew is able to see; the breathing apparatuses — the scuba tanks, the submersibles, and the flouro-carbonated water — push the boundaries of where humans are capable of going. The crew of the *Montana* and the grunts on the oil rig were all able to exist happily at extreme depths because they were encased in a protective technology that flips the Terminator on its head: machine outside, human in. When Lindsey encounters the aliens and touches their gliding ship, she tries to describe her experience to Bud. She tells him that the aliens weren't riding around in a tin can, the kind that humans would build. "It was a machine, but it was alive; it was like a dance of light."[60]

Ripley driving the armored tank into the station to rescue the soldiers from the aliens is another case in point. The wire-tripping device in *Strange Days* extends the visual experience of the ROV and sends the senses into a virtual romp, firing someone else's neurons. When the wire-tripping device is used as a weapon, it signifies the dangers inherent in how and to what extent we use technology. Two characters have their brains scrambled by an over-amplification of the SQUID's playback.

In *Aliens*, remote robot sentries are set up to guard the perimeter. Equipped with sensors, they automatically shoot when something — any-thing — moves, for as long as their ammo holds out, protecting the platoon. Ripley, however, sets the standard for the human in the machine when she leaps into the power loader and draws on its mechanical heft and strength to defeat the deadly, multi-mouthed alien queen. Ripley sits somewhere between Laura (*Xenogenesis*), who churned her arms to make her exo-skeleton move, and Quaritch, who barely had to make a micro-gesture and his AMP suit would do just that — amplify his movement and its power tenfold. Ripley, who confronts the seriously scary queen mother alien in her trusty yellow hunk of metal, motivated the power loader with joystick technology; the swivel of her thumb could direct its massive pincerlike arms to squeeze one of the alien's heads, or could blast flames at the big bug.

In yet another example of the melding of the machine and the man, we have the character of Logan Cale, a cyber-journalist, played by Michael Weatherly, who befriends Max and saves her life in the final episode of the *Dark Angel* series. Logan is shot in the opening episode and loses the use of his legs. When Max's DNA, which at first is helpful, turns deadly to Logan, he procures mechanized leg braces from Manticore, the company responsible for creating the transgenics and mutants in the first place. These hydraulic leg braces not only enable Logan to perambulate, but give his legs super strength so that he can jump several stories high and kick powerfully enough to do his enemies serious damage.[61]

Othering

The opposition between the human and the machine is simply one specific form of the generic strife between any "us" and any "them" — the ten-dency we have to distance ourselves from what we perceive as different or threatening, from what we consider "other." In almost every film of Cameron's, this estrangement is played out, sometimes resulting in the transformation of the ways in which characters see the "other," sometimes not. The refrain of the "other" that is hinted at in almost all of his films becomes fully orchestrated in *Avatar*.

We have looked at the us/them of the human/machinic in *Xenogenesis*, the two Terminator films, *Aliens*, and *Avatar*, but it also arises in some other flavors in others of Cameron's films. If we follow the trajectory from *Aliens* to *Avatar*, it lines up nicely with what we might imagine was Cameron's own transformation. He articulates an arc that moves from the reifying, power-over paradigm of Western civilization — fear and hatred of the other as exemplified in *Aliens*— to a circumspect relationship which shifts and fluctuates instead of fixes, in which the "other," the Na'vi in this case, reveals what is healing, positive, and redemptive and ultimately is embraced.

Aliens portrays the conflict as bare bones with the most underdeveloped resolution. The aliens are bad, perhaps even evil. And the humans — who are of course good — are all about blowing them off of the face of the planet they inhabit and out of the universe. Even in *Aliens*, however, there are hints of a less than clear divide between the *us* and the *them*. Burke represents another "them"— the corporate, greedy, "let's make a profit" them that returns in *Avatar* with a vengeance. Burke distances himself from the army grunts and from Ripley at every turn. When Lieutenant Gorman is incapacitated, Ripley points out that the chain of command puts Corporal Hicks in charge. Horrified, Burke insists that a grunt like the corporal isn't fit to make the call to demolish what he maintains is a multi-million-dollar installation. In no uncertain terms we have the grunt versus the corporate lackey, military versus civilian, hands dirty versus hands clean. Burke, like Selfridge to follow, is responsible for the deaths of hundreds of beings. But Burke is even willing to take direct action against Ripley when he feels threatened by her stance. After his unsuccessful attempt to kill Ripley by releasing the facehuggers in the locked lab where she sleeps, she is quick to point out that even the aliens, as despicable as they are, aren't "fucking each other over for a percentage."[62]

It would be oversimplifying to label the sides simply the "haves" against the "have-nots," although that is clearly the case in *Titanic*. There is nothing subtle about the stratification of classes on that ship and its impact on who lived and who didn't as memorialized in story and in song. The *Dark Angel* series blatantly pits the mutants/transgenics against the humans who created them, the humans who fear them, and the humans who want to destroy them. In *Strange Days*, we are given the corruption of a police state at the turn of the century versus the poor, disenfranchised, and disgruntled populace of L.A. In *The Abyss*, Cameron exploits the tension between the tightly knit group of grunts who work on the oil platform and the highly skilled, highly trained elite Navy SEALs. The oil platform workers are laid back, unorthodox, down to earth. The SEALs are painted as by the book, tight-assed, and as Lindsey notes, "about as much fun as a tax-audit."[63] These close-up tensions are backgrounded by the antagonisms between the United States and Russia, another major figure of an us and a them which in *The Abyss* is used to artic-ulate hostility born simply of misunderstanding and misinformation.

When the humans encounter the underwater aliens, they understand them immediately to be simply "not us." Cameron turns the tables in this film — which followed on the heels of *Aliens*— when he shows that these aliens see the human race as potentially dangerous and unworthy of existence. As the NTIs prepare to send out a series of monolithic tidal waves that would destroy the major cities of the world, they become aware of Bud's self-sacrifice to ensure that the nukes in the abyss are disarmed. After the NTIs rescue him from drowning they present him with a watery slide show of sorts, presenting images of war, of nuclear explosions, of starvation, of atrocities. When he asks them why they changed their minds and pulled back the tidal waves to spare the human race, they show him the words of what he thought would be his final message to Lindsey: "Knew this was one way ticket but you know I had to come. Love you wife."[64]

Transformation

In *The Abyss*, it is the aliens whose vision is transformed, who come to see the humans more clearly in all their complexity and in the end are willing to rescue Bud and all of the workers on the platform. The figure of transforma-tion infuses and enlivens much of Cameron's work. *Avatar* refines this theme of the hero's quest, but Cameron had been playing with and fine-tuning it for years prior to this. Cameron has a soft spot for the loser, the wounded, the trapped, the traumatized, and places them in circumstances — often beyond their control — which provide the vehicle for healing, for freedom, for release. Sarah Connor is an innocent, perky waitress who suddenly finds herself the target of a determined, maniacal Terminator. She is hunted down and then rescued by a man who asks her to believe that he comes from a future in which the Earth has been destroyed and in which her not-yet-born son has become the pivotal hope of humankind. By the time we meet her in the sec-ond Terminator film, she is a militant warrior, fanatically protecting the life of her ten-year-old son. She has gone so far in the direction of keeping him safe that she no longer has access to her human connection to him. She has become almost a machine herself. It is only when it comes to destroying the last Skynet chip that paradoxically the Terminator cracks her machinelike shell. He demonstrates that he has learned the value of human life. He insists, despite John's despair and his direct order, that Sarah destroy him too, since his brain is the repository of the last Skynet chip. The film ends with Sarah speaking of a renewed sense of hopefulness. Her experience of the machine that learns to care and sacrifices himself for the benefit of humankind suggests to her the possibility that humans might be able to learn this lesson as well.

Ripley finds herself awakened after her almost six-decade-long hyper-sleep, traumatized and suffering from a form of PTSD. She learns that in her long absence, her daughter has not only grown up but has died at the age of 66 and she has missed not only her daughter's 11th birthday—by which date she had promised to return—but her entire life. The grief and trauma are unwieldy, and she suffers from nightmares, waking in a cold sweat night after night. She is mistrustful of everyone, but particularly of Bishop, the synthetic being. Through their encounter with the aliens on the terra-formed planet, she is forced to come to grips with her own "alienation," forced to rely on other beings, including Hicks and Bishop, to be able to successfully rescue Newt. Her relationship with the little girl transforms and heals her, and the necessity of acting on Newt's behalf enables Ripley to move through her own trauma.

When we first meet Max of the TV series *Dark Angel*, she has been living on her own, having successfully escaped from Manticore, the secret government facility where she was being held, ten years earlier. While she never gives up searching for her peers who also escaped, she is a loner who trusts no one and has no concern for bettering the world that had been thrown into chaos when terrorists set off a "pulse" weapon that destroyed all the electronics worldwide. She first meets Logan when she tries to steal a statue from him. Fascinated by her strength, speed and agility, Logan tries to persuade her to join his activist efforts. Max is uninterested. But as the series progresses, she changes. In part due to his example—Logan is shot and paralyzed trying to protect a witness—Max comes to take her proper role as leader, as defender of the mutants/transgenics, and as someone who has learned to be part of something larger than herself.

Strange Days' Lenny is portrayed as a loser. An ex-cop—we get the feeling not by choice—he is a con man and a big talker, hawking his wares to make ends meet. He has lost the love of his life, and while he doesn't do drugs, he is addicted to the past. He spends his time reliving moments with his ex, Faith, by wire-tripping. His relationship with Mace appears one-sided: he takes and she gives. He demonstrates no respect for her, interferes with her work—he hijacks one of her limo clients so that he can sell some wire-trip tapes—and thinks only about how he is going to be able to get to Faith, to convince her to come back to him. When Mace tries to help him see the way he is living, he argues that he can't help loving Faith, even if his feelings aren't returned. While his pathetic-ness may cause confusion over why Mace even bothers with him, we are given a flashback that sheds a sliver of light on her attachment to him. He was the police officer on the scene during the arrest of her husband, and when she came home and found him in her house, he was taking care of her son, Zander, protecting him from the mayhem engendered by his father. In that moment we see that perhaps there is something buried and unreachable that Lenny has to offer.

Whether it is the betrayal of his friend Max, the brutal deaths he witnesses on the snuff tapes that come into his possession, the shock of the stab wound in the back, or Mace's bravery and commitment to seeking retribution, by the movie's end, Lenny is returned to something resembling his former compassionate and altruistic self. When one of the dirty cops attempts to shoot Mace, Lenny shields her with his body. The film ends not only with a promise of hope for the millennium, but also for Lenny and Mace. He is finally able to see her and what she has been offering all along.

By her own admission, Rose felt that as she boarded the *Titanic*, she was boarding not the ship of dreams, but a slave ship taking her home in chains. The metaphor old Rose uses to describe her feelings was that she saw herself standing at a great precipice without anyone there to pull her back. When she does step over the railing at the stern of the ship and readies herself to jump, it is Jack who is there, promising to jump if she jumps, ready to pull her back. When her fiancé presents her with the "heart of the ocean," the astounding blue diamond necklace, she feels her fate is sealed. While he tells her that it is a token of his feelings for her, she sees it is a shackle.

When Jack manages to snatch her from her walk on the promenade deck and declare his love for her, she emphatically refuses him, taking one last stab at accepting her station and responsibilities. But soon after she denies him she is struck by the vision of the small girl in the dining room, sitting ramrod rigid, smoothing her napkin elegantly with white-gloved hands, and the limitations of life ahead become unbearable. This is illustrated only too clearly in the scene where her mother is literally pulling the strings of Rose's corset so tightly that she can no longer breathe. Cameron emphasizes Rose's lot as a woman with few choices, while at the same time underscoring her mother's skewed values. Prostituting her daughter is preferable, she makes plain, to having to part with their "fine things" with their "memories."[65]

Jack sees that Rose's spirit is in jeopardy. And while she reminds him that it isn't his job to save her, when she decides that the life that awaits her is the wrong life, she finds Jack on the prow of the ship. The antithesis of her corset tightening, in this iconic scene Rose stands suspended in the air with sky and sea all about her, endless space. Her arms extend outward and she declares, "I'm flying!" pointing to the possibility of her freedom ahead.[66]

When she asks Jack to draw her nude with just her diamond around her neck, she is transforming not only herself, but the object of her imprisonment as well. She leaves the drawing in the safe for her fiancé with a note suggesting that now he can keep her — a facsimile any way — locked up in the safe just the way he would like. The heart of the ocean metamorphoses from her fetter to the key to her freedom. And while in her youth she was adamant that it was not Jack's job to save her, the older Rose testifies that Jack Dawson indeed did save her, "in every way that a person could be saved."[67] In a montage of her personal photos, Cameron reveals the life of adventure — deep-sea fishing, horseback riding by the roller coaster in Santa Monica, piloting a plane — that Rose ended up living instead of the life her mother had prescribed.

Love Is All You Need

Interestingly in both *True Lies* and *The Abyss*, the story does not center on a broken individual becoming transformed and experiencing redemption, but instead on a broken relationship. The double life Harry is leading has left Helen feeling isolated and neglected, as well as dissatisfied with what she is able to accomplish in her life. As a result of her own subterfuge she causes a crisis of faith on Harry's part. When the curtain of duplicity falls away revealing the truth of their situation, the underlying love they still feel for one another resurfaces and is rekindled. When their daughter is threatened, Harry's secret life is blown wide open as he comes to her rescue. Their family becomes whole again, if still somewhat quirky.

In the early scenes of *The Abyss* we are presented with the broken marriage of Lindsey and Bud. On the verge of a divorce and brimming with hostility toward one another, neither is pleased to be in the situation where they are forced to work together in close quarters under life-threatening circumstances. But in fact, the very real threat of nuclear destruction, of alien intervention, of the crazy Lieutenant Coffey about to blow them sky high, dwarfs their differences and the damage done to their marriage. As they each face their spouse's imminent death, the tensions between them pale, and their connection is revitalized and deepened after all.

There is no doubt that Cameron loves his machines, his aliens, the exploding of glass buildings, and the shearing of metal in action-packed car chases. But underlying his fascination with doubling and dissembling, with losers and their journeys to self-actualization, is his love of love. It is, in no uncertain terms, love that drives his stories, love that reaches out just like his 3-D SimulCam and touches audiences. And while it may be bittersweet and certainly less than perfect, Cameron's portraits of love include those that transgress traditional boundaries, engender the manifestation of great courage in the face of tremendous risks, and above all in the process transform the lovers.

It is love that brings Kyle Reese across time to find Sarah Connor and make love to her, conceiving their son John. It is love that drives Ellen Ripley to risk life and limb, to confront her fears and the acid-blooded aliens, and to rescue Newt and carry Hicks to safety. It is love that propels Sarah Connor to fight against her incarceration and drugging, to stay strong so that she can once again be a mother to John. And it is love that brings John and the Terminator to break her out of the asylum. It is some kind of love — for John, for humanity even — that motivates the Terminator to convince Sarah and John to destroy him so that the human race can endure.

It was love that gave Lindsey the courage to let herself drown, to trust that Bud would get her back to the oil platform quickly enough to revive her, and it was love that moved Bud to agree to dive to the deadly depths to disarm the nuke, believing it would be a dive from which he would not return. It was witnessing this love-motivated sacrifice that changed the NTIs assessment of what humans were capable of and resulted in their decision to divert the devastating tidal waves. It was Mace's steadfastness, her devotion to Lenny, that brought him back from the brink of destruction to realize his own affection for her. And it was Mace's love for humanity and her belief in the power of redemption that gave her the courage to risk her own life to bring the corrupt cops down. Transgressing racial boundaries, their kiss at the conclusion of the movie and the beginning of the millennium is a kiss of possibility, of hope for the future, of tolerance, of change.

Rose and Jack's love defied the odds and broke through rigid class taboos. Their clear-sighted and some might argue naïve desire — if Jack had lived, how would they have survived? Would Rose have been so easily able to let go of the luxury and comfort she was used to? — gave them the courage to face their potentially imminent deaths. Cameron articulates his interest in exploring how people thrown into a situation over which they have no control — a sinking ship, a flooding oil platform, an impending nuclear holocaust, a deadly race of aliens, being flown to a far-off moon and transposed into the body of an alien — confront and surmount their circumstances.[68] If his films are any indication, they can face their lives in more meaningful ways if in that process they also love.

It could be the love of a child, of a person of a different race or species, the love of someone from whom they have become estranged, the love of a planet, the love of all forms of life. While perhaps this might smack of cliché, there is a power and truth to this maxim which points to why it has become clichéd in the first place. Its power lies in the fact that this portrayal of love links to the spectator who has also loved, much like Jake linking to his avatar. This connection, this identification, is at the heart of cinema, at the heart of all storytelling. And while there are no certainties — Rose risks everything to be with Jack and he dies in the icy water by her side; Max and Logan hold each other's hands through the barrier of protective gloves; Lenny and Mace's kiss is a mere glimmer of what the new century might hold — Cameron paints a picture in which love is a driving force for change, for a shift in what we are given to see, and the way in which we are able to see it.

While it is in the last scene of *Terminator 2* that Sarah Connor articulates her hope for a future, a hope that is born in the heart of a machine — and here we might sit up and take notice of another Tin Man with a heart!— it is in the last scene of *The Terminator* that there is a visual signification of the filmic arena that Cameron has inhabited, perfected and staked out as his own. Sarah Connor is pregnant with John and in Mexico. She fills up the gasoline tank of her Jeep and heads down a two-lane highway as a storm is imminent. The lighting is dramatic. On the left side of the screen we see the dark and threatening storm clouds approaching. On the right the sky is blue, the mountains in the distance brightly lit and tinted pink. The red Jeep on the black tarmac bifurcates the landscape. In the driver's seat the pregnant Connor, conveying fecundity, creativity, new life and possibility, straddles the light and the dark. Both are visible on the horizon, both are contained within the frame.

It is this interstice that Cameron excavates, the space between light and dark, between human and machine, between technology and nature, between chick flick and action-packed adventure, between self and other, between old-fashioned storytelling and new-fangled technology. Cameron's cinematic frame is large enough to contain it all. As Sarah drives into an unknown future, the thunder roars, a driving techno beat comes up, and the credits start to roll. Like Faith, we know that the movie is over, but we also know that the story isn't.

Notes

Introduction

1. David Brooks, "The Messiah Complex," *New York Times*, January 7, 2010, http://www.ny times.com/2010/01/08/opinion/08brooks.html.
2. Manohla Dargis, "A New Eden, Both Cosmic and Cinematic," *New York Times*, December 18, 2009, http://movies.nytimes.com/2009/12/18/movies/18avatar.html.
3. Betsy Schiffman, *Daily Finance*, April 26, 2010, http://srph.it/dcVkSW.
4. Christian Metz, "The Imaginary Signifier, [Excerpts]," in *Narrative, Apparatus, Ideology*, ed. Philip Rosen (New York: Columbia University Press, 1986).
5. With thanks to Professor Paul Chafe, English Department, Ryerson University, Toronto, for this particular lens.

Chapter One

1. Laura Mulvey, "Visual Pleasure and Narrative Cinema," in *The Routledge Critical and Cultural Theory Reader*, ed. Neil Badmington and Julia Thomas (New York: Routledge, 2008).
2. Rosalind Galt, "The Obviousness of Cinema," *World Picture* 2 (Autumn 2009), http://english.okstate.edu/worldpicture/WP_2/PDF%20Docs/GaltPDF.pdf.
3. See Thomas Lamarre, *The Anime Machine: A Media Theory of Animation* (Minneapolis: University of Minnesota Press, 2009), 26.
4. M. Merleau-Ponty, "The Intertwining — the Chiasm," in *The Continental Aesthetics Reader*, ed. Clive Cazeaux (London: Routledge, 2000), 164.
5. See Paul Crowther, "The Experience of Art: Some Problems and Possibilities of Hermeneutical Analysis," *Philosophical and Phenomenological Research* 43, no. 3 (March 1983), and Martin Heidegger, *The Origin of the Work of Art*, ed. Clive Cazeaux, trans. Albert Hofstadter, in *The Continental Aesthetics Reader* (London: Routledge, 2000).
6. David Brooks, "The Messiah Complex," *New York Times*, Op-Ed Column, January 7, 2010, http://www.nytimes.com/2010/01/08/opinion/08brooks.html.
7. *Avatar*, DVD, directed by James Cameron (USA: Twentieth Century–Fox Film Corporation, Dune Entertainment, Ingenious Film Partners, 2009).
8. This is one of many instances that have been cited to emphasize the badly written dialog in the film. I personally thought it was intentionally trite, tongue in cheek.
9. See Chapter Four for an in-depth investigation of the narrative structure of *Avatar*.
10. Susan Sontag, *On Photography* (New York: Picador, 1973), 8.
11. Stephen Houlgate, "Vision, Reflection and Openness: The 'Hegemony of Vision' from a Hegelian Point of View," in *Modernity and the Hegemony of Vision*, ed. David Michael Levin (Los Angeles: University of California Press, 1993).
12. John Dewey, *Art as Experience* (New York: Perigee Books, 1934).

13. David Michael Levin, ed., *Sites of Vision: The Discursive Construction of Sight in the History of Philosophy* (Cambridge, MA: MIT Press, 1999).

14. Martin Jay, "Scopic Regimes of Modernity," in *Vision and Visuality,* ed. Hal Foster (New York: New Press, 1988), 3.

15. Martin Heidegger, *Being and Time,* trans. Joan Stambaugh (Albany: State University of New York, 1996), 15.

16. Clive Cazeaux, "Theorizing Theory and Practice," *Point: Art and Design Journal* 7 (1999), 26–31.

17. Heidegger, *Being and Time,* 65.

18. Ibid.

19. *Avatar,* DVD, directed by James Cameron (USA: Twentieth Century–Fox Film Corporation, Dune Entertainment, Ingenious Film Partners, 2009).

20. Ibid.

21. Ibid.

22. Ibid.

23. See Robert Heinlein, *Stranger in a Strange Land* (New York: Putnam, 1961).

24. *Avatar.*

25. Daniel Mendelsohn, "The Wizard: *Avatar,*" *New York Review of Books,* March 25, 2010, http://www.nybooks.com/articles/archives/2010/mar/25/the-wizard.

26. Carrie Rickey, "Previewing the Oscars 2010," *On Point,* March 5, 2010, WBUR, http://onpoint.wbur.org/2010/03/05/the-oscars-2010.

27. *Avatar.*

28. Merleau-Ponty, "The Intertwining — the Chiasm," 166.

29. Ibid., 167.

30. Ibid., 165.

31. Rorty doesn't seem to be disturbed by the inherent paradox in choosing to adopt this term as a replacement for the "epithet" *relativist,* which he seems to deplore.

32. Richard Rorty, *Philosophy and Social Hope* (London: Penguin, 1999), 47. His list here includes William James, Friedrich Nietzsche, Donald Davidson, Jacques Derrida, Hilary Putnam, Bruno Latour, John Dewey, and Michel Foucault.

33. Ibid.

34. Ibid.

35. Mendelsohn, "The Wizard: *Avatar.*"

36. Terry Gross. "James Cameron: Pushing the Limits of Imagination," *Fresh Air,* February 18, 2010, http://www.npr.org/player/v2/mediaPlayer.html?action=1&t=1&islist=false&id=123810319&m=123847924.

37. It is worth noting here that Cameron was not the first to utilize "flux" in this way. In the *Back to the Future* movies, it is the "flux capacitor" that enables time travel.

38. *Avatar.*

39. Ibid.

40. "Making a Scene: *Avatar,*" Fox Movie Channel, Sam Hurwitz Productions, http://www.hulu.com/watch/110975/making-a-scene-avatar.

Chapter Two

1. Online Etymology Dictionary, http://www.etymonline.com/index.php?term=technology.

2. Sven Birkerts, *The Gutenberg Elegies* (New York: Faber & Faber, 2006), xii.

3. Matt Richtel, "Growing Up Digital, Wired for Distraction," *New York Times,* November 21, 2010, A1, A20.

4. Martin Kemp, *The Science of Art: Optical Themes in Western Art from Brunelleschi to Seurat* (New Haven, CT: Yale University Press, 1990), 169.

5. M. Heidegger, "The Question Concerning Technology," in *Martin Heidegger: Basic Writings,* ed. D. F. Krell (New York: HarperCollins, 1953), 312.

6. Ibid., 312.

7. Ibid., 318.

8. Ibid., 315.

9. Ibid., 316.

10. Heidegger, *Being and Time*, 49.

11. D. M. Levin, *The Philosopher's Gaze: Modernity in the Shadows of Enlightenment* (Berkeley: University of California Press, 1999), 48.

12. Cazeaux, "Theorizing Theory and Practice," 26–31.

13. Levin, *The Philosopher's Gaze*, 182. The brackets are Levin's, and he footnotes this quote from Heidegger: "The Question Concerning Technology," in *The Question Concerning Technology and Other Essays* (New York: Harper & Row, 1977), 28.

14. Eric Norden, "Marshall McLuhan: A Candid Conversation with the High Priest of Popcult and Metaphysician of Media," *Playboy*, March 1969, http://www.nextnature.net/2009/12/the-playboy-interview-marshall-mcluhan.

15. Ibid.

16. Ibid.

17. Cazeaux, "Theorizing Theory and Practice," 29.

18. Heidegger, "The Question Concerning Technology" (1953), 317.

19. Ibid., 317.

20. Ibid., 318.

21. Ibid., 318.

22. Ibid., 320.

23. Ibid., 321.

24. "'Wired Magazine' Co-Founder's Tech Advice for Academics," interview with Kevin Kelly, Jeff Young, *Chronicle of Higher Education*, November 9, 2010, http://chronicle.com/article/Audio-Tech-Therapy-Wired/125229.

25. Ibid., 322.

26. Ibid., 333.

27. Ibid., 340.

28. Norden, "Marshall McLuhan," 340.

29. Heidegger, "The Question Concerning Technology" (1953), 330.

30. Mordecai Roshwald, *Dreams and Nightmares: Science and Technology in Myth and Fiction*, eds. Donald E. Palumbo and C. W. Sullivan (Jefferson, NC: McFarland, 2008).

31. M. Heidegger, *Discourse on Thinking* (New York: Harper & Row, 1966), 56.

32. Gary Westfahl, "All Energy Is Borrowed," *Locus Online*, December 20, 2009, http://www.locusmag.com/Reviews/2009/12/all-energy-is-borrowed-review-of-avatar.html.

33. Ibid.

34. Dennis Danvers, *Circuit of Heaven* (New York: Avon, 1998).

35. *Pandorapedia: The Official Field Guide*, http://www.pandorapedia.com/human_operations/rda/the_avatar_program.

36. Heidegger, "The Question Concerning Technology" (1953), 324.

37. Birkerts, *Gutenberg Elegies*, xiii.

Chapter Three

1. Thomas Lamarre, *The Anime Machine: A Media Theory of Animation* (Minneapolis: University of Minnesota Press, 2009).

2. Ibid., 15.

3. Ibid., 27.

4. Ibid., 31.

5. Ibid., 31.

6. Lev Manovich, *The Language of New Media*, (Cambridge, MA: MIT Press, 2001), 302.

7. Jeff Foster, *The Green Screen Handbook: Real World Production Techniques* (Indianapolis, IN: Sybex, 2010), 12.

8. "The Making of *Mary Poppins*," http://www.youtube.com/watch?v=E9LVywDGrdI&feature=related.

9. In his caustic review of *Avatar* in the *New Statesman* online, Slavoj Žižek flippantly suggests that the film should be compared to *Roger Rabbit*, because it was a hyper-real blend of animation and live action. Žižek misses what is important about *Avatar* entirely, but he inadvertently connected these two films based on the application of the technology.

10. "The Making of *Who Framed Roger Rabbit*," 1988, Thames, http://www.youtube.com/watch?v=JTxwGNeVUw0&feature=related.

11. Ibid.

12. John Belton, "Digital Cinema: A False Revolution," in *Film Theory and Criticism*, ed. Leo Braudy and Marshall Cohen (New York: Oxford University Press, 2004), 902.

13. Manovich, *The Language of New Media*, 302.

14. Lamarre, *The Anime Machine*, 35.

15. Industrial Light and Magic website, http://www.ilm.com.

16. Ibid.

17. *The Making of* Jurassic Park, Part 2, video, directed by John Schultz, http://www.youtube.com/watch?v=dmOTHb6JBMM&feature=related.

18. Ibid.

19. Brian Knep, Craig Hayes, Rick Sayre, and Tom Williams, "Dinosaur Input Device," in *Proceedings of the SIGCHI Conference on Human Factors in Computing Systems* (CHI '95), ed. Irvin R. Katz, Robert Mack, Linn Marks, Mary Beth Rosson, and Jakob Nielsen (New York: ACM Press/Addison-Wesley, 1995), 304–309. doi:10.1145/223904.223943, http://dx.doi.org/10.1145/223904.223943.

20. Ibid.

21. Ann Dils, "The Ghost in the Machine: Merce Cunningham and Bill T. Jones," *PAJ: A Journal of Performance and Art* 24 (2002).

22. Ibid.

23. See also Anne Friedberg, *The Virtual Window, from Alberti to Microsoft* (Cambridge, MA: MIT Press, 2006), and Brian Massumi, *Parables for the Virtual: Movement Affect Sensation* (Duke University Press, 2002).

24. Simon Vreeswijk, "A History of CGI in Movies," http://www.stikkymedia.com/articles/a-history-of-cgi-inmovies.

25. Industrial Light and Magic website, http://www.ilm.com.

26. See Lamarre, *The Anime Machine*, 112.

27. Clive Thompson, "The Undead Zone: Why Realist Graphics Makes Humans Look Creepy," *Slate*, June 9, 2004, http://www.slate.com/id/2102086.

28. Marissa Brooks, "A Walk in the Valley of the Uncanny," *Damn Interesting*, May 24, 2007, http://www.damninteresting.com/a-walk-in-the-valley-of-the-uncanny.

29. "*Lord of the Rings*, Rendering Gollum," http://www.youtube.com/watch?v=4ul3zwO8W50.

30. "Exclusive Interview with James Cameron," Anne Thomas with *Popular Mechanics*, http://www.popularmechanics.com/technology/digital/visual-effects/4339455.

31. *Avatar Mirrors Emotion with Motion Capture*, video, *WiredVideo*, http://www.huffingtonpost.com/2010/02/03/making-of-avatar-video-cr_n_446323.html.

32. *James Cameron's* Avatar, DVD Collector's Edition, "Capturing Avatar: Interview with Director, James Cameron," produced by Laurent Bouzereau and Thomas C. Grane (Twentieth Century–Fox Home Entertainment, 2009).

33. Ibid.

34. Avatar *Mirrors Emotion with Motion Capture*.

35. Ibid.

36. "Making a Scene: *Avatar*," video, *Fox Movie Channel*, http://www.hulu.com/watch/110975/making-a-scene-avatar.

37. Ibid.

38. Ibid.

39. "Exclusive Interview with James Cameron."

40. Ibid.

41. Ibid.

42. Ibid.

43. Maurice Merleau-Ponty, "The Film and the New Psychology," in *Sense and Non-Sense*, trans. H. Dreyfus and P. Dreyfus (Evanston, IL: Northwestern University Press, 1964), 48–59.

44. Ibid., p. 52.

45. Ibid., p. 53.

46. "Exclusive Interview with James Cameron."

47. Ibid.

48. "Avatar's Cameron-Pace 3D Camera Rig Review," *Gadget PrOn*, G4TV, http://g4tv.com/attackoftheshow/gadgetpr0n/71878/avatars-cameron-pace-3d-camera-rig-review.html.

49. Manohla Dargis, "A New Eden, both Cosmic and Cinematic," *New York Times*, December 18, 2009, http://movies.nytimes.com/2009/12/18/movies/18avatar.html.

50. Daniel Mendelsohn, "The Wizard: *Avatar*," *New York Review of Books*, March 25, 2010, http://www.nybooks.com/articles/archives/2010/mar/25/the-wizard.

51. Terry Gross. "James Cameron: Pushing the Limits of Imagination," *Fresh Air*, February 18, 2010, http://www.npr.org/player/v2/mediaPlayer.html?action=1&t=1&islist=false&id=12381 0319&m=123847924.

52. Avatar SimulCam, http://www.youtube.com/watch?v=OsSqq7E3vPc.

53. "Exclusive Interview with James Cameron."

54. Ibid.

55. "Making a Scene: *Avatar*."

56. Ibid.

57. Ibid.

58. Avatar *Mirrors Emotion with Motion Capture*.

59. Ibid.

60. Ibid.

61. Ibid.

Chapter Four

1. Noel Carroll, "From Philosophical Problems of Classical Film Theory: The Specificity Thesis," in *Film Theory and Criticism*, ed. Leo Braudy and Marshall Cohen, 6th ed. (New York: Oxford University Press, 1988), 332.

2. Kirby Ferguson, *Everything Is a Remix*, 2011, http://www.everythingisaremix.info/?p=58.

3. Mark Feeney, "'Avatar' Is Powered by Many Influences — for Better and Worse," *Boston Globe*, January 10, 2010, http://www.boston.com/ae/movies/articles/2010/01/10/avatar_is_power ed_by_many_influences_for_better_and_worse.

4. Daniel Mendelsohn, "The Wizard: *Avatar*," *New York Review of Books*, March 25, 2010, http://www.nybooks.com/articles/archives/2010/mar/25/the-wizard.

5. Gary Westfahl, "All Energy Is Borrowed," *Locus Online*, December 20, 2009, http://www.locusmag.com/Reviews/2009/12/all-energy-is-borrowed-review-of-avatar.html.

6. Scott Mendelsohn, "*Avatar*: The 3D IMAX Experience," *Salon.com*, December 16, 2009, http://open.salon.com/blog/scott_mendelson/2009/12/15/open_salon_review_avatar_the_3d_imax_experience_2009.

7. Tom Gunning, "Narrative Discourse and the Narrator System," in *Film Theory and Criticism*, ed. Leo Braudy and Marshall Cohen, 6th ed. (New York: Oxford University Press, 1991), 470.

8. Gerard Genette, *Narrative Discourse: An Essay in Method* (Ithaca, NY: Cornell University Press, 1980), 25.

9. Ibid., 29.

10. Westfahl, "All Energy Is Borrowed."

11. Ibid.

12. See Westfahl, "All Energy Is Borrowed," and Christopher Cokinos, "Science and Empathy in James Cameron's *Avatar*: A Response to Gary Westfahl," *New York Review of Science Fiction*, February 2010.

13. Mendelsohn, "The Wizard: *Avatar*."

14. David Brooks, "The Messiah Complex," *New York Times*, January 7, 2010, http://www.nytimes.com/2010/01/08/opinion/08brooks.html.

15. Mendelsohn, "*Avatar*: The 3D IMAX Experience."

16. Terry Gross, "Pushing the Limits of Imagination," *Fresh Air*, February 18, 2010, http://www.npr.org/player/v2/mediaPlayer.html?action=1&t=1&islist=false&id=123810319&m=123 847924.

17. Joseph Campbell, *The Hero with a Thousand Faces* (Princeton, NJ: Princeton University Press, 2004).

18. Will Wright, "The Structure of Myth and the Structure of the Western Film," in *Cultural*

Theory and Popular Culture, ed. John Storey, 3rd ed. (Englewood Cliffs, NJ: Pearson/Prentice Hall, 1975), 304.

19. Campbell, *The Hero with a Thousand Faces*.

20. Ibid., 12.

21. Clifford Simak, *City* (New York: Ace Books, 1952).

22. Ibid.

23. Deleted Scenes, *James Cameron's* Avatar, Collector's Edition.

24. Deleted Scenes, *James Cameron's* Avatar, Collector's Edition.

25. Thanks to Jonathan Foltz, "Technological Malaise," paper presented at the 42nd Annual Northeast Modern Languages Association Convention, New Brunswick, New Jersey, April 7–10, 2011.

26. With gratitude to Erin Andrews, "Race, Nationality and Arthropods: District 9's South African Science Fiction," paper presented at the Pop Culture Association/American Culture Association National Conference, San Antonio, Texas, April 2011.

27. Wright, "The Structure of Myth," 303.

28. Ibid., 304.

29. Ibid., 306.

30. Ibid., 312.

31. Ibid.

32. Stuart Hall, "The Spectacle of the 'Other,'" in *Representation: Cultural Representations and Signifying Practices*, ed. Stuart Hall (Thousand Oaks, CA: Sage, 1997), 235.

33. Roland Barthes, *Image, Music Text*, trans. Stephen Heath (New York: Hill and Wang, 1977), 52.

34. Graeme Turner, *Film as a Social Practice* (London: Routledge, 1999), 97.

35. John Podhoretz, "Avatarocious: Another Spectacle Hits an Iceberg and Sinks," *Weekly Standard*, December 28, 2009, http://www.weeklystandard.com/Content/Public/Articles/000/000/017/350fozta.asp.

36. Ibid.

37. *James Cameron's* Avatar, Collector's Edition.

38. Alan Menken, composer, and Stephen Schwartz, lyricist, "Colors of the Wind," in *Pocahontas* (Walt Disney Feature Animation, 1995).

39. Slavoj Žižek, "Return of the Natives," New Statesman.com, March 4, 2010, http://www.newstatesman.com/film/2010/03/avatar-reality-love-couple-sex.

40. Max Ajil, "Žižekk on Avatar," *Pulse*, March 19, 2010, http://pulsemedia.org/2010/03/19/zizek-on-avatar.

41. Ken Hillis, "From Capital to Karma: James Cameron's *Avatar*," *Postmodern Culture* 19, no. 3 (2009). Interestingly, Dr. Hillis wrote his article for the journal *Postmodern Culture* in May of 2009, well in advance of *Avatar*'s theatrical release, so one must assume it was based on a reading of the screenplay of the film.

42. Ibid.

43. Ibid.

44. Ibid.

45. Ibid.

46. Ibid.

47. Brooks, "The Messiah Complex."

48. Ibid.

49. Ibid.

50. Ibid.

51. David Bordwell, "Classical Hollywood Cinema: Narrational Principles and Procedures," in *Narrative, Apparatus, Ideology*, p. 21 (New York: Columbia University Press, 1986).

52. Ibid.

53. Campbell, *The Hero with a Thousand Faces*.

54. Mendelsohn, "The Wizard: *Avatar*."

55. Ibid.

56. Brooks, "The Messiah Complex."

57. Gross, "Pushing the Limits of Imagination."

58. Manohla Dargis, "Floating in the Digital Experience," *New York Times*, January 3, 2010.

59. Mendelsohn, "*Avatar*: The 3D IMAX Experience."

60. David Harvey, *The Condition of Postmodernity* (Oxford: Basil Blackwell, 1989).

61. Robert Heinlein, "Science Fiction: Its Nature, Faults and Virtues," in *Turning Points: Essays on the Art of Science Fiction*, ed. Damon Knight (New York: Harper & Row, 1959).

62. Bordwell, "Classical Hollywood Cinema," 19.

63. Ibid., 18.

64. Ibid.

65. Rosalind Galt, "The Obviousness of Cinema," *World Picture* 2, http://www.worldpicture journal.com/WP_2/Galt.html.

66. Ibid.

67. Ibid.

68. Ibid.

69. Mendelsohn, "*Avatar*: The 3D IMAX Experience."

70. Bordwell, "Classical Hollywood Cinema," 18.

71. Christian Metz, "The Imaginary Signifier, [Excerpts]," in *Narrative, Apparatus, Ideology*, ed. Philip Rosen (New York: Columbia University Press, 1986).

72. Mendelsohn, "*Avatar*: The 3D IMAX Experience."

73. *James Cameron's* Avatar, Collector's Edition.

74. Ibid.

75. Manohla Dargis, "Floating in the Digital Experience."

76. Susan Sontag, "The Decay of Cinema," *New York Times*, February 25, 1996, http://part ners.nytimes.com/books/00/03/12/specials/sontag-cinema.html.

77. Ibid.

78. Ibid.

Chapter Five

1. Christian Metz, "The Imaginary Signifier, [Excerpts]," in *Narrative, Apparatus, Ideology*, ed. Philip Rosen (New York: Columbia University Press, 1986).

2. See Anne Friedberg, *The Virtual Window, from Alberti to Microsoft*, (Cambridge, MA: MIT Press, 2006).

3. See E. Panofsky, *Perspective as Symbolic Form* (New York: Zone Books, 1991); J. Crary, *Techniques of the Observer: On Vision and Modernity in the 19th Century* (Cambridge, MA: MIT Press, 1992); K. Harries, *Infinity and Perspective* (Cambridge, MA: MIT Press, 2001); Friedberg, *The Virtual Window, from Alberti to Microsoft*; Hubert Damisch, *The Origin of Perspective*, trans. John Goodman (Cambridge, MA: MIT Press, 1995); and of course Leon Battista Alberti, *On Painting and on Sculpture: The Latin Texts of De Pictura and De Statua*, trans. Cecil Grayson (London: Phaidon, 1972).

4. Friedberg, *The Virtual Window, from Alberti to Microsoft*, 5.

5. Stephen Heath, "Narrative Space," in *Narrative, Apparatus, Ideology*, ed. Philip Rosen (New York: Columbia University Press, 1986), 404.

6. Maurice Merleau-Ponty, *Sense and Non-Sense*, trans. H. Dreyfus and P. Dreyfus (Evanston, Ill: Northwestern University Press, 1964), 48–59.

7. Thomas Lamarre, *The Anime Machine: A Media Theory of Animation* (Minneapolis: University of Minnesota Press, 2009), xix.

8. See Heath, *Narrative Space*, 404.

9. Tom Gunning, "Narrative Discourse and the Narrator System," in *Film Theory and Criticism*, ed. Leo Braudy and Marshall Cohen, 6th ed. (New York: Oxford University Press, 1991), 475.

10. Jacques Lacan, *The Four Fundamental Concepts of Psychoanalysis*, trans. A. Sheridan (London: Hogarth Press, 1977), 93.

11. F. Nietzsche, "On Truth and Lie in an Extra-Moral Sense," in *The Continental Aesthetics Reader*, ed. C. Cazeaux (London: Routledge, 2000), 53–62.

12. Harries, *Infinity and Perspective*, 43.

13. Ludwig Wittgenstein, *Philosophical Investigations* (Malden, MA: Blackwell, 1953).

14. G. C. Spivak, "Translator's Preface," in *Of Grammatology* (Baltimore, MD: Johns Hopkins University Press, 1974), ix–lxxxvii.

15. Harries, *Infinity and Perspective*, 49.

16. Ibid., 32.

17. Jean-Louis Baudry, "Ideological Effects of the Basic Cinematographic Apparatus," in *Film Theory and Criticism*, ed. Leo Braudy (New York: Oxford University Press, 2004), 355.

18. Harries, *Infinity and Perspective*, 69.

19. John Berger, "Ways of Seeing," (New York: Viking, 1972), 16.

20. Panofsky, *Perspective as Symbolic Form*, 66.

21. Harries, *Infinity and Perspective*, 76.

22. Aldous Huxley, *The Art of Seeing* (London: Chatto and Windus, 1943) in Paul Virilio, *The Vision Machine* (Bloomington: Indiana University Press, 1994).

23. Ibid.

24. Ibid., 13.

25. See "Cezanne's Doubt" in G. A. Johnson, *The Merleau-Ponty Aesthetics Reader: Philosophy and Painting* (Evanston, IL: Northwestern University Press, 1993).

26. Lamarre, *The Anime Machine*, 5. For an extensive treatment of this print, see K. Harries, *Infinity and Perspective* (Cambridge, MA: MIT Press, 2001), and Anne Friedberg, *The Virtual Window, from Alberti to Microsoft* (Cambridge, MA: MIT Press, 2006).

27. Heath, *Narrative Space*, 397.

28. Jean-Louis Comolli, "Technique and Ideology: Camera, Perspective, Depth of Field" (parts 3 and 4), in *Narrative, Apparatus, Ideology*, ed. Philip Rosen (New York: Columbia University Press, 1986).

29. Timothy Corrigan and Patricia White, *The Film Experience: An Introduction* (Boston, MA: Bedford/St. Martin's, 2004), 456.

30. Baudry, *Ideological Effects of the Basic Cinematographic Apparatus*, 357.

31. Ibid., 356.

32. Virilio, *The Vision Machine*, 13.

33. Ibid., 13.

34. Baudry, *Ideological Effects of the Basic Cinematographic Apparatus*, 357.

35. Ibid., 360.

36. Jean Mitry, *Esthetique et psychologie du cinema* (Paris: Presse Univeritaires de France, 1965), 179.

37. Ibid., 360.

38. Friedberg, *The Virtual Window, from Alberti to Microsoft*, 143.

39. Metz, "The Imaginary Signifier, [Excerpts]," 252.

40. See Friedberg, *The Virtual Window, From Alberti to Microsoft*, 178.

41. Ibid.

42. Ibid., 179.

43. Ibid.

44. Baudry, *Ideological Effects of the Basic Cinematographic Apparatus*, 364.

45. Ibid., 362.

46. Jean-Louis Baudry, "The Apparatus: Metapsychological Approaches to the Impression of Reality in Cinema," in *Film Theory and Criticism*, ed. Leo Braudy (New York: Oxford University Press, 2004), 212.

47. Noel Carroll, in his essay, dismantles Baudry's theory, point by point, underscoring the disanalogies that undermine Baudry's logic. In relation to what purpose the analogy to Plato's allegory might serve, Carroll points out that Baudry has torn the story out of its historical context and treats it as a fantasy, "ripe for psychoanalysis." Carroll understands the use of the parable to support a belief that the recent invention of cinema really manifests "long standing transhistorical and instinctual desire of the sort that psychoanalysis is fitted to examine," asserting that the archaic wish underlying cinema is atavistic. In addition, Carroll points to the involuntary nature of the chained inhabitants of Plato's cave and the voluntary stillness of the average moviegoer. See Noel Carroll, "From Mystifying Movies: Jean-Louis Baudry and 'The Apparatus'" in *Film Theory and Criticism*, ed. Leo Braudy and Marshall Cohen (New York: Oxford University Press, 2004).

48. Rose, *Visual Methodologies*, 115.

49. C. Cazeaux, ed., *The Continental Aesthetics Reader* (New York: Routledge, 2000), 495.

50. Rose, *Visual Methodologies*, 115.

51. Baudry, *Ideological Effects of the Basic Cinematographic Apparatus*, 363.

52. Ibid., 364.

53. Metz, "The Imaginary Signifier, [Excerpts]," 251.

54. Ibid., 249.
55. Ibid.
56. Ibid., 252.
57. With thanks to Chris Dilworth, "Wake Up! Watch It! Yaa!: Competing Cognitivist Metaphors in Cameron's *Avatar*," paper presented at the Northeast Modern Languages Association Conference, University of Rutgers, New Jersey, April 2011.
58. Ibid., 254.
59. Ibid.
60. Ibid., 250.
61. Ibid., 255.
62. See pages xxx and xxx in this volume.
63. Dilworth, "Wake Up! Watch It! Yaa!," 255.
64. Ibid., 255.
65. Kaja Silverman, "Suture [Excerpts]," in *Narrative, Apparatus, Ideology*, ed. Philip Rosen (New York: Columbia University Press, 1983), 219.
66. Ibid., 220.
67. Ibid., 221.
68. Maurice Merleau-Ponty, *The Visible and the Invisible*, ed. Claude Lefort, trans. Alphonso Lingis (Evanston, IL: Northwestern University Press, 1968), 54.
69. Griselda Pollock, *Differencing the Canon: Feminist Desire and the Writing of Art's Histories* (London: Routledge, 1999), 8.
70. Slajov Žižek, "The Return of the Natives," *New Statesman*, March 4, 2010.
71. Ibid.
72. Ibid.
73. Friedberg, *The Virtual Window, from Alberti to Microsoft*, 84.
74. Ibid., 84.
75. Dargis, "Floating in the Digital Experience."
76. Ibid.
77. Ibid.
78. Heath, *Narrative Space*, 261.
79. Baudry, *The Apparatus: Metapsychological Approaches to the Impression of Reality in Cinema*, 221.
80. Ibid.
81. Ibid., 116.
82. Metz, "The Imaginary Signifier, [Excerpts]," 253.
83. See N. Carroll, "From Mystifying Movies: Jean-Louis Baudry and 'The Apparatus,'" in *Film Theory and Criticism*, ed. Leo Braudy and Marshall Cohen (New York: Oxford University Press, 1988), for a cogent counterargument to Baudry's apparatus theory.
84. Baudry, *The Apparatus: Metapsychological Approaches to the Impression of Reality in Cinema*, 226.
85. "James Cameron: Dream," James Lipton interview, on *Inside the Actors Studio*, Bravo, http://www.hulu.com/watch/130518/inside-the-actors-studio-james-cameron-dream.

Chapter Six

1. Susan Sontag, "The Decay of Cinema," *New York Times*, February 25, 1996, http://partners.nytimes.com/books/00/03/12/specials/sontag-cinema.html.
2. Ibid.
3. *Killing Us Softly 3: Advertising's Image of Women*, DVD, directed by Sut Jhally (Media Education Foundation, 2010).
4. Stuart Hall, *Representation: Cultural Representations and Signifying Practices* (Thousand Oaks, CA: Sage, 1997), 15.
5. Ibid., 236.
6. Ibid., 236.
7. Ibid., 236.
8. "Man in the Wall," *Bones*, Fox Network, November 15, 2005.

9. Ibid.

10. Ibid.

11. Ibid.

12. Ibid.

13. Hall, *Representation*, 236.

14. Ibid., 254.

15. Ibid.

16. Ibid., 236.

17. Michael Rogin, *Blackface, White Noise: Jewish Immigrants in the Hollywood Melting Pot* (Berkeley: University of California Press, 1996), 86.

18. Ibid., 89.

19. Ibid., 86.

20. Ibid., 119.

21. Ibid.

22. Hall, *Representation*, 236.

23. Ibid., 259.

24. Ibid.

25. See Chapter Two, this volume.

26. Teresa de Lauretis, "Through the Looking Glass," in *Narrative, Apparatus, Ideology*, ed. Philip Rosen (New York: Columbia University Press, 1984), 368.

27. Wesley Morris, "Elastic Fantasy Defies Fixed Ideas About Race, Identity: In a Virtual World, James Cameron's Message Is Quite a Stretch," *Boston Globe*, January 10, 2010.

28. Manohla Dargis, "A New Eden, Both Cosmic and Cinematic," *New York Times*, December 18, 2009, http://movies.nytimes.com/2009/12/18/movies/18avatar.html.

29. Courtland Milloy, "*Avatar* Is Part of Important Discussion About Race," *Washington Post*, December 23, 2009.

30. Vanessa E. Jones, quoting Nalo Hopkinson, in "Race, the Final Frontier: Black Science-Fiction Writers Bring a Unique Perspective to the Genre," *Boston Globe*, July 31, 2007, http://www.boston.com/ae/books/articles/2007/07/31/race_the_final_frontier.

31. *James Cameron's* Avatar, Collector's Edition.

32. Ibid.

33. Morris, "Elastic Fantasy Defies Fixed Ideas."

34. Robert E. Kelly, January 14, 2010, "'*Avatar*': Blue Ewoks Save the Amazon from Blackwater Inc.," *Asian Security Blog*, http://asiansecurityblog.wordpress.com/2010/01/14/avatar-blue-ewoks-save-the-amazon-from-blackwater-inc.

35. David Brooks, "The Messiah Complex," *New York Times*, January 7, 2010, http://www.nytimes.com/2010/01/08/opinion/08brooks.html.

36. Jesse, December 24, 2009, comment on Remington Smith, "Avatar Totally Racist, Dude," *The Filmsmith Blog: A Place for Film Fans*, December 17, 2009, http://thefilmsmith.com/2009/12/17/avatar-totally-racist-dude.

37. Nalo Hopkinson, *Midnight Robber* (New York: Warner Books, 2000).

38. Amy Bloom, "Branching Out: Throw Open the Doors to a New Kind of Love and Family," *O, the Oprah Magazine*, July 2011, http://www.oprah.com/spirit/Advantages-of-Non-Traditional-Families-Unconventional-Families.

39. James Cameron, "James Cameron: Before *Avatar* … a Curious Boy," TED Talk, March 2010, http://www.ted.com/talks/james_cameron_before_avatar_a_curious_boy.html.

40. "Desert Grassland Whiptail Lizard" entry, *Wikipedia*, http://en.wikipedia.org/wiki/Desert_Grassland_Whiptail_Lizard D. Crews, and K.T. Fitzgerald, "'Sexual' Behavior in Parthenogenetic Lizards (Cnemidophorus)," *Proceedings of the National Academy of Sciences* 77, no. 1 (1980): 499–502.

41. Bloom, "Branching Out."

42. Milloy, "*Avatar* Is Part of Important Discussion About Race."

43. Ibid.

44. "Deane," January 13, 2010, comment on Remington Smith, "*Avatar* Totally Racist, Dude," *The Filmsmith Blog: A Place for Film Fans*, December 17, 2009, http://thefilmsmith.com/2009/12/17/avatar-totally-racist-dude.

45. Milloy, "*Avatar* Is Part of Important Discussion About Race."

46. Annalee Newitz, "When Will White People Stop Making Movies Like 'Avatar'?" *IO9 Blog*,

December 18, 2009, http://io9.com/5422666/when-will-white-people-stop-making-movies-like-avatar.

47. Newitz, "When Will White People Stop?"
48. Ibid.
49. Ibid.
50. Morris, "Elastic Fantasy Defies Fixed Ideas."
51. Ibid.
52. "'Avatar' a Box Office Hit, But Some Say It's Racist," *Tell Me More*, interview with Courtland Milloy and Wesley Morris, NPR, December 28, 2009, http://www.npr.org/templates/story/story.php?storyId=121968796.
53. Ibid.
54. Eric Ribellarsi, "Avatar: Condescending Racism or a Story of Transformation and Struggle?" *The Fire Collective: Fight Imperialism, Rethink Experiment*, December 21, 2009, http://thefirecollective.org/Art-Culture/avatar-condescending-racism-or-a-story-of-transformation-and-struggle.html.
55. "Palestinians Stage Avatar-Inspired Political Protest," *Blastr.com: The SyFy Online Network*, February 12, 2010, http://blastr.com/2010/02/palestinians-stage-avatar.php.
56. Scott Edelman, "Latest Avatar-Inspired Political Protest? Save the Apes!" *Blastr.com: The SyFy Online Network*, February 24, 2010, http://blastr.com/2010/02/latest-avatar-inspired-political-protest-save-the-apes.php.
57. Jo Piazza, "Avatar-Induced Depression: Coping with the Intangibility of Pandora," requoted from CNN.com, March 18, 2010, http://www.huffingtonpost.com/2010/01/12/avatar-induced-depression_n_420605.html?view=print.
58. Mitchell Silver, "Our Morality: A Defense of Moral Objectivism," *Philosophy Now*, no. 83 (2011).
59. Rabbi Fred Guttman, "A Jewish Reflection on the Spiritual Message of 'Avatar,'" Ethics Daily.com, January 8, 2010, http://www.ethicsdaily.com/a-jewish-reflection-on-the-spiritual-message-of-avatar-cms-15477.
60. Thanks to Bob Zellan for sharing Rabbi Guttman's online post with me.
61. Rabbi Fred Guttman, "A Jewish Reflection on the Spiritual Message of 'Avatar.'"
62. Judith Butler, "Giving an Account of Oneself," *Diacritics* 31, no. 4 (2001): 28.
63. Ibid.
64. Ibid.
65. Ibid.
66. Ibid.
67. Ibid.
68. Ibid.
69. With gratitude to Jennifer Miller for pointing me in the direction of Butler in Jennifer Miller, "Jake Sully and Judith Butler: The Disorienting *Avatar* as a Model for Understanding Self and Other," paper presented at the Northeast Modern Languages Association Conference, University of Rutgers, New Jersey, April 2011.
70. Gary Westfahl, "All Energy Is Borrowed," *Locus Online*, December 20, 2009, http://www.locusmag.com/Reviews/2009/12/all-energy-is-borrowed-review-of-avatar.html.
71. Ibid.
72. Robert McRuer, "As Good as It Gets: Queer Theory and Critical Disability," *GLQ* 9, nos. 1–2 (Durham, NC: Duke University Press, 2003), 80.
73. Fatema Ahmen, "Stalinist Self-Criticism," *London Review of Books Blog Reports*, April 9, 2010, http://www.lrb.co.uk/blog/2010/04/09/fatema-ahmed/stalinist-self-criticism.
74. Slavoj Žižek, "Return of the Natives," New Statesman.com, March 4, 2010, http://www.newstatesman.com/film/2010/03/avatar-reality-love-couple-sex.
75. Ibid.
76. Ibid.
77. Ibid.
78. Ibid.
79. McRuer, "As Good as It Gets," 79.
80. Harry, "Harry Reviews *Avatar* at Last," *Ain't It Cool*, December 18, 2009, http://www.aintitcool.com/node/43430.
81. Ibid.

82. With gratitude to Briana Martino for sharing Robert McRuer's article with me.

83. McRuer, "As Good as It Gets," 85.

84. Ibid.

85. *Avatar.*

86. Ibid.

87. Malinda Lo, "Native Women Are Not Trophies," MalindaLo.com, December 21, 2009, http://www.malindalo.com/2009/12/note-to-james-cameron-native-women-are-not-trophies.

88. de Lauretis, *Through the Looking Glass*, 362.

89. Ibid., 364.

90. Laura Mulvey, "Visual Pleasure and Narrative Cinema," in *The Routledge Critical and Cultural Theory Reader*, ed. Neil Badmington and Julia Thomas (New York: Routledge, 2008), 203.

91. Ibid.

92. Ibid.

93. See Chapter Three in this volume for a detailed exploration of performance capture.

94. With appreciation to Jennifer Nesbitt for sharing Jennifer Nesbitt, "For Women, Pleasures of *Avatar* Dearly Bought," paper presented at the Northeast Modern Languages Association Conference, University of Rutgers, New Jersey, April 2011.

95. Nesbitt, "For Women, Pleasures of *Avatar* Dearly Bought."

96. Daniel Mendelsohn, "The Wizard: *Avatar*," *New York Review of Books*, March 25, 2010, http://www.nybooks.com/articles/archives/2010/mar/25/the-wizard.

97. Nesbitt, "For Women, Pleasures of *Avatar* Dearly Bought."

98. Ibid.

99. Ibid.

100. Ibid.

101. Mendelsohn "The Wizard: *Avatar*."

102. Ibid.

103. *The Jazz Singer*, DVD, directed by Alan Crosland (Warner Brothers, 1927).

104. *The Jazz Singer.*

105. *The Jazz Singer.*

106. Rogin, *Blackface, White Noise*, 116.

107. Mendelsohn, "The Wizard: *Avatar*."

108. See Chapter Five.

109. Rogin, *Blackface, White Noise*, 116.

110. Ibid.

111. Ibid., 92.

112. Ibid., 102.

113. Ibid., 94.

114. Ibid., 80.

115. *The Jazz Singer.*

116. Ibid.

117. Ibid.

118. Rogin, *Blackface, White Noise*, 89.

119. Ibid., 102.

120. Ibid., 103.

121. Ibid.

122. Ibid., 30.

123. Ibid., 105.

Chapter Seven

1. Manohla Dargis, "A New Eden, Both Cosmic and Cinematic," *New York Times*, December 18, 2009, http://movies.nytimes.com/2009/12/18/movies/18avatar.html.

2. Ibid.

3. "AFI's 10 Top 10," *American Film Institute Web Site*, http://www.afi.com/100Years.

4. Dana Goodyear, "A Man of Extremes: The Return of James Cameron," *New Yorker*, October 26, 2009, http://www.newyorker.com/reporting/2009/10/26/091026fa_fact_goodyear?printable=true&currentPage=all.

5. Wesley Morris, "Elastic Fantasy Defies Fixed Ideas About Race, Identity: In a Virtual World, James Cameron's Message Is Quite a Stretch," *Boston Globe*, January 10, 2010.

6. James Cameron, "James Cameron: Before *Avatar* ... a Curious Boy," TED Talk, March 2010, http://www.ted.com/talks/james_cameron_before_avatar_a_curious_boy.html.

7. Ibid.

8. "James Cameron," Internet Movie Database, http://www.imdb.com/name/nm0000116.

9. Ibid.

10. Goodyear, "A Man of Extremes."

11. Ibid.

12. Ibid.

13. Daniel Mendelsohn, "The Wizard: *Avatar*," *New York Review of Books*, March 25, 2010, http://www.nybooks.com/articles/archives/2010/mar/25/the-wizard.

14. Ibid.

15. Peter Wollen, "From Signs and Meaning in the Cinema: The Auteur Theory," in *Film Theory and Criticism*, ed. Leo Braudy and Marshall Cohen, 6th ed. (New York: Oxford University Press, 1969), 565.

16. See Chapter Three.

17. Wollen, "From Signs and Meaning in the Cinema," 565.

18. Ibid.

19. Ibid.

20. Ibid.

21. Goodyear, "A Man of Extremes."

22. Andrew Sarris, "Notes on the Auteur Theory in 1962," in *Film Theory and Criticism*, ed. Leo Braudy and Marshall Cohen, 6th ed. (New York: Oxford University Press, 1962), 562.

23. Ibid., 562.

24. Ibid., 563.

25. Ibid.

26. Goodyear, "A Man of Extremes."

27. Joshua Davis, "James Cameron's New 3-D Epic Could Change Film Forever," *Wired*, November 17, 2009, http://www.wired.com/magazine/2009/11/ff_avatar_cameron.

28. Goodyear, "A Man of Extremes."

29. *The Making of* Terminator, video, directed by Drew Cummings, http://video.google.com/videoplay?docid=-6199341931899559783.

30. Ibid.

31. *Bug Hunt: Creature Design*, video, *Aliens—The Making of: Creature Design* (part 2/25) (1986; Twentieth Century–Fox Home Entertainment, 2003), http://www.youtube.com/watch?v=c300 wmQ5d-g&feature=related.

32. David Chute, *The Abyss* (1989), *Rotten Tomatoes*, http://www.rottentomatoes.com/m/abyss.

33. Peter Travers, *The Abyss* (1989), *Rotten Tomatoes*, http://www.rottentomatoes.com/m/abyss.

34. *Under Pressure: The Making of* The Abyss, video, directed by Ed. W. Marsh (Twentieth Century–Fox, 1993), http://www.youtube.com/watch?v=gUYDj2Ge28o&NR=1.

35. Ibid.

36. Cameron, "James Cameron: Before *Avatar* ... a Curious Boy."

37. *Strange Days*, Internet Movie Database, http://www.imdb.com/title/tt0114558/trivia.

38. Ibid.

39. Andrew Sarris, "Notes on the Auteur Theory in 1962," 578.

40. *The Abyss*, DVD, directed by James Cameron (Twentieth Century–Fox Film Corporation, Pacific Western, Lightstorm Entertainment, 1989).

41. *Under Pressure: The Making of* The Abyss.

42. *Two Orphans: The Making of* Aliens, http://www.youtube.com/watch?v=9S7Jc3xu630.

43. *The Making of* Terminator 2: Judgment Day, Part 2, produced by David G. Hudson and Ed Marsh (1991; Carolco Pictures, 2001), http://www.youtube.com/watch?v=5doqIiCAJ-g&feature=related.

44. *Heart of the Ocean: The Making of* Titanic, directed by Ed W. Marsh, 1997, http://www.youtube.com/watch?v=8MZ4WaBlZ9g.

45. *The Making of* Terminator 2: Judgment Day, Part 2.

46. Goodyear, "A Man of Extremes."

47. See Chapter Three. As of this writing Cameron's headgear was adopted in the making of

the *Rise of the Planet of the Apes* and was used in the performance capture of Andy Serkis who also played Gollum in *The Lord of the Rings*.

48. Wollen, *From Signs and Meaning in the Cinema*, 565.

49. Cameron, "James Cameron: Before *Avatar* ... a Curious Boy."

50. *Strange Days*, DVD, directed by Kathryn Bigelow (Twentieth Century–Fox Film Corporation, 1995).

51. Ibid.

52. Carrie Rickey, "Previewing the Oscars 2010," *On Point*, WBUR Boston Public Radio (Boston, MA: WBUR, March 5, 2010), http://onpoint.wbur.org/2010/03/05/the-oscars-2010.

53. *James Cameron's* Avatar, DVD, Collector's Edition.

54. *The Abyss*.

55. *James Cameron's* Avatar, DVD, Collector's Edition.

56. "Creator James Cameron on *Terminator*'s Origins, Arnold as Robot, Machine Wars," as told to Steve Daly, *Wired*, March 23, 2009, http://www.wired.com/entertainment/hollywood/magazine/17-04/ff_cameron.

57. *The Terminator*, DVD, directed by James Cameron (Hemdale Film, Cinema 84, Euro Film Funding, Pacific Western, 1984).

58. *Terminator 2: Judgment Day*, DVD, directed by James Cameron (Carolco Pictures, Pacific Western, Lightstorm Entertainment, 1991).

59. Ibid.

60. *The Abyss*.

61. Cameron was also instrumental in the character creation of the TV series *The Terminator: The Sarah Connor Chronicles*. This series, written by Josh Friedman, builds on *Terminator* and is rife with human/machinic interplay.

62. *The Abyss*.

63. *Aliens*, DVD, directed by James Cameron (1986; Twentieth Century–Fox Film Corporation, 1991 Special Edition).

64. *The Abyss*.

65. *Titanic*, DVD, directed by James Cameron (Twentieth Century–Fox Film Corporation, Paramount Pictures, Lightstorm Entertainment, 1997).

66. Ibid.

67. Ibid.

68. *The Making of* Terminator.

Bibliography

Barthes, R. *Image, Music, Text*. Translated by Stephen Heath. New York: Hill and Wang, 1977.

Baudry, Jean-Louis. "The Apparatus: Metapsychological Approaches to the Impression of Reality in Cinema." In *Film Theory and Criticism*, edited by Leo Braudy. New York: Oxford University Press, 2004.

_____. "Ideological Effects of the Basic Cinematographic Apparatus." In *Film Theory and Criticism*, edited by Leo Braudy. New York: Oxford University Press, 2004.

Berger, J. *Ways of Seeing*. New York: Viking Press, 1972.

Birkerts, Sven. *The Gutenberg Elegies*. Boston: Faber and Faber, 2006.

Bordwell, David. "Classical Hollywood Cinema: Narrational Principles and Procedures." In *Narrative, Apparatus, Ideology*. New York: Columbia University Press, 1986.

Braudy, Leo, and Marshall Cohen, eds. *Film Theory and Criticism*. New York: Oxford University Press, 2004.

Butler, Judith. "Giving an Account of Oneself." *Diacritics* 31, no. 4 (2001): 22–40.

Campbell, Joseph. *The Hero with a Thousand Faces*. Princeton, NJ: Princeton University Press, 2004.

Carroll, N. "From Mystifying Movies: Jean-Louis Baudry and 'the Apparatus.'" In *Film Theory and Criticism*, edited by Leo Braudy and Marshall Cohen. New York: Oxford University Press, 1988.

_____. "From Philosophical Problems of Classical Film Theory: The Specificity Thesis." In *Film Theory and Criticism*, edited by Leo Braudy and Marshall Cohen. New York: Oxford University Press, 1988.

Cazeaux, C. "Theorizing Theory and Practice." *Point: Art and Design Journal* 7 (1999): 26–31.

_____, ed. *The Continental Aesthetics Reader*. New York: Routledge, 2000.

Comolli, Jean-Louis. "Technique and Ideology: Camera, Perspective, Depth of Field" (Parts 3 and 4). In *Narrative, Apparatus, Ideology*, edited by Philip Rosen. New York: Columbia University Press, 1986.

Corrigan, Timothy, and Patricia White. *The Film Experience: An Introduction*. New York: Bedford/St. Martin's, 2004.

Crary, J. *Techniques of the Observer: On Vision and Modernity in the 19th Century*. Cambridge, MA: MIT Press, 1992.

Crowther, Paul. "The Experience of Art: Some Problems and Possibilities of Hermeneutical Analysis." *Philosophical and Phenomenological Research* 43, no. 3 (March 1983).

Danvers, Dennis. *Circuit of Heaven*. New York: Avon Books, 1998.

de Lauretis, Teresa. "Through the Looking Glass." In *Narrative, Apparatus, Ideology*, edited by Philip Rosen. New York: Columbia University Press, 1984.

Dewey, John. *Art as Experience*. New York: Perigee Books, 1934.

Friedberg, Anne. *The Virtual Window, from Alberti to Microsoft*. Cambridge, MA: MIT Press, 2006.

Galt, Rosalind. "The Obviousness of Cinema." *World Picture* 2 (Autumn 2009). http://english.okstate.edu/worldpicture/WP_2/PDF%20Docs/GaltPDF.pdf.

Genette, Gerard. *Narrative Discourse: An Essay in Method.* Ithaca: Cornell University Press, 1980.
Gunning, Tom. "Narrative Discourse and the Narrator System." In *Film Theory and Criticism*, edited by Leo Braudy and Marshall Cohen. New York: Oxford University Press, 1991.
Hall, Stuart. *Representation: Cultural Representations and Signifying Practices.* Thousand Oaks, CA: Sage, 1997.
_____. "The Spectacle of the 'Other.'" Chap. 4 in *Representation: Cultural Representations and Signifying Practices*, edited by Stuart Hall. Thousand Oaks, CA: Sage, 1997.
Harries, K. *Infinity and Perspective.* Cambridge, MA: MIT Press, 2001.
Harvey, David. *The Condition of Postmodernity.* Oxford: Basil Blackwell, 1989.
Heath, Stephen. "Narrative Space." In *Narrative, Apparatus, Ideology*, edited by Philip Rosen. New York: Columbia University Press, 1986.
Heidegger, M. *Being and Time.* Albany: State University of New York, 1996.
_____. *Discourse on Thinking.* New York: Harper & Row, 1966.
_____. *The Origin of the Work of Art.* Edited by Clive Cazeaux, translated by Albert Hofstadter. *The Continental Aesthetics Reader.* New York: Routledge, 2000.
_____. "The Question Concerning Technology." In *Martin Heidegger: Basic Writings*, edited by D. F. Krell. New York: HarperCollins, 1953.
Heinlein, Robert. "Science Fiction: Its Nature, Faults and Virtues." In *Turning Points: Essays on the Art of Science Fiction*, edited by Damon Knight. New York: Harper & Row, 1959.
Hillis, Ken. "From Capital to Karma: James Cameron's Avatar." *Postmodern Culture* 19, no. 3 (2009).
Hopkinson, Nalo. *Midnight Robber.* New York: Warner Books, 2000.
Houlgate, Stephen. "Vision, Reflection and Openness: The 'Hegemony of Vision' from a Hegelian Point of View." In *Modernity and the Hegemony of Vision*, edited by David Michael Levin. Los Angeles: University of California Press, 1993.
Jay, Martin. "Scopic Regimes of Modernity." In *Vision and Visuality*, edited by Hal Foster. New York: New Press, 1988.
Johnson, G. A. *The Merleau-Ponty Aesthetics Reader: Philosophy and Painting.* Evanston, IL: Northwestern University Press, 1993.
Kemp, Martin. *The Science of Art: Optical Themes in Western Art from Brunelleschi to Seurat.* New Haven: Yale University Press, 1990.
Lamarre, Thomas, *The Anime Machine: A Media Theory of Animation.* Minneapolis: University of Minnesota Press, 2009.
Levin, David Michael. *The Philosopher's Gaze: Modernity in the Shadows of Enlightenment.* Berkeley: University of California Press, 1999.
_____, ed. *Sites of Vision: The Discursive Construction of Sight in the History of Philosophy.* Cambridge, MA: MIT Press, 1999.
McRuer, Robert. "As Good as It Gets: Queer Theory and Critical Disability." *GLQ* 9:1–2 (2003).
Merleau-Ponty, Maurice. "The Intertwining-the Chiasm." In *The Continental Aesthetics Reader.* New York: Routledge, 2000.
_____. *The Visible and the Invisible.* Translated by Alphonso Lingis, edited by Claude Lefort. Evanston, IL: Northwestern University Press, 1968.
Metz, Christian. "The Imaginary Signifier." In *Film Theory and Criticism*, edited by Leo Braudy and Marshall Cohen. New York: Oxford University Press, 2004.
Mitry, Jean. Esthetique et psychologie du cinema. Paris: Presse Univeritaires de France, 1965.
Mulvey, Laura. "Visual Pleasure and Narrative Cinema." In *The Routledge Critical and Cultural Theory Reader*, edited by Neil Badmington and Julia Thomas. New York: Routledge, 2008.
Nietzsche, F. "On Truth and Lie in an Extra-Moral Sense." In *The Continental Aesthetics Reader*, edited by C. Cazeaux. New York: Routledge, 2000.
Panofsky, E. *Perspective as Symbolic Form.* New York: Zone Books, 1991.
Pollock, G. *Differencing the Canon: Feminist Desire and the Writing of Art's Histories.* New York: Routledge, 1999.
Rogin, Michael. *Blackface, White Noise: Jewish Immigrants in the Hollywood Melting Pot.* Berkeley: University of California Press, 1996.
Rorty, Richard. *Philosophy and Social Hope.* London: Penguin, 1999.
Rose, G. *Visual Methodologies.* Thousand Oaks, CA: Sage, 2001.

Rosen, Philip, ed. *Narrative, Apparatus, Ideology.* New York: Columbia University Press, 1986.

Roshwald, Mordecai. *Dreams and Nightmares: Science and Technology in Myth and Fiction.* Critical Explorations in Science Fiction and Fantasy. Series editors Donald E. Palumbo and C. W. Sullivan. Jefferson, NC: McFarland, 2008.

Sarris, Andrew. "Notes on the Auteur Theory in 1962." In *Film Theory and Criticism*, edited by Leo Braudy and Marshall Cohen. New York: Oxford University Press, 1962.

Silver, Mitchell. "Our Morality: A Defense of Moral Objectivism." *Philosophy Now* 83 (2011).

Silverman, K. "Suture [Excerpts]." In *Narrative, Apparatus, Ideology*, edited by Philip Rosen. New York: Columbia University Press, 1983.

Simak, Clifford. *City.* New York: Ace Books, 1952.

Sontag, Susan. "The Decay of Cinema." *New York Times*, February 25, 1996.

_____. *On Photography.* New York: Picador, 1973.

Spivak, G. C. "Translator's Preface." In *Of Grammatology*. Baltimore: Johns Hopkins University Press, 1974.

Turner, Graeme. *Film as a Social Practice.* London: Routledge, 1999.

Virilio, Paul. *The Vision Machine.* Bloomington: Indiana University Press, 1994.

Wittgenstein, L. *Philosophical Investigations.* Malden, MA: Blackwell, 1953.

Wollen, Peter. "From Signs and Meaning in the Cinema: The Auteur Theory." In *Film Theory and Criticism*, edited by Leo Braudy and Marshall Cohen. New York: Oxford University Press, 1969.

Wright, Will. "The Structure of Myth and the Structure of the Western Film." In *Cultural Theory and Popular Culture*, edited by John Storey. Englewood Cliffs, NJ: Pearson/Prentice Hall, 1975.

Index